AMERICAN POETS OF THE 20TH CENTURY

NOTES

including
- *Life of the Author*
- *Chief Works*
- *Discussion and Research Topics*
- *Selected Bibliography*
- *Glossary*

by
Mary Ellen Snodgrass, M.A.
University of North Carolina, Greensboro

D0962858

Cliffs
NOTES INC.

Editor	Consulting Editor
Mary Goodwin	*Greg Tubach*

CONTENTS

Analyzing Poetry 5

    The Context of the Poem 5
    The Style 6
    The Title 6
    Repetition 6
    The Opening and Closing Lines 7
    The Passage of Time 7
    The Speaker 7
    Names of Characters 8
    Basic Details 8
    Culture 8
    Fantasy versus Reality 8
    The Mood and Tone 8
    Themes 9
    Rhythm 9
    Use of the Senses 10
    Imagery 10
    Language 10
    Supplemental Materials 11
    Drawing Conclusions 11

Edgar Lee Masters 12

Edward Arlington Robinson 16

Robert Frost 22

Amy Lowell 31

Carl Sandburg 36

Wallace Stevens 41

William Carlos Williams 47

Ezra Pound 53

Hilda Doolittle (H. D.) 60

Robinson Jeffers 66

Marianne Moore 71

T. S. Eliot 75

John Crowe Ransom 83

Edna St. Vincent Millay... 91
Jean Toomer 97
Louise Bogan 102
Hart Crane 107
Allen Tate 115
Sterling Brown... 119
Langston Hughes 124
Countée Cullen.. 131
Elizabeth Bishop 137
John Berryman... 143
Randall Jarrell... 148
Gwendolyn Brooks 154
Robert Lowell 159
Richard Wilbur... 166
James Dickey... 171
Denise Levertov 177
A.R. Ammons 180
Allen Ginsberg... 184
W. S. Merwin 190
James Wright... 195
Anne Sexton 199
Adrienne Rich 206
Sylvia Plath 211
Amiri Baraka... 218
Wendy Rose.. 222
Joy Harjo 225
Rita Dove.. 230
Cathy Song 236
General Bibliography.. 239
Glossary.. 241
Index 245

ANALYZING POETRY

Poetry is a compact language that expresses complex feelings. To understand the multiple meanings of a poem, readers must examine its words and phrasing from the perspectives of rhythm, sound, images, obvious meaning, and implied meaning. Readers then need to organize responses to the verse into a logical, point-by-point explanation. A good beginning involves asking questions that apply to most poetry.

THE CONTEXT OF THE POEM

Clear answers to the following questions can help establish the context of a poem and form the foundation of understanding:

- Who wrote the poem? Does the poet's life suggest any special point of view, such as a political affiliation, religious sect, career interest, musical talent, family or personal problems, travel, or handicap—for example, H. D.'s feminism, Amiri Baraka's radicalism, T. S. Eliot's conversion to Anglicanism, William Carlos Williams' career as a physician, A. R. Ammons' training in chemistry, Amy Lowell's aristocratic background, John Berryman's alcoholism, or Hart Crane's homosexuality?
- When was the poem written and in what country? Knowing something about the poet's life, times, and culture helps readers understand what's in a poem and why.
- Does the poem appear in the original language? If not, readers should consider that translation can alter the language and meaning of a poem.
- Is the poem part of a special collection or series? Examples of such series and collections include Edna St. Vincent Millay's sonnets, Carl Sandburg's Chicago Poems, or Rita Dove's triad, "Adolescence—I, II, and III."
- Does the poem belong to a particular period or literary movement? For example, does the poem relate to imagism, confessional verse, the Beat movement, the Harlem Renaissance, the Civil Rights era, the American Indian renaissance, or feminism?

THE STYLE

Into what category does the poem fit — for example, Carl Sandburg's imagism in "Fog" or Gwendolyn Brooks' epic "The Anniad"? Readers should apply definitions of the many categories to determine which describes the poem's length and style:

- Is it an epic, a long poem about a great person or national hero?
- Is it a lyric, a short, musical verse?
- Is it a narrative, a poem that tells a story?
- Is it a haiku, an intense, lyrical three-line verse of seventeen syllables?
- Is it confessional? For example, does it examine personal memories and experiences?

THE TITLE

- Is the title's meaning obvious? For example, does it mention a single setting and action, such as W. S. Merwin's "The Drunk in the Furnace" or James A. Wright's "Autumn Begins in Martins Ferry, Ohio"?
- Does it imply multiple possibilities? For example, Jean Toomer's "Georgia Dusk," which refers to a time of day as well as to dark-skinned people.
- Does it strike a balance, as in Rita Dove's "Beulah and Thomas"?
- Is there an obvious antithesis, as with Robert Frost's "Fire and Ice"?
- Is there historical significance to the title? For example, Robert Lowell's "The Quaker Graveyard in Nantucket."

REPETITION

Readers should read through a poem several times, at least once aloud. If it is a long poem, such as Allen Ginsberg's *Howl* or Hart Crane's *The Bridge*, readers should concentrate on key passages and look for repetition of specific words, phrases, or verses in the poem.

- Why is there a repeated reference to the sea in Robinson Jeffers's poetry?
- Why does the pronoun "we" recur in Gwendolyn Brooks' "We Real Cool"?
- Why does Edgar Lee Masters reprise epitaphs for *Spoon River Anthology*?

If readers note repetition in the poem, they should decide why certain information seems to deserve the repetition.

THE OPENING AND CLOSING LINES

- Does the poet place significant information or emotion in these places? For example, when reading Marianne Moore's "Poetry," readers may question the negative stance in the opening lines.
- Does the poet intend to leave a lasting impression by closing with a particular thought? For example, why does Langston Hughes' "Harlem" lead to the word "explode"?

THE PASSAGE OF TIME

- Can readers pin down a time frame? What details specify time?
- Does the poet name a particular month or season, as with Amy Lowell's "Patterns"?
- Is there a clear passage of time, as with the decline of the deceased woman in Denise Levertov's "Death in Mexico"?
- How long is the period of time? Are there gaps?

THE SPEAKER

- Who is the speaker? Is the person male or female?
- Does the voice speak in first person (I, me, my, mine), for example, John Berryman's "Huffy Henry"?
- Does the speaker talk directly to a second person, as with Adrienne Rich's "Diving into the Wreck"?
- Is the voice meant to be universal—for example, applicable to either sex at any time or place?

NAMES OF CHARACTERS

- Does the name of a character suggest extra meaning, such as Eben Flood (an alcoholic) in Edwin Arlington Robinson's "Mr. Flood's Party" and T. S. Eliot's prissy protagonist in "The Love Song of J. Alfred Prufrock"?

BASIC DETAILS

- Is the poet deliberately concealing information from the readers, as with the source of depression in Robert Lowell's "Skunk Hour"?
- Why does the poet leave out significant facts? Are readers supposed to fill in the blanks, for example, the relationship between mother and daughter in Cathy Song's "The White Porch" or the perplexity of a modern tourist in Allen Tate's "Ode to the Union Dead"?

CULTURE

- Does the poem stress cultural details, such as the behavior, dress, or speech habits of a particular group or a historical period or event — for instance, the death of an airline stewardess in James Dickey's "Falling"?
- Are any sections written in dialect, slang, or foreign words, as with the Deep South patois of Sterling Brown's "Ma Rainey"?

FANTASY VERSUS REALITY

- Is the poem an obvious fantasy, as is the case with the intense confrontation in Sylvia Plath's "Daddy" and the setting of Rita Dove's "Geometry"?

THE MOOD AND TONE

- What is the mood of the poem? Is it cheerful or jolly like limericks? Is it mysterious, provocative, zany, ominous, festive, fearful, or brooding, as with Randall Jarrell's "Sad Heart at the Supermarket"? Does the mood change within the body of the work, as with Joy Harjo's "The Woman Hanging from the Thirteenth Floor Window"? Why does the mood shift? Where does the shift begin?

- What is the poet's tone? Is it satiric, serious, mock serious, playful, somber, brash, or teasingly humorous, as with Robert Frost's "Departmental: The End of My Ant Jerry"? Does the poet admire, agree with, ridicule, or condemn the speaker, as in the touch of mock heroic in Richard Wilbur's "The Death of a Toad"? Is there an obvious reason for the poet's attitude, as suggested by the suffering in James Dickey's "Angina"? Does the poet withhold judgment, as is the case with the epitaphs of Edgar Lee Masters' *Spoon River Anthology*?

THEMES

Locating and identifying theme is crucial to understanding dominant ideas; theme is the poem's essence.

- Is the subject youth, loss, renewal, patriotism, nature, love? Are there several themes? How do these themes relate to each other?
- Is the poet merely teasing or entertaining or trying to teach a lesson, as do Robinson Jeffers' "Hurt Hawks" and Marianne Moore's "The Mind Is an Enchanted Thing"?
- Does the poet emphasize the theme by means of onomatopoeia, personification, or controlling images?

RHYTHM

- Is there a dominant rhythm? Does it dance, frolic, meander, slither, or march? Is it conversational, like a scene from a drama? Is it a droning monologue, as found in a journal, diary, or confessional?
- Does the rhythm relate to the prevalent theme of the poem? Or does it seem at odds with the theme?
- Does the rhythm increase or decrease in speed, as does Ezra Pound's *Hugh Selwyn Mauberley: Life and Contacts*? Why?

USE OF THE SENSES

- Does the poem stress sense impressions—for example, taste, touch, smell, sound, or sight? Are these impressions pleasant, unpleasant, or neutral?
- Does the poet concentrate on a single sense or a burst of sensation, as in Wallace Stevens's "Peter Quince at the Clavier" or Elizabeth Bishop's "The Fish"?

IMAGERY

- Are there concrete images or pictures that the poet wants readers to see?
- Are the pictures created by means of comparisons—for instance, metaphor or simile? Do inanimate objects take on human traits (personification)? Does the speaker talk to inanimate objects or to such abstract ideas as freedom?

LANGUAGE

- Does the poet stress certain sounds, such as pleasant sounds (euphony) or harsh letter combinations (cacophony), as demonstrated by Wendy Rose's title "Academic Squaw"?
- Are certain sounds repeated (alliteration, sibilance), as in the insistent *a* sounds in Amiri Baraka's "A Poem for Willie Best"?
- Are words linked by approximate rhyme, like "seem/freeze," or by real rhyme, such as "least/feast"? Is there a rhyme scheme or sound pattern at the ends of lines, as with the interlocking rhymes of Robert Frost's "Stopping by Woods on a Snowy Evening"? Does rhyming occur within a line (internal rhyme), as in "black flak" in Randall Jarrell's "The Death of the Ball Turret Gunner"?
- Is there onomatopoeia, or words that make a sound that imitates their meaning, such as swoosh, ping pong, ricochet, clangor, plash, wheeze, clack, boom, tingle, slip, fumble, or clip-clop, as with the verb "soar" in Edna St. Vincent Millay's "On Thought in Harness"?

SUPPLEMENTAL MATERIALS

- Has the editor included any preface, explanatory notes, or concluding comments and questions; for example, T. S. Eliot's dedication of *The Waste Land* or Wendy Rose's use of epigraphs?
- Are there notes and comments in a biography, poet's letters and essays, critical analyses, Web site, or anthology, such as biographical footnotes to Anne Sexton's "Sylvia's Death" and the many commentaries on Hart Crane's *The Bridge*?
- Is there an electronic version, such as the poet reading original verse on the Internet? Are there notes on the record jacket, cassette box, or CD booklet, as found on recordings of Adrienne Rich's feminist verse?

DRAWING CONCLUSIONS

After answering the questions presented in this introduction, readers should paraphrase or restate the poem in everyday words, as though talking to someone on the telephone. A summary of the poem should emphasize a pattern of details, sounds, or rhythm. For example, do various elements of the poem lead readers to believe that the poet is describing an intense experience? Is the poet defining something, such as parenthood, risking a life, curiosity, marriage, religious faith, or aging, as in Denise Levertov's "A Woman Alone"? Is the poet telling a story event by event? Does the poet want to sway the reader's opinion, as Louise Bogan does in "Evening in the Sanitarium"?

Before reaching a conclusion about the meaning of a poem, readers should summarize their personal responses. Are they emotionally moved or touched by the poem? Are they entertained or repulsed, terrified or stirred to agree? Do words and phrases stick in their memory? How has the poet made an impression? And most important, why?

EDGAR LEE MASTERS
(1868–1950)

One of America's most cited poets, Edgar Lee Masters pioneered the psychological character study. A neglected, one-book poet offhandedly admired for his *Spoon River Anthology* (1915), a collection of poetic laments spoken by different characters, he maintained his appeal through repeated anthologizing of his curt, often grimly regretful verse monologues. He is considered a transitional figure at the beginning of the twentieth century who drew on his readings of English Romantic poets, including Wordsworth, Keats, Shelley, and Browning, as well as the Americans Ralph Waldo Emerson and Walt Whitman, for a massive output of essay, drama, novel, biography, and history. Masters, a maverick by nature, refused to be drawn into arguments about criticism and poetic styles of writing. Rather, he consciously chose everyday naturalistic truths over dense poetic complexities.

Masters was a native of Garnett, Kansas, who grew up in Petersburg and Lewistown, Illinois, in grass country near Spoon River. During hard times, the family lived comfortably on handouts of clothing, firewood, apples, and root vegetables from his grandfather's farm, which Masters cherished as an oasis from an unhappy home life. In boyhood, he displayed an interest in publishing by working as a reporter, printer's helper, and storywriter and verse writer for magazines.

Masters struggled to hold on to literature, his heart's aim, as did the figures in the Spoon River cemetery. Masters dutifully read law with his father because his father, disdainful of poetry, insisted that his son study law; he achieved bar certification in 1891. He joined a Chicago law firm allied with attorney Clarence Darrow and specialized in labor and industrial casework. After his marriage to Helen Jenkins, mother of their three children, he often visited Spring Lake, Wisconsin, where he established a sizable farm and he escaped his life as a lawyer.

While successfully pursuing legal work and supporting populist political candidates in Chicago, Masters submitted unoriginal poems to Chicago newspapers. He also published *A Book of Verses* (1889), a derivative work of *belles lettres*, and an anti-war pamphlet, *The Constitution and Our Insular Possessions* (1900), later collected in *The New Star Chamber and Other Essays* (1904). For a decade, he worked on a series of plays, including *Maximilian* (1902), *Althea* (1907), *The Trifler* (1908), *The Leaves of the Tree* (1909), *Eileen* (1910), *The Locket* (1910), and *The Bread of Idleness* (1911). During this time, Masters was acquainted with novelist Theodore Dreiser, editor Harriet Monroe, and poets Amy Lowell, John Masefield, Vachel Lindsay, and Carl Sandburg.

Under the influence of editor William Marion Reedy, Masters gave up artsy poetry and initiated a characteristic style and subject choice that improved with succeeding poems. He produced a collection of self-revelatory verse epitaphs, *Spoon River Anthology*, drawing on settings and ordinary people he remembered from his youth in Lewiston. The work, a landmark American microcosm comprised of free verse satires of former residents of Illinois, appeared under the pseudonym Webster Ford in Reedy's *St. Louis Mirror* from May 1914 to January 1915 before it was published in a stand-alone volume. The cleverly arranged verse soliloquies, naturalistic in their probing of the sterility of village life, earned him the 1916 Levinson Prize and a critical deluge that ranged from the highest praise to outright castigation.

In 1920, two years after the publication of *Toward the Gulf*, a collection of lyrical ballads, Masters abandoned law to become a full-time poet, taking up residence in New York's Chelsea Hotel. A later anthology, *The New Spoon River* (1924), criticized urbanism and helped to bracket the poet into the limited category of caustic satirist ridiculing city life.

In 1926, Masters remarried Ellen F. Coyne and withdrew from the literary circuit. Throughout the 1930s, Masters' various works — such as *Poems of the People* (1936); subsequent prose, including biographies of Abraham Lincoln, Vachel Lindsay, Walt Whitman, and Mark Twain; and an autobiography, *Across Spoon River* (1936)— failed to alter the public perception of him as a dull, ponderous, but essentially courteous curmudgeon. Despite a lack of popularity, Masters continued to publish: A late poetry collection, *Illinois Poems* (1941), contains the title "Petersburg," recapturing a boyhood residence; *The Sangamon* (1942) lauds the beauties of the American Midwest. Masters died in a nursing home in Melrose Park, Pennsylvania, on March 5, 1950. He was buried in nearby Oakland Cemetery. His Petersburg home became a museum.

CHIEF WORKS

In *Spoon River Anthology*, Masters creates a symbol for democracy at the town cemetery when he "buries" long-past residents, such as the town marshal, druggist, physician, and a housewife, side-by-side. Residents like "Elmer, Herman, Bert, Tom, and Charley" lie alongside one unknown person and 245 identified graves on the hill above Spoon River. Their passing, equally egalitarian, juxtaposes fates such as fever and accident with brawling, jail, childbirth, and a suspicious fall from a bridge. The lamentations, griefs, and woes about death give place to a comforting blessing, "All, all are sleeping, sleeping, sleeping on the hill." The narrative concludes with a dramatic epilogue that blends a checker game and Beelzebub's oratory with the reassuring blessing of the sun and Milky Way. To a four-line homily written in old-school puritan moralizing—"Worship thy power, / Conquer thy hour, / Sleep not but strive, / So shalt thou live"—the poet claims the last word: "Infinite Law, / Infinite Life."

"Petit, the Poet" (1915), one of the best of Masters' nonjudgmental epitaphs, speaks the poet's after-death faith in the lines, "Life all around me here in the village." A repetitious craftsman (tick, tick, tick), Petit, named for the smallness of his vision, regrets the "little iambics" of his life's work. To characterize spiritual poverty and poetic tedium, Masters imprisons elegant verse style in a confining "dry pod." To further minimize the "triolets, villanelles, rondels, rondeaus, / Ballades by the score," the simile "like mites in a quarrel" reduces them to ridicule. When his spirit is freed from the outworn snows and roses of Horace and François Villon, Petit is at last able to hear "Homer and Whitman" roaring in the pines.

One of Masters' enduring characterizations of determination, "Lucinda Matlock" (1915) spins a tightly interconnected strand of meeting and marrying her husband and bearing their children. Locked into a pattern of nurturing, Lucinda devotes herself, over a seventy-year marriage, to raising children, nursing, and gardening. Now at age 96, she upbraids the young for their crankiness. Masters typifies Lucinda's prairie-rich philosophy with the oft-quoted aphorism, "It takes life to love Life."

"Doc Hill" is melodramatic compared to the other more restrained confessions in *Spoon River Anthology*. It focuses on the good deeds performed in compensation for a sad home life. Affectionately known as "Doc," the title character has always been afraid to sever his fruitless, disastrous relationships with a spiteful wife and ruined son. Although Masters does not criticize or judge Doc's wife and son, he implies the too-late sorry wisdom of looking out from the grave at the firm devotion of Em Stanton.

Although "Serepta Mason" is in the same vein, it is less successful than "Doc Hill" at expressing regret. Unlike Lucinda Matlock, who ventured out of the village and met new people, Serepta harbors resentment against villagers who saw only her stunted side. The epitaph slips into overblown language with the poet's conclusions about "the unseen forces / That govern the processes of life." More touching is the lament of a historical figure, Anne Rutledge, Abraham Lincoln's beloved, who speaks with the patriotism of Walt Whitman, "Bloom forever, O Republic, / From the dust of my bosom!"

DISCUSSION AND RESEARCH TOPICS

(1) Summarize the range of personal credos in segments of Masters' *Spoon River Anthology*.

(2) Trace evidence of Masters' heartland speech and characterizations in Sherwood Anderson's *Winesburg, Ohio*, Hamlin Garland's *Main-Traveled Roads*, or Sinclair Lewis's *Main Street* or *Babbitt*.

(3) Contrast Masters' Spoon River portraiture with that of Edwin Arlington Robinson's "Richard Cory," "Miniver Cheevy," "Mr. Flood's Party," or "Luke Havergal."

(4) Discuss the absence of meaningful human relationships in Masters' poetry.

SELECTED BIBLIOGRAPHY

MASTERS, EDGAR LEE. *Spoon River Anthology*. New York: Macmillan, 1921.

ZWICK, JIM. "Anti-Imperialist Writings by Edgar Lee Masters." home.ican.net/~fjzwick/masters/

———. "Edgar Lee Masters: *Spoon River Anthology*." www.outfitters. com/illinois/fulton/masters.html

EDWIN ARLINGTON ROBINSON (1869–1935)

The rare poet to succeed critically and financially, Edwin Arlington Robinson rejected the twentieth century's liberalized verse forms. His diverse application of traditional forms to the close-clipped, unconsciously cynical character study distinguished him in an era of rash experimentation. Only Robert Frost surpassed Robinson in Pulitzer Prize-winning volumes. Skilled at creating sustained ironies, Robinson preserved the best in nineteenth-century rationalism and respect for the individual—in particular, losers who cope daily with failure and falter without having attained their full potential. To criticism that his poetry was exceedingly depressing, he cryptically replied, "The world is . . . a kind of spiritual kindergarten, where millions of bewildered infants are trying to spell God with the wrong blocks."

Robinson was born in Head Tide, Maine, on December 22, 1869, and his poetry reflects the tastes and outlook of the New Englanders of Gardiner, where he grew up. A writer from age 11, he excelled at Latin and English. However, in 1893, after two years at Harvard, Robinson no longer had the money to stay in school and returned home to care for his ailing father. Following his father's death and a brother's mismanagement of family funds, he settled among family to write and play his violin and clarinet.

Robinson was distraught after the death of his mother from diphtheria in 1896 and left Maine permanently. He worked briefly at Harvard as a secretary and as a subway agent in New York City, then resettled in Peterborough, New Hampshire, at the MacDowell artist colony, where he stayed until 1935. His self-publication, *The Torrent and the Night Before* (1896), reissued as *The Children of the Night* (1897), demonstrates a gripping, dramatic seriousness, particularly in "Richard Cory" and "Luke Havergal," two of his more frequently anthologized and recited poems. Robinson's blank verse, influenced by his celibacy, agnosticism, binge drinking, and withdrawal from friends, showcases his pervasive distrust of humanity.

A turning point for Robinson occurred with *Captain Craig* (1902), which he wrote while living in midtown Manhattan. The volume found favor with President Theodore Roosevelt, who offered Robinson first a consular post in Mexico, then a job at the

New York Custom House. For four years, Robinson lived in a Greenwich Village townhouse and profited from the undemanding customhouse post, which gave him time to rewrite and refine spare verbal portraits that became his trademark. He served on the Poet's Guild with Robert Frost, Edwin Markham, and Vachel Lindsay and wrote full time from 1910 until his death in 1935.

Robinson, who was influenced by Thomas Hardy's romanticism and the naturalism of Emile Zola, refused to freelance, teach, or otherwise lower his literary standards. While living in Staten Island, New York, he completed two plays, *Van Zorn* (1914) and *The Porcupine* (1915). He lived off an inheritance and trust fund while earning three Pulitzer Prizes for poetry for *Collected Poems* (1922), *The Man Who Died Twice* (1925), and a trilogy, *Lancelot* (1920), *Tristram* (1927), and *Modred* (1929), a popular verse narrative that restates romantic situations from Arthurian lore. In addition, Robinson received acclaim for *The Town Down the River* (1910), which he dedicated to Roosevelt, *The Man Against the Sky* (1916), *The Three Taverns* (1920), source of "Mr. Flood's Party," and the biography of a hate-driven man, *Avon's Harvest* (1921), which the poet once characterized as a "dime novel in verse." In all, he published twenty-eight works.

After his death from stomach cancer at a New York Hospital on April 6, 1935, Robinson was cremated, his ashes interred in Gardiner, and a plaque erected on Church Square commemorating his writings about Tilbury Town. Posthumous works include *King Jasper* (1935), an allegory of the Industrial Age he proofread only hours before his death; an anthology, *Collected Poems*, issued in 1937; and *Selected Letters* (1940), a glimpse into his private, self-concealing correspondence. His papers are housed at the University of New Hampshire.

CHIEF WORKS

A speaker for the dispossessed, Robinson achieved greatness with "Miniver Cheevy" (1910), a frequently anthologized portrait of a shortsighted malcontent, often taken for the poet himself. Like Cliff Klingenhagen, Fleming Helphenstine, and John Evereldown, the name "Miniver," perhaps a combination of "minimum" and "achieve," sets the main character apart from the ordinary

New Englander. The poet selected a complex quatrain stanza with an alternating rhyme scheme that conveys order and control. He overleaps the constraints of a simple four-beat line with lengthenings—"When swords were bright and steeds were prancing"—and ominous shortenings, "Could he have been one."

The autumnal note of longing that anchors the tone of the poem derives from the speaker's sighings for past valor and the distant settings and legendary figures found in classic literature. To Miniver's dismay, the warriors of Troy and Arthurian Camelot give place to the humdrum khaki of modern warfare. Such mundane figures have no place in his extensive fantasies. Lost in daydreams, he accepts fate, foreshadowed by a cough, and embraces alcohol as his only escape.

"Luke Havergal" (1896), a somber, incantatory address, dramatizes a suicidal mood brought on by the loss of a lover. In the poet's words, the poem is "a piece of deliberate degeneration . . . which is not at all funny." The text, composed in iambic pentameter couplets, echoes with double beats spoken by a ghost. The poet creates beautiful lines with a single protracted rhyme in Havergal/ wall/fall/call and skies/eyes/flies/paradise/skies for a rhyme scheme of aabbaaaa. The subject, deprived of his love, faces physical and spiritual oblivion, symbolized by the western gate, which faces the setting sun. Colored with the fall reds of climbing sumac, the wall is the final barrier that separates Luke from death, where he hopes to reunite with his beloved. In lines 20 and 21, the poet states the crux of his dilemma: "Yes, there is yet one way to where she is, / Bitter, but one that faith may never miss." The poem's final line impels Luke to a dread decision with two commands. The second, with some exasperation, orders, "But go!" and observes that trust is the seeker's only hope.

"Richard Cory," a sober piece from the same collection as "Luke Havergal," is a poem filled with implied meanings. The poem's title invests the character with "richness at the core" and makes a connection with Richard the Lion-Hearted. Additional references to a crown, imperial slimness, and glittering step imply that Cory stands out among "We people on the pavement" like a king appearing before his subjects. Characteristic of Cory's situation as separate from everyone else is the necessary separation between royalty and commoner, which, for Cory, symbolizes the desperate solitude of his life.

Robinson chooses a disarmingly simple form for the poem. Composed in iambic pentameter, the four quatrains rhyme abab and come down cleanly on masculine end rhymes — for example, town/him/crown/slim. The transitional "So" in the fourth stanza shifts the poem's focus from Richard Cory to the laboring class, which has its own mundane difficulties. The surprise of suicide achieved by one bullet to the head suits the "calm summer night," which masks the turmoil of Cory's life.

"Eros Tuarannos" (1916) is a complex psychological portrait. At its heart is an obsessive female attracted to a no-good man whom she can't live with but fears living without. Taking its title from the domineering god of sexual love, the poem depicts the woman's "blurred sagacity," a diminished sense of acceptance in taste and behavior. By the end of the third stanza, she achieves a flawed victory and "secures him," the Judas figure. The declining action, epitomized by "The falling leaf," makes its painful downward slide as she comes to grips with illusions. In a home where "passion lived and died," she must admit that she has made her own hell.

An unusual feature in "Eros Tuarannos" is stanza five, which intrudes with a sanctimonious "we," who perceives hard truths about unbalanced marriages. Gliding on with the easeful rhyme scheme of ababccbb, the final stanza distances observer from observed as the rhymes pound out striven/given/driven, a commentary on doom. With a considerable amount of self-satisfaction, the "we" speaker chooses to "do no harm," but to leave the distraught wife to battle the forces she has challenged. As though willing herself to failure, she becomes her own Judas by betraying her finer instincts.

Robinson's most debated title, "Mr. Flood's Party" (1920), is a more generous verse told in gracious lines that lull at the same time that they reveal. The text epitomizes one of Robinson's hard-bitten losers, Eben Flood, and reflects Robinson's firsthand knowledge of two derelict older brothers, one an alcoholic and the other a drug addict. The poem describes a public nuisance who lets drink drive him away from the hospitality and home life that once filled him with hope. Like a mirthful drinker, he hoists his spirits to "the bird . . . on the wing," a suggestion of the state of flux typical of human interactions. Too late "winding a silent horn," he makes empty gestures, like the French epic figure of Roland sounding the alarm when it is too late for rescue. The sounds of the final two stanzas reiterate plaintive oo's and oh's in do, too, moons, loneliness, alone, below, opened, and ago. Well under the influence of a night's drinking, Eben gazes up at a double moon, an emblem of instability and duplicitous face.

The social climate of Tilbury Town in the final four lines is ambiguous. Either Flood is ostracized for carousing or else has outlived old friends and is now an unknown consoling himself with drink. Composed in tight octets linked by masculine end rhymes in a pattern of abcb in conversational iambic pentameter, the poem speaks with third-party knowledge of the events that have estranged Eben from his neighbors. The mellow sot approaches sentimentality by watching over his jug in token of the fact that "most things break." He toasts himself "for auld lang syne" and contemplates the nothingness of no place to return to and no hope for a better future.

DISCUSSION AND RESEARCH TOPICS

(1) Summarize regional touches in Robinson's poems. Compare his insight into New Englanders with that of Robert Lowell, Edna St. Vincent Millay, and Robert Frost.

(2) Contrast the tone and atmosphere of Robinson's "Luke Havergal" with Edgar Allan Poe's "Lenore," "Ulalume," or "Annabel Lee."

(3) Discuss Robinson's characterization of women in "Eros Tuarannos."

(4) Compare Robinson's apparent obsession with losers to that of novelists Edith Wharton and John Steinbeck.

(5) Compare Robinson and Edgar Lee Masters in the use of somber tone.

SELECTED BIBLIOGRAPHY

"Children of the Night." www.mirrors.org.sg/pg/etext95/chnit10.txt

"Edwin Arlington Robinson." *Contemporary Authors.* Gale Research. galenet.gale.com

"Edwin Arlington Robinson." tqd.advanced.org/2847/authors/robinson.htm

"Edwin Arlington Robinson." wwwsc.library.unh.edu/specoll-mancoll.robinson.htm

PARISH, JOHN E. "The Rehabilitation of Eben Flood." *English Journal* (September 1966): 696-699.

ROBINSON, EDWIN ARLINGTON. *Tilbury Town.* New York: Macmillan, 1953.

UNTERMEYER, LOUIS. "E. A. R.: A Remembrance." *Saturday Review,* April 10, 1965, 33–34.

ROBERT FROST (1874–1963)

Robert Lee Frost, New England's cherished poet, has been called America's purest classical lyricist and one of the outstanding poets of the twentieth century. Although he is forever linked to the stone-pocked hills and woods of New England, he was born in San Francisco, California, on March 26, 1874. His parents, school headmaster William Prescott Frost and teacher Margaret Isabelle Moodie, had left New England because of post–Civil War politics. After his father's death from alcohol abuse and tuberculosis in May 1885, Isabelle, accompanied by her son and newborn daughter, Jeanie, returned the body to his New England home in Lawrence, Massachusetts, and remained in the East because she lacked the money to return to San Francisco.

Educated at Lawrence High School, Frost thrived in English and Latin classes and discovered a common thread in Virgil's poetry and the romantic balladry of his Scottish ancestors. His grandfather enticed him to enter pre-law at Dartmouth in 1892, but Frost ended any hope of a legal career in the first months. His first published work, "My Butterfly: An Elegy" (1894), earned him a check from the *New York Independent* and precipitated a self-published collection, *Twilight* (1894). He married Elinor Miriam White, his high school sweetheart, in 1895, and dedicated himself to poetry.

Frost sought further education in Harvard's classics department and, in 1898, joined his mother as a teacher at her private school. When symptoms of consumption necessitated a move to the country, he situated his family on a poultry farm in Derry, New Hampshire, purchased by his grandfather. Frost did little during a six-month depression that resulted from his son Elliott's death from cholera and his mother's hospitalization with cancer. At the farm he kept hens, a cow, and a horse, and established a garden and orchard; ultimately, the farm rejuvenated him. But Frost never profited from his labor and suffered annually from hay fever.

From 1900 to 1905, while scrimping along on a $500 annuity from his grandfather's will, Frost produced bucolic verse that enlarged on his experiences with Yankee gentry. Simultaneously, he worked at cobbling shoes, farming, and editing the *Lawrence Sentinel*. A failure at farming, for the next six years he supported his family by teaching at the nearby Pinkerton Academy before moving to Plymouth, New Hampshire, to teach education and psychology at the State Normal School.

To achieve his original goal of writing serious poetry, Frost, at his wife's suggestion, gambled on a break with the past. In 1912, he sold the farm and used the money to move to England. During a three-year self-imposed exile in Beaconsfield, Buckinghamshire, he scraped for cash. He came under the influence of poet Rupert Brooke and published *A Boy's Will* (1913), followed by the solidly successful *North of Boston* (1914), which contains "Mending Wall," "The Death of the Hired Man," "Home Burial," and "After Apple-Picking."

Frost returned to the United States on borrowed funds at the beginning of World War I. He settled in Franconia, New Hampshire, where he soaked up New England culture. Seated in his Morris chair with his lapboard in place, the farmer-poet looked out on the New England landscape as he wrote *Mountain Interval* (1916) and the beginnings of *New Hampshire: A Poem with Notes and Grace Notes* (1923), which contains "Fire and Ice" and "Stopping by Woods on a Snowy Evening," an American masterwork. Because he was newly popular on the commercial market, Frost violated his seclusion in New England to serve as his own agent and fan club to keep himself financially afloat.

A distinguished new literary voice and member of the National Institute of Arts and Letters, Frost found himself in demand and began giving readings across the United States. He served the University of Michigan as poet in residence and was honored with the title Fellow in Letters at both Harvard and Dartmouth. In addition to one drama, *A Way Out* (1929), he steadily contributed to the New England poetic canon with *West-Running Brook* (1928), *A Further Range* (1936), *A Witness Tree* (1942), *A Masque of Reason* (1945), *Steeple Bush* (1947), *A Masque of Mercy* (1947), *How Not to Be King* (1951), and *And All We Call American* (1958).

Frost's works found favor with readers worldwide. He won the Pulitzer Prize for poetry in 1924 and again in 1931, 1937, and 1943, a sad series of years that saw the deaths of his sister Jeanie in a mental institution, his favorite daughter Marjorie of puerperal fever, his wife Elinor from heart disease, and his son Carol, who committed suicide with a deer rifle. In addition to receiving a gold medal and membership from the American Academy of Arts and

Letters, the United States Senate accorded Frost a citation of honor in 1950, and Vermont named a mountain for him. In his declining years, he wintered in Florida. In 1948, he returned to Amherst, where he lived until his death from a pulmonary embolism on January 29, 1963. He was eulogized at Amherst's Johnson Chapel, where his ashes were buried in the family plot in June of 1963.

CHIEF WORKS

"The Pasture," published in 1913, displays Frost's first-person amiability as well as his delight in a homeowner's country chores. In familiar farm surroundings, he speaks from the farmer's point of view in an easy iambic pentameter. His diction, containing seven contractions in eight lines, is the simple wording of an ordinary, earth-centered fellow. The pattern of masculine end-sounds, rhyming abbc deec, is characteristic of Frost, who ties the relaxed, confident quatrains together with a disarmingly uncomplicated repetition and rhyme.

In identical meter but without rhyme, "Mending Wall," written in 1914 after Frost's visit to the Scottish highlands, ventures beyond mundane observation to muse over the effects of stone boundaries on relationships. In neighborly fashion, the speaker joins a next-door landowner (identified as Frost's French-Canadian neighbor, Napoleon Guy) at an appointed time to "walk the line," a seasonal chore that calls for repairing the damage to the land by rabbit hunters and winter heaving—the alternate freezing and thawing above the frost line. The reference to the inevitability of destruction alludes to Matthew 24:2 ("There shall not be left here one stone upon another, that shall not be thrown down"), Christ's prophecy that Herod's temple in Jerusalem will eventually fall.

In an offhand parable, the speaker mischievously challenges a prevailing attitude toward neat divisions, expressed in the home-spun revelation that "Good fences make good neighbors." To the speaker's way of thinking, an orchard poses no hazard to a pine woodlot, but the neighbor persists in the tradition of replenishing fallen stones. The forceful action suggests that tradition is an adversary not easily overthrown.

"Home Burial," written in 1914, presents an engrossing, intensely empathetic scenario. The title suggests both a home graveyard and a household buried in unrequited grief. In the action, a perplexed husband asks his wife to "let me into your grief," perhaps a reference to Elinor Frost's devastation at the death of son Elliott. In the poem's fictional setting, the husband responds to his mournful wife's inability to cope with the death of their child by putting up a false cover of business as usual. Departing the confines of blank verse through extensive enjambment, the carry-over lines and double caesuras ["-how could you?-"] press the poem's two main characters into a halting, real-life confrontation. Added to this personal drama is the couple's view through the upstairs window of a fresh burial plot that stands out among older gravestones. The husband, who resents his wife's refusal to share her suffering with him, defuses a confrontation by sitting at the top of the stairs while his wife frowns her disapproval.

To buoy his 116-line poem, Frost elaborates on the husband's and wife's motivations for their behavior. At the heart of the domestic confrontation is the indelicate word "rot," which the husband, carelessly utters after digging an infant-sized grave. The wife, named "Amy" (from the Latin word for love), uses her emotions about her child's death as a weapon against her husband—and, ironically, against herself. Given to stiff-necked silence and withdrawal, she threatens to abandon him in order to escape their separate emotional difficulties in dealing with death. The pacing refuses to drop to a mutually satisfying resolution as the husband, whose muscular hand dug the hole and mounded the gravel, resorts to force if need be to keep his marriage from disintegration and public shame. The realism of harsh words hanging in the air suggests a situation that Frost had witnessed or been party to—perhaps his own troubled marriage to a tight-lipped woman or an anticipation of the marital difficulties of his daughters.

"The Death of the Hired Man," also written in 1914, pits wife and husband in a confrontation over infirmity and self-esteem. As Mary and Warren tiptoe around a touchy subject—old Silas' return to the farm on the pretense of performing short-term labor—they debate indirectly the same question of values that fuels "Home Burial." Mary, who shelters tender feelings, wants Warren to lower his voice to spare Silas the insult of Warren's disdain for him. As for the question of having Silas ditch the meadow, an unnecessary task, Mary assures Warren that the ruse is a "humble way to save [Silas'] self-respect."

The couple's low-key debate featuring the dynamics of feminine mode versus masculine mode resurrects the confrontation between actively doing and passively existing. Like the husband in "Home Burial," Warren is a doer. His physicality clashes on prickly occasions when he can't see the logic in merely being a friend to Silas. The opposite of Warren is Mary, who recognizes that Silas feels outclassed by Harold Wilson, the self-important collegian, whose academic accomplishments outrank Silas' skill in bunching hay into "big birds' nests." At the crux of the confrontation, Mary speaks Frost's most beloved aphorism: "Home is the place where, when you have to go there, / They have to take you in."

The homely, almost stumbling cadence conceals the altruism of Mary's gift of grace. Lest the reader doubt Frost's poetic thrust, he ends with three linked images—"the moon, the little silver cloud, and she"—a metaphorical preface to Warren's squeeze on the hand and somber announcement that Silas has died.

Another of Frost's contemplative literary moments illumines "The Road Not Taken," a teasing conundrum written in 1916, when the poet was trying to succeed at farming and publishing. This somewhat stoic poem, characterizing a momentous, life-altering resolution, profits from the poet's blend of delight and wisdom. The speaker recalls once choosing one of two forks in a road through the woods. Settling for the less-worn fork, the traveler notes, with some regret, that normal momentum would cause him to press ahead, thus negating a return trip to try the other path.

The poem stops shy of dramatizing the speaker's choice of which road to take. Frost deliberately hedges on the speaker's emotion by whittling down differences in the two roads with "just as fair," "perhaps," and "about the same." Anticipating nostalgia over missed chances, the speaker acknowledges that the morning's decision "has made all the difference" but leaves the reader with no tangible clue to an interpretation, good or bad.

In "Birches," a fanciful monologue, the poem's speaker expresses a Twain-like nostalgia for carefree boyhood and tree-climbing. The 59-line poem triggers a memory—bent trees jog the poet's recall of a boy's mischievous but normal pastime. Indulging in digression, the speaker notes that ice storms have the same effect on birches and that the glass-like shards falling on the ground below suggest the shattering of heaven's crystal dome, a symbol of divine perfection. Restored to the original train of thought after "Truth broke in / With all her matter of fact," the speaker returns to reliving boyhood in the country, where a skilled birch-bender could subdue trees with the same care as a hand requires to fill a cup to the brim without spilling.

The philosophical gist of "Birches" begins in line 41, where the speaker identifies himself as a rural lad given to birch-bending. Now burdened with frustration characterized as a walk in a "pathless wood," a cobweb tickling the face, and a tearing eye that has met the lash of a limb, the speaker remains in the land of metaphor by envisioning an escape. To avoid an adulthood "weary of considerations," he pictures a respite—a swing outward from reality. Accentuating his point is the italicized word "Toward," which reminds the reader that the speaker isn't ready for heaven. Earth is his true home. Even with everyday miseries, being earthbound in "the right place for love" suits human nature.

In 1923, at the height of his appeal, Frost composed "Stopping by Woods on a Snowy Evening," one of America's most memorized poetic treasures. He wrote it about an early period of personal frustration and considered it his "best bid for remembrance." The rhyme scheme—aaba, bbcb, ccdc, dddd, like that in "The Pasture"—couples a flow of action and thought over four stanzas, ending in a gently repetitive refrain. Restful and placid, the action of watching woods being covered with snow is elusively simple. This simplicity is reinforced by the graceful yoking of tactile, auditory, and visual imagery with euphonious, drowsy *-eep* sounds in sweep, deep, keep, and sleep, and alliterated *l* sounds in lovely, sleep, and miles.

Dramatically, the poem builds to a climax and then makes its way down to resolution. At its heart, line 8 implies a tension: Is this the "darkest evening of the year" because it is December 22, the winter solstice, or because of some emotional turmoil in the viewer's spirit? Is the poem a veiled death wish? Whatever the reader's interpretation, the speaker reassures that a stock-still moment of contemplation of the "dark and deep" is normal and up-lifting, for the figure decides to continue toward a preset goal or destination.

Note that the title contains the pun "evening," which means both post-sunset hours and a balancing or leveling. December 22, the shortest day of the year, is a traditional folk holiday that cele-brates the equalizing of day and night. Beginning on December 23, winter begins its annual decline and days get longer as the seasons shift toward spring. After the speaker's pause, the morbid lure of snow-decked woods returns to an emotional balance as melan-choly gives place to jangling harness bells and mental demands of "miles to go," which could refer to physical miles or unfinished tasks or responsibilities to family or job. The end of the ambiguous couplet, "before I sleep," could preface a night's rest or an eternal sleep—death—that concludes a satisfyingly challenged life.

"Departmental: The End of My Ant Jerry" is a verse animal fa-ble. Composed by Frost when he was 62 years old, the poem takes its title from Rudyard Kipling's "Departmental Ditties" and demon-strates a blend of tweakish humor and mock-heroic form. The comic eulogy lauds the "selfless forager" in intentionally inept rhyme and a truncated rhythm that limps along in mockery of staid Homeric epic style. The elevation of Jerry, a victim of bu-reaucratic bumblers, visualizes him lying in state—embalmed in ichor and enshrouded in a petal—in the state's ennobling gesture to his role as citizen. Rigidly formal in style and protocol, the poem establishes the city's soullessness as the twiddly funeral director completes the ceremony in a semblance of decorum.

DISCUSSION AND RESEARCH TOPICS

(1) Apply Frost's vision of childhood in "Birches" to the realistic details of Edna St. Vincent Millay's "Sonnets from an Ungrafted Tree." Then determine how retrospect clouds the speaker's memory of the loneliness of a country boy living too far from town to play baseball, but how, in his isolation, he made a one-person game of swinging on trees.

(2) Analyze the complex shift from strict pentameter in Frost's "Fire and Ice." Contrast the compression of lines, rhymes, and enjambment with the more leisurely vernacular of the verse dramas "The Death of the Hired Man" and "Home Burial."

(3) Determine why the patriotism and dynamics of "The Gift Outright" suited the stirring public occasion of John F. Kennedy's January 1961 presidential inauguration. Select other appropriate works of Frost's canon that would ennoble a formal state occasion.

(4) Contrast the quirky logic of Frost's "Departmental: The End of My Ant Jerry" with the straightforward contemplation of death in "Out, Out-" and "Fire and Ice." Compare Frost's style of humor with that of Ogden Nash, Dorothy Parker, James Thurber, Cornelia Otis Skinner, or Edward Lear.

(5) Discuss the husband and wife's relationship in "Home Burial." Is one character more at fault than the other for the couple's inability to communicate meaningfully?

SELECTED BIBLIOGRAPHY

BURNSHAW, STANLEY. *Robert Frost Himself*. New York: George Braziller, 1986.

FROST, ROBERT. *Collected Poems, Prose, & Plays*. New York: Literary Classics, 1995.

MAXSON, H. A. *On the Sonnets of Robert Frost: A Critical Examination*. Jefferson, N. C.: McFarland, 1997.

MEYERS, JEFFREY. *Robert Frost: A Biography*. Boston: Houghton Mifflin, 1996.

MORRISON, KATHLEEN. *Robert Frost: A Pictorial Chronicle*. New York: Holt, Rinehart & Winston, 1974.

SKOW, JOHN. "The Roads Taken." *Time,* August 12, 1974, 74.

THOMPSON, LAWRANCE, and R. H. WINNICK. *Robert Frost, the Later Years, 1938–1963.* New York: Holt, Rinehart & Winston, 1976.

———. *Robert Frost, the Years of Triumph, 1915–1938.* New York: Holt, Rinehart & Winston, 1970.

———, eds. *Selected Letters of Robert Frost.* New York: Holt, Rinehart and Winston, 1964.

UNGER, LEONARD, ed. *Seven Modern American Poets.* Minneapolis: University of Minnesota Press, 1967.

WALSH, JOHN EVANGELIST. *Into My Own: The English Years of Robert Frost.* New York: Grove Press, 1988.

AMY LOWELL (1874–1925)

Noted modernist and imagist Amy Lawrence Lowell was a consummate lecturer and conversationalist, as well as a joker and friend-maker among the great literary figures of her day. She enhanced her promotion of imagism as a viable alternative to traditional forms with the composition of over 600 poems. The sheer volume of verse mars her canon by the inclusion of mediocre works among such masterpieces as "Patterns" and "The Sisters," a defense of female artistry. Until feminist criticism defended her place among early-twentieth-century poets, she was largely neglected, in part because homophobic critics rejected her bisexual and lesbian views on human relationships.

Amy Lowell was one of the prestigious Massachusetts Lowells and was a relative of James Russell Lowell, the first editor of *Atlantic Monthly*. She was born on February 9, 1874, in Brookline to aristocratic parents, Katherine Bigelow Lawrence and Augustus Lowell. Lowell's mother tutored and educated her, and she completed a basic education at private schools in Boston and Brookline. Much of her learning derived from self-directed reading in the family's vast library. At age 13, to aid a charity, she published a volume of juvenilia, *Dream Drops, or Stories from Fairyland* (1887), a token of the late-blooming artistry yet to emerge.

Lowell traveled across Europe before settling in the family manor, Sevenels, in 1903. Lowell published her first sonnet, "A Fixed Idea," in *Atlantic Monthly* in 1910, followed by three more submissions and the translation of a play by Alfred de Musset, staged at a Boston theater.

Acclaimed for Keatsian verse in *A Dome of Many-Colored Glass* (1912), Lowell stopped mimicking other poets' styles in 1914 and developed an independent voice, in part influenced by Ezra Pound, H. D., Robert Frost, D. H. Lawrence, and Harriet Monroe, editor of *Poetry: A Magazine of Verse*. Following positive reception of her experimental "polyphonic prose," her term for free verse, in *Sword Blades and Poppy Seeds* (1914), she published in *The Bookman*, a respected New York monthly, and edited *Some Imagist Poets, 1915–1917* (1917). A landmark work that sets the parameters of imagism, *Some Imagist Poets* names six requisites for imagism:

- To employ common language that is precisely suited to the phrase
- To search out new rhythms to express new moods
- To welcome all subjects to the field of topics
- To quell vagueness with exact images
- To produce hard, clear verse free of confusion and distortion
- To compress thought as though distilling the essence of meaning

Lowell's own output in the new poetry genre of imagism included *Men, Women and Ghosts* (1916), *Can Grande's Castle* (1918), *Pictures of the Floating World* (1919), which contains some of her best short works, and *Legends* (1921), a critically successful collection of narrative verse.

Lowell earned a reputation for violating conservative standards by flaunting her obesity, swearing, smoking cigars, and having a same-sex lover, actress Ada Dwyer Russell, with whom Lowell remained all her life. In addition to poetry, she published translations in *Six French Poets: Studies in Contemporary Literature* (1915), collected critical essays in *Tendencies in Modern American Poetry* (1917) and satire in *A Critical Fable* (1922), a reprise of *Fable for Critics*, written by her illustrious New England ancestor, James Russell Lowell. For *Fir-Flower Tablets* (1921), a detailed collection of miniatures, she joined Florence Ayscough to translate Chinese verse into "chinoiseries," restatements of Asian idiom in English.

During a period when she experienced eye strain and glandular imbalance, Lowell labored on a two-volume centennial biography, *John Keats* (1925). A substantial contribution to English criticism, the work began as a Yale address and flowered into exhaustive research. Historians blame the rigor of the insightful study for Lowell's sudden death from cerebral hemorrhage on May 12, 1925, in Brookline. She was buried at Mount Auburn Cemetery. Her posthumous volumes include *What's O'Clock* (1925), which earned a Pulitzer Prize for poetry, *East Wind* (1926), *Ballads for Sale* (1927), *Poetry and Poets* (1930), and *Complete Poetical Works* (1955).

CHIEF WORKS

In 1916, Lowell published her masterwork, "Patterns," a tense, almost frenzied free verse minidrama spoken in first person. The speaker, traumatized by the news that her fiancé has been killed in combat, attends a formal dance. Dressed in the constrictive gown, powdered wig, and jeweled fan of the eighteenth century, she contrasts the natural colors and configurations of daffodils and squills, bulbs that flower in spring. Tears sprung from pent-up emotions parallel the silent shedding of blossoms from a lime tree.

In the poem's second stanza, the poet enlarges the dual droplets to include a parallel "plashing of waterdrops / In the marble fountain," a rhythmic "dripping [that] never stops," symbolic of the grief she will never escape. As though casting off the constraints of fashion and social propriety, she fantasizes about meeting her lover among the hedges. By supplanting a silver and pink gown with the flesh hues of her own body, she envisions a passionate chase in which the man, graced by reflected light from "sword-hilt and buckles," stumbles after her as though held back by the trappings of military rank. At the climax, complex interweavings of grief and dreamlike seduction are emotionally too much for the speaker to handle, threatening in line 57 to overwhelm the dreamer.

Lowell develops the narrative with romantic plotting in lines 60 through 71. After receiving a standard wartime communication, the speaker begins a rhythmic pacing, replicated in the juxtaposition of short and long lines. Stiffly clad in "correct brocade," she sees herself upright among the blooms. To dramatize loss, she relives the blessing of sunlight, rhyming "And I answered, 'It shall be as you have said.' / Now he is dead."

Line 91 retreats from past and present to predict the flow of seasons, each with its characteristic flowers and weather. Locked in a prim celibacy, the speaker regrets that war has negated passion. The closing couplet, suited to the charged atmosphere of tumbling emotions, crackles with defiance of the feminine role of mourner and the masculine world that wastes good men in war.

"Madonna of the Evening Flowers," set at Sevenels and composed in honor of Ada Russell in 1919, is an opulent piece that displays Lowell's deft verbal abilities. The three-part text moves from simple description to sensuous impressionism. Composed in un-rhymed cadence, it draws energy from visual profusion, including oak leaves feathered by the wind and late afternoon sun reflected off mundane objects—books, scissors, and a thimble. From an unassuming domestic still life, the central stanza follows the seeker into a religious vision sanctified by the pure heart of the unnamed "you." Color and sound mount into a surreal chiming of bell-shaped garden flowers, which enrich the holy setting with connections between their common name, Canterbury bells, with the cathedral and shrine in southeastern England.

The final stanza injects a playful note of miscommunication. The speaker, who stands transfixed by mystic thoughts, discounts the gardener's mission to assess growth, spray, and prune. Enraptured in wonder, the speaker shuts out sounds to absorb the aura of the gardener, whom the steepled larkspur transforms into the Virgin Mary, traditionally clad in blue as a symbol of devotion. Lowell concludes the poem with a kinesthetic gesture by turning sight into sound; the color and shape of the bell-blossoms evolve into an organ swell, a traditional anthem, a Te Deum ([We praise] thee, God) of worship and adoration.

Similarly majestic, "Venus Transiens" [Venus Crossing Over] (1919), replete with Renaissance awe at female grace, derives its title and drama from Sandro Botticelli's painting depicting Venus rising from the sea, a mythic birth of beauty out of sea foam. Again, Lowell wreathes her subject in silver and blue, colors that reflect the light of sea and sky. The sands on which the speaker stands anchor her to the real world while the waves and sky uplift her beloved to a sublime, exalted state. The viewer stands apart from subject, as though the human element is permanently distanced from the divine.

DISCUSSION AND RESEARCH TOPICS

(1) Compare Amy Lowell's praise of female beauty with that of Wordsworth, Byron, Keats, and the Pre-Raphaelites.

(2) Refute Amy Lowell's statement in "The Sisters" that women who write poetry are "a queer lot." Comment on her choice of Sappho and Elizabeth Barrett Browning as models.

(3) Apply Amy Lowell's six precepts of imagism to her poems "Lilacs" and "Night Clouds" as well as to the works of three American imagists: H. D.'s "Lais" or "Heat," e. e. cummings's "Buffalo Bill's," "in Just-," or "i was considering how," and William Carlos Williams' "Nantucket" or "Flowers by the Sea." Determine which works fit the constraints without compromising lyricism and aesthetic grace.

(4) Discuss the role of fantasy in Amy Lowell's poetry.

SELECTED BIBLIOGRAPHY

"Amy Lowell." www.aristotle.net/~sehudnall/amylowell.htm

"Amy Lowell." *Contemporary Authors.* Gale Research. galenet.gale.com

DAVIDSON, CATHY N., and LINDA WAGNER-MARTIN. "Amy Lowell." *The Oxford Companion to Women's Writing in the United States.* New York: Oxford University Press, 1995.

CARL SANDBURG (1878–1967)

Acclaimed America's people's poet, Carl August Sandburg spoke directly and compellingly of the worker, a vigorous, enduring composite character who embodied Sandburg's free-verse portraits of democracy's inhabitants. Some audiences were bowled over by Sandburg's engagingly slangy phrasing and shadowy figures; the poet's massive correspondence linked him to the personalities of his day, including socialist Lincoln Steffens, actor Gary Cooper, President Lyndon Johnson, and editor Harry Golden, Sandburg's traveling buddy. Others, like Robert Frost, were repulsed by Sandburg's folksy affectation. Frost once described his contemporary as "the most artificial and studied ruffian the world has had." The description was not without merit.

Sandburg was born of Swedish ancestry in Galesburg, Illinois, on January 6, 1878. He was the son of a semiliterate laborer, rail blacksmith August Johnson, and Clara Anderson. His family chose the name Sandburg to separate them from a confusing neighborhood of Johnsons. Sandburg later boasted of the bold X that served his immigrant father as an honorable signature.

A restless vagabond, Sandburg ended formal schooling and his job as morning milk deliverer at age 13 to take other hands-on jobs, including bootblack, newsboy, hod carrier, kitchen drudge, potter's and painter's assistant, iceman, and porter at Galesburg's Union Hotel barbershop. For four months in 1897, he traveled the railroads and washed dishes at various hotels. After a brief residency at West Point in 1899, Private Charlie Sandburg fought for eight months in Puerto Rico with the Sixth Regiment of the Illinois Volunteers during the Spanish-American War. With the encouragement of an army comrade, he attended Lombard College for four years but quit before receiving a degree.

Sandburg was fortunate in gaining the support of Philip Green Wright, an English professor who printed Sandburg's first poetry collection, *In Reckless Ecstasy* (1904), on a basement press. In Milwaukee in 1907, while organizing the Wisconsin Social Democrat Party, Sandburg met Lillian "Paula" Steichen, his mate of nearly sixty years and mother of their daughters, Janet, Margaret, and Helga. During the period known as the Chicago Renaissance, he was secretary to Emil Seidel, Milwaukee's first socialist mayor, and then he took various writing jobs. During World War I, Sandburg served the Newspaper Enterprise Associates as Stockholm correspondent. Upon return, he wrote editorials for the Chicago *Daily News* and settled on Lake Michigan in Harbert, east of Chicago, and, in 1919, in Elmhurst.

Sandburg published his famous "Chicago" in 1914 in *Poetry: A Magazine of Verse*, and produced pulsing, realistic verse set in America's urban industrial complex, which he idealized as a brusque, up-and-coming national treasure. His steady outpouring—*Chicago Poems* (1916), *Corn Huskers* (1918), *Smoke and Steel* (1920), *Slabs of the Sunburnt West* (1922), *Good Morning, America* (1928), and *The People, Yes* (1936), which lauds the vigorous folk hero Pecos Bill—resulted in *Complete Poems* (1950), winner of the 1951 Pulitzer Prize for poetry. In addition, he staked out new territory with a cross-cultural collection of folk ballads, *The American Songbag* (1927). The work derives from his voice-and-guitar platform presentations. He also published a polemical memoir, *The Chicago Race Riots* (1919), three children's stories—*Rootabaga Stories* (1922), *Rootabaga Pigeon* (1923), and *Potato Face* (1930)—and an American saga, *Remembrance Rock* (1948), his only novel.

Sandburg was a lifelong collector of Lincolniana. He was living at Chickaming Goat Farm in Harbert while lecturing, collaborating with P. M. Engle on *Mary Lincoln: Wife and Widow* (1932), and completing a six-volume *Life of Abraham Lincoln*, composed of the two-part *The Prairie Years* (1926) and the four-part *The War Years* (1939). The work was a solid success, acquiring instant readership and universal admiration, and it won him the 1940 Pulitzer Prize for history and the Saturday Review of Literature award in history and biography. After numerous summers of touring to earn ready cash with recitations and folk songs plucked out on his banjo and guitar, Sandburg's last years brought the secure notoriety of the people's poet. He published memoirs of his coming of age in *Always the Young Strangers* (1953).

Following a crippling seizure in 1965, Sandburg inaccurately predicted that he would survive to a year divisible by eleven. He was bedridden his last two years, and he relied on his wife as spokesperson until his death at home from a second heart attack on July 22, 1967. He was eulogized at the nearby St. John in the Wilderness Episcopal Church; his and Paula's ashes are buried in Galesburg beneath Remembrance Rock.

CHIEF WORKS

Sandburg's poem "Chicago" is self-consciously artless—a brash, assertive statement of place. In 1914, the poem thrust him into national prominence as a modernist poet and image-maker for the laboring class. A rambunctious portrait of a flourishing urban center, the poem makes a vigorous proletarian thrust with its initial images of a butcher, tool maker, harvester, and freight handler. Outside the pre-modern niceties of predictable line lengths and rhyme, the poet ignores scholars and entrepreneurs as he surges toward the city skyline. With crudely forceful, startling figures, he mines the verbal subsoil for the source of Chicago's raw energy and steadying optimism. He applauds its ample frame, personified as a muscular, essentially male pair of shoulders, but balances his realistic assessment by chastising the urban penchant for vice and crime.

As though addressing an individual, Sandburg personifies the city as a brutal depriver of women and children, who perform a lesser role as victims dependent on man-sized protection and support. He confronts the attacker who would vilify his "alive," "coarse," "strong," and "cunning" city, a "tall bold slugger" of a metropolis. The forces that undergird Chicago's permanence founder on the edge of honesty and respectability, implying that too much gentility saps a growing nation, depriving it of the underworld heft essential to progress. To further the image of growth, the poet piles up present participles, beginning with a dog lapping and moving briskly through "building, breaking, rebuilding." With a return to the opening stanza, Sandburg repeats the skills of the burly, uncompromising city, the sources of its might. By its nature, the poem itself becomes one of the enduring homegrown products of America's "second city."

A persistent contrast to "Chicago" is "Fog" (1916), which is often a companion piece in anthologies. An American haiku, the poem captures a phenomenon of nature in a second natural image. A feral image of sinuous grace, the diminutive cat shape perches over the skyline before soundlessly creeping away. The silky presence relieves the gathering fog of menace as it unifies the harbor and city streets under one silent, soft-furred cloud. Simple, yet rich in brooding, elusive mysticism, the figure compels the reader to draw conclusions from personal experience with both fog and cats.

In 1918, at the end of World War I, Sandburg produced "Grass," a savagely realistic, calm poem, more heavily symbolic and less spontaneous than his imagist verse. A familiar theme in world literature, the idea of creeping cemetery grass uniting all wars dates to ancient Mediterranean verse. By speaking through the persona of grass, Sandburg captures the impersonal work of nature: the vivid green blades conceal from passersby the destruction of three wars—Napoleonic battles, the American Civil War, and World War I. By naming cities forever linked to carnage, Sandburg reminds the reader that, once inflicted on humanity, war leaves an indelible history as grass reclaims battle grounds and turns them into burial places. Although veiled by spreading root structure, the events remain in memory, a prologue to subsequent wars.

DISCUSSION AND RESEARCH TOPICS

(1) Characterize the sturdy American figures in Sandburg's "I Am the People, the Mob," "Psalm of Those Who Go Forth Before Daylight," and "Chicago," with the New Englanders in Robert Frost's poems, Chicagoans in Gwendolyn Brooks' ghetto pictures, Harlemites in Langston Hughes' poems, and Midwesterners in Edgar Lee Masters' *Spoon River Anthology.*

(2) Analyze the imagism of Frost's "Grass" or "Fog," H. D.'s "Pear Tree," and William Carlos Williams' "Red Wheelbarrow." Determine which of the verses depends most heavily on sense impressions.

(3) Contrast "Chicago" and "Fog" in terms of nature images. Which of the two poems ends more jubilantly?

(4) How is Sandburg's "Grass" more realistic than his other poems?

SELECTED BIBLIOGRAPHY

"American Troubadour." *Time,* July 28, 1967, 68.

GOLDEN, HARRY. "Carl's Letters." *Charlotte Observer,* 29 September 1968, 6F.

———. "Golden's Sandburg." *Charlotte Observer,* 23 July 1967, 6B.

MITGANG, HERBERT. "Carl Sandburg." *Saturday Review,* 12 August 1967, 18–19.

SANDBURG, CARL. *The Letters of Carl Sandburg.* New York: Harcourt, Brace & World, 1968.

STEIN, RITA. *A Literary Tour Guide to the United States: South and Southwest.* New York: William Morrow, 1979.

WEEKS, BILL. "Poet's Mountain Home Unique." *Charlotte Observer,* 4 October 1998, 7G.

WALLACE STEVENS
(1879-1955)

Wallace Stevens was the literary anomaly—the rather humdrum insurance company executive who, with the publication of a single volume, *Harmonium*, rose to dominance among American aesthetes, the seekers of beauty in art. Pervasive in his shimmering lines are a naturalism and awe that overstep the pessimism that stymied the post–World War I generation. Long into his career, his officemates were surprised to learn that "Wally" was capable of writing such lush, elegantly textured poems, but the critical world had long ranked his verse within the growing modernist canon. Stevens earned respect from literary colleagues for whimsical ironies, skepticism, and the sensuous, ever-shifting intricacy of his vision.

Stevens was born in Reading, Pennsylvania, on October 2, 1879, the son of teacher Margaretha Catherine Zeller and attorney Garrett Barcalow Stevens. He studied privately at St. John's Evangelical Lutheran parochial school before entering high school, where he excelled at oratory and classics and wrote for the school newspaper. During three years at Harvard, 1897 to 1900, he contributed to the *Harvard Advocate* and edited the *Harvard Monthly*. He initiated an unsuccessful career in journalism at the *New York Tribune* before enrolling at New York Law School in 1901 and entering a partnership with Lyman Ward in 1904. Stevens married Elsie Viola Kachel; they had one daughter, Holly, and lived in midtown New York from 1909 to 1916. Disdaining American dependence on cars, he began a lifelong habit of walks that took him as far as Greenwich, Connecticut.

After settling into the legal department of the Hartford Accident and Indemnity Company in 1916, Stevens rose to the vice presidency. He was an amateur poet for ten years and earned a reputation for roaming the streets in all weather while composing. Beginning in 1913, he pursued publication in many literary magazines and journals. Like other poets of the era, he was discovered by Harriet Monroe, editor of *Poetry*, who made room for the four-stage *Phases* in a 1914 war issue. After earning the magazine's $100 prize a second time for the verse play *Three Travellers Watch a Sunrise* (1915), he saw his one-act work produced at New York's Provincetown Theatre.

Although Stevens produced a second play, *Carlos Among the Candles* (1920), first in Milwaukee, then at New York's Neighborhood Playhouse, he discounted drama as his life's work. He contributed to anthologies for ten years before seeing his poems collected in a volume. With the assistance of critic Carl Van Vechten and publisher Alfred A. Knopf, he issued a first collection, *Harmonium* (1923), which brought negligible royalties. He followed with *Ideas of Order* (1935), *Owl's Clover* (1936) (winner of a poetry prize from *Nation*), *The Man with the Blue Guitar* (1937), *Parts of a World* (1942), *Notes Toward a Supreme Fiction* (1942), which espouses his personal philosophy, and *Transport to Summer* (1947). Two collections, *The Auroras of Autumn* (1950) and *The Necessary Angel* (1951), earned him the Bollingen Prize, a National Book Award, and a gold medal from the Poetry Society of America.

By studying early twentieth-century poets, Stevens achieved his place among modern poets shortly before his death with *Complete Poems of Wallace Stevens*, which took a second National Book Award and a Pulitzer Prize. After his demise from cancer on August 2, 1955, in Hartford, and interment at Cedar Hill Cemetery, eulogies linked the two halves of his life, informing startled colleagues of his importance to twentieth-century American literature.

CHIEF WORKS

An early display of Stevens' expertise, "Peter Quince at the Clavier" (1923) employs a four-part symphonic form to intone modernist dissonance. A hymn to impermanence, the musical stanzas, each in its distinctive rhythm and line length, arise from the playing on a Renaissance keyboard instrument by a rustic laborer, the director of the masque "Pyramus and Thisbe," which concludes William Shakespeare's *A Midsummer Night's Dream*. Through a graphic scenario, his thoughts on the effects of music on the spirit draw an analogy with the beauty of Susanna, whose naked loveliness stirred the elders to pry into her private bliss. With a pun on *bass/base,* the poet ridicules the throb of passion in the old men that produces "pizzicati of Hosannas," a reference to the plucking of strings to produce a lightly separated flow of melody.

In Stanza 2, Stevens slows the four beats of the previous tetrameter to an emotionally composed two-beat dimeter interspersed with triplets or trimeter. The crescendo of drama replaces fluctuating strings with the clamor of cymbals and horns. Resuming a four-beat line, he elongates the lifting of lamps, by which ineffectual Byzantine attendants, arriving too late to be of help, disclose the elders leering at Susanna's nakedness. Departing from the legend, the poet closes with an ode to beauty, noting that the details of the story are secondary to the importance of beauty itself. Although Susanna's admirable physique could not last, the memory of her loveliness survives "Death's ironic scraping," leaving a memory as clear as the sweep of a bow over a viol. That, insists the poet, is the constant of art.

Derived from an agnostic era, "Sunday Morning" (1923), a 120-line blank verse statement of the conflict between faith and poetry, voices Stevens' long-running personal debate on the existence of God. The verbal music wraps the speaker in a sustaining melody. Content in her reverie, she avoids Christian ritual and traditions and questions, "What is divinity if it can come / Only in silent shadows and in dreams?" She finds spiritual renewal in "balm or beauty of the earth," which challenges trite, worn-out concepts of heaven.

Foremost in the speaker's doubt about an afterlife is the absence of completion, which she depicts as fruit that never ripens and rivers that never find the sea. Without death, she declares, mystical beauty has no aim, no fulfillment. The speaker exalts "the measures destined for her soul," a primitive concept that the absorption of the body into nature is a more appropriate form of immortality than heaven. Stanza 7 asserts that art, represented by human chanting, encapsulates history, that is, "whence they came and whither they shall go." Rounding out the poem is a return to the vision of wings, which bear "casual flocks of pigeons" to their graceful demise, emphasized by the alliteration of "Downward to darkness." As though enfolding a small portion of life, the span, unlike Christian images of up-stretched flight, embrace earth in their final moments.

In line with the thinking of "Sunday Morning," Stevens' "The Emperor of Ice-Cream" (1923) continues the thread of logic that death is an essential element of life. In two octaves bizarrely joyous in rhythm and tone, he arranges imperatives—call, bid, let bring, let be—to the attendants of the dead as the droll funereal rites take shape. The piling up of death images frames the finality of passage as well as an end to posturing, an end to desire. In a line that demystifies ritual grief, the cigar roller whips up "concupiscent curds" in kitchen cups, a lengthening of hard-edged cacophonies of alliterated K sounds to express the artificiality of mourning. Modern standards of grief take shape in the wenches' "usual" dress and boys bearing floral arrangements in discarded newspaper. However well performed, none of these actions stops the finality of death.

For good reason, Stevens repeats the title image in lines 8 and 16. The notion of decay, embodied in the dresser lacking knobs, expands with the image of failed pride, which the dead woman once depicted in embroidery as a peacock's spread tail. The feet of the deceased, grotesquely callused and oddly removed from the attendants' scurrying, symbolize the cold, unresponsive state of the corpse, now made dumb by the absence of speech. Like the bird's tail in stitchery, the "horny" feet have surrendered any connection with sexual desire or function. When the body is arranged and the lamp lighted, Stevens insists that earthly sway belongs to the emperor of ice cream, a theatrical mockery of permanence.

Celebrating poet and verse, "The Idea of Order at Key West" (1936) expresses Stevens' concept of art by dramatizing an unassuming singer lofting a song to the sea. The poet proposes an outlandish rearrangement of the usual romantic notions of the majestic sea: As though imposing artistic order on nature, the singer reduces the sea to "merely a place by which she walked to sing," uplifting herself by creating melody. In the poet's expanded view, the singer represents "the single artificer of the world," a station that elevates her above nature's "constant cry" with the imaginative ordering of notes into musical phrasing.

In lines 33 to 34, the poet-speaker, certain that the sea is not a mask or source of imitation for the singer, begins a series of hyperboles that place high value on the creative power of artistry. As the poem shifts away from the singer, the poet-speaker challenges philosopher Ramon Fernandez to explain another enigma—how light orders and arranges something so vast and insuperable as darkness. The implication is that mysticism poses no answer that can be expressed in human terms. In its final five-line stanza, an emotional "Oh" introduces a prayerful apostrophe to order amid chaos. The poet, content with the limitations of human art, stops short of reconciling philosophy with art.

DISCUSSION AND RESEARCH TOPICS

(1) Contrast T. S. Eliot and Wallace Stevens in their depictions of post-Christian doubts about an afterlife in paradise. Cite lines that establish differences of opinion about the place of art as spiritual sustenance.

(2) Contrast John Keats' "Ode on a Grecian Urn" to Stevens' "Anecdote of the Jar." Summarize the difference between the romantic view and that of the modernist.

(3) Explain how Stevens' obtuse "Thirteen Ways of Looking at a Blackbird" (1923) ponders varied perceptions of reality. Account for the bird's lasting influence on the observer.

(4) Account for Stevens' depiction of a moment of passionate confrontation with nature in "The Idea of Order at Key West."

(5) After reading Stevens' "Sunday Morning," discuss the speaker's attitude about God. Does the speaker ultimately believe that God exists?

(6) Discuss Stevens' theme that death is an essential element of life. Cite passages in his poetry that support this view.

SELECTED BIBLIOGRAPHY

BORROFF, MARIE, ed. *Wallace Stevens: A Collection of Critical Essays*. Englewood Cliffs, NJ: Prentice-Hall, 1963.

"Hartford Friends and Enemies of Wallace Stevens." www.wesleyan.edu/wstevens/stevens.html

MORSE, SAMUEL FRENCH. *Wallace Stevens: Poetry as Life*. New York: Pegasus, 1970.

"The Poet in Two Worlds." www.cwrl.utexas.edu/~mmaynard/316s/paper3/tomi/

STEVENS, WALLACE. *The Collected Poems of Wallace Stevens*. New York: Alfred A. Knopf, 1955.

UNGER, LEONARD, ed. *Seven Modern American Poets*. Minneapolis: University of Minnesota Press, 1967.

"Wallace Stevens." *Contemporary Authors*. Gale Research. galenet.gale.com

WILLIAM CARLOS WILLIAMS (1883–1963)

A much admired homebody whose verse captures humanistic truths, William Carlos Williams managed a forty-one-year career in medicine alongside a considerable contribution to modern literature. His background as a jazz disciple allied him with poets Hart Crane, Jean Toomer, Wallace Stevens, and e. e. cummings, all proponents of variable meter. Unlike the more flamboyant, Europeanized literary experimenters of the age, he remained tethered to small-town American life. Rebelling against the nihilism and academic elitism of modern art, the substance of his work returned poetry to the common citizen.

Born on September 17, 1883, in Rutherford Park, New Jersey, Williams was a first-generation American. His studies at the Château de Lançy in Geneva and the Lycée Condorcet in Paris did little to alter his New World identity. In his late teens, he discovered the works of Walt Whitman and John Keats and began imitating their style. Because of rigid upbringing, he established the stable career that his parents expected and relegated writing to off-hours relaxation as a form of mental and spiritual liberation.

Williams entered professional studies at the University of Pennsylvania Medical School, where he met fellow students Ezra Pound and H. D. From them, he acquired a delight in the unfettered creativity of free verse. After switching from dentistry and obtaining an M.D. in 1906, Williams interned in New York City slums at the French Hospital and the Nursery and Child's Hospital. He completed an advanced degree in pediatrics from the University of Leipzig and settled into practice. He married Florence "Flossie" Herman, with whom he had two sons, William and Paul.

Williams operated a medical practice in his Rutherford home from 1910 to 1952 and delivered some 2,000 infants, while maintaining a second-floor studio for his writing. From lines scribbled on prescription pads and typed while he rested between patients, he submitted polished human-centered verse to magazines and journals. He published his first stand-alone volume in 1909 as *Poems*, an unremarkable start privately printed at a cost of $50. *The*

Tempers (1913) was the first of many verse collections grounded in the vital vernacular of ordinary folk.

Williams maintained a slow, steady evolution into a significant spokesman for localism and the American idiom. Like Frost, he began to focus on everyday figures and objects. He developed mythic and classic allusions without straying from a workaday intent. In *Transitional* (1915), he moved into free verse, a venue that suited his contemporary flow of *Al Que Quiere!* [*To Him Who Seeks*] (1917), *Kora in Hell: Improvisations* (1920), *Sour Grapes* (1921), and *In the American Grain* (1925), the culmination of his intense study of national themes and attitudes. He followed with *Collected Poems* (1934), *An Early Martyr and Other Poems* (1935), *Adam & Eve & the City* (1936), *Complete Collected Poems* (1938), *The Broken Span* (1941), and *Journey to Love* (1956), but published nothing that elevated his literary reputation among average readers. Angered by the success of more erudite poets, he founded alternative magazines to provide a voice for populist poems. In addition to writing verse, he translated the work of Philippe Soupault and published four novels, three collections of short fiction, four anthologies of essays, a libretto, a play, a volume of letters, and an autobiography. At the height of his artistry, he composed a personal epic, *Paterson*, published in four installments from 1946 to 1951. In 1963, *Pictures from Brueghel and Other Poems* (1962) earned him the Pulitzer Prize and a gold medal from the American Academy of Arts and Letters.

Williams suffered a heart attack in 1948; in 1951, he transferred his practice to his son. In 1952, during the McCarthy era, Williams served only a few months as national poetry consultant, an appointment marred by accusations that his poem "Russia" was pro-Communist. Public humiliation and the failure of the literary community to support him precipitated a stroke, followed by diminished sight. He died at home in his sleep on March 4, 1963, and he was buried at Hillside Cemetery in Lyndhurst, New Jersey.

Williams, the maverick genius, is remembered for mentoring poets Allen Ginsberg and Kay Boyle and for influencing Robert Lowell, Charles Olson, and Denise Levertov. A posthumous collection, *The William Carlos Williams Reader*, was issued in 1966; a fiction anthology, *William Carlos Williams: The Doctor Stories*, appeared in 1984. Libraries at the University of Buffalo and Yale house his personal papers.

CHIEF WORKS

Heavy with implications, "The Young Housewife" (1920) displays Williams' penchant for freezing a moment in time. The unnamed subject is distantly erotic in the poet-speaker's fantasy of her in a negligee or standing at the curb without a corset. She captures his attention by lifting her arms to tame an errant strand of hair. Retreating into metaphor, the observer rolls soundlessly by in his car as though deliberately distancing himself from her housewifely chores. The brief tension in crushing dried leaves derives from his declaration in lines 9 and 10 that she is a dried leaf. Drama emerges from the demands of housekeeping, which wither the beauty of a woman walled up in the wooden cubicle of "her husband's house" and only occasionally freed to the outdoors to dicker with tradesmen.

From the same period, "Portrait of a Lady" (1920) ventures more openly into erotic contemplation, a subject that embroiled Williams in domestic conflict with his wife, who harbored no illusions about his fidelity. The poet-speaker attempts to locate the source of female loveliness by fluctuating between metaphor and artistic representations of womanhood. Moving downward from thighs to ankles, his mind debates breaching the "shore," a euphemism for propriety. At the poem's climax in line 15, sand at the lips yanks the admirer earthward. After he returns to the polite abstraction of apple blossom petals, his better judgment urges him to write sedate, nonsexual verse.

Williams excited debate about American imagism with "The Red Wheelbarrow" (1923). Some analysts question whether it achieves the purpose of poetry. Others declare it a purist classic of imagism for its haiku-like form, simplified beauty, and muted tension. Depersonalized of poultry owner or user of the wheelbarrow, the poem rivets attention on a specific still life. The stark depiction of red and white and the glazing of rain are the substance of the visual scene, but the poetic tension resides in the first line, "so much depends." Williams gives force to the brief observation with the pointed suggestion that humble farm life is a precarious existence, often made or broken on primitive equipment and the amount and pattern of rainfall.

With a botanist's meticulous eye, Williams composed "Queen Anne's Lace" (1923), a minutely detailed, impressionistic study of the small white blooms that form the compact flower head known as Queen Anne's lace. A member of the carrot family, it is a standard among American wildflowers and thus often overlooked as nothing special. The poet's transformation of the white flower into sexual stirring demonstrates a ready embrace of beauty and passion.

Williams, a master of surprise, disarms the reader with a fresh approach to sexual attraction. The irony of the flower's "taking / the field by force" reverses the romantic notion of femininity compromised by heavy-handed male passion. As though examining a human patient, the poet-speaker imagines arousing the flower to "the fibres of her being." Implicit in his reverie is the inborn flaw, the purple center that mars the unblemished whiteness of each stalk. Williams expresses its uniqueness in an optical corollary: If the flower were totally white, the field would vanish in the unity of color. As it exists in nature, the flower's modified purity halts the scene from "[going] over" into the nothingness of perfection.

"Spring and All" (1923), one of Williams' most anthologized poems, abandons normal sentence structure to string together surreal impressions of an emerging season. The setting, on an unremarkable drive to "the contagious hospital," suggests the contagion of emergence, which will soon spark "upstanding" twigs, leaves, and shoots of myriad types to spring back to life. Similarly contagious is his anticipation of an end to the sterile lifelessness of late winter and his joy in nature's constant state of flux. The ambiguity of "they" in line 16 expands the thrust of inanimate life to include humanity as well. By allying the uncertainty of birth in "the cold, familiar wind," he implies that newborns also quicken, "grip down and begin to awaken."

Like a scene from a film, "Danse Russe" [Russian Dance] illustrates the two sides of Williams' life—the creative and the mundane. With dispassionate observation, his nervous, short lines establish the household rhythm in the family's sleep, a bland, non-threatening peace. In wild counterpoint, the rush of activity in the north room characterizes the disquiet that inflames and compels the poet, whose nudity suggests an unflinching study of self. Line 12 speaks the blunt truth of the poet's singularity—a loneliness that sets him apart from satisfied domesticity. Like a closet dervish, he can pull the shades and relish a moment of pride in rebellion without openly challenging his family's serene conventionality.

"This Is Just to Say" (1934), which is less structured than the poems of the 1920s, illustrates Williams' ability to strike to the heart of meaning with a single, deft phrase. The first-person admission of eating plums intended for someone's breakfast begs for understanding. Building on sibilance and concluding on "so cold," the poem implies that sweet, fruity taste contrasts the coldness of a human relationship that forbids sharing or forgiveness for a minor breach of etiquette.

As though reprising Christmas tradition in a momentary conflagration, "Burning the Christmas Greens" (1944) is a sensory encounter that overlays green boughs with the red flame that devours them. Gathered at the "the winter's midnight," a metaphor for the winter solstice, when day and night are equal in length, the armloads of hemlock serve their purpose and give place to bare mantle and walls when Christmas passes. The color tensions—green fronds heavy with snow, green transformed to red fire, then to black and white ash—unite human observers in the wonder of a post-Christmas ritual. In a retreat to pagan, pre-Christian paradox, the flame stands up from the grate like "shining fauna," a description of the people as well. In an act that tips the balance of the solstice, they become one with all nature in their rise to passion and return in death to simple elemental matter. Williams implies that nature refrains from balance with a constant shifting to extremes.

DISCUSSION AND RESEARCH TOPICS

(1) Select several imagistic works by Williams, such as "The Red Wheelbarrow" or "Burning the Christmas Greens," that alter substance with a flash of surprise or an unforeseen gestalt. Compare his visual method to that of Salvador Dali, Jackson Pollock, Edward Hopper, Willem De Kooning, Marcel Duchamp, and other painters, sculptors, and muralists of his day.

(2) Summarize Williams' commentary on art in "The Desert Music." Contrast his purpose to that of T. S. Eliot, Hart Crane, Ezra Pound, or Marianne Moore.

(3) Compare Williams' view of the ugliness, monotony, and crassness of everyday life with similar themes and subjects in Tennessee Williams' *The Glass Menagerie*, O. E. Rolvaag's *Giants in the Earth*, Theodore Dreiser's *Sister Carrie*, Robert Frost's "'Out, out . . .,'" and Sherwood Anderson's *Winesburg, Ohio*.

(4) How does Williams elicit eroticism in "Portrait of a Lady"?

(5) Is Williams' "The Red Wheelbarrow" poetry or not? Defend your answer.

SELECTED BIBLIOGRAPHY

JACQUES, GEOFFREY. *Free Within Ourselves: The Harlem Renaissance.* New York: Franklin Watts, 1996.

LITZ, A. WALTON, and CHRISTOPHER MACGOWAN, eds. *The Collected Poems of William Carlos Williams.* New York: New Directions, 1986.

MILLER, J. HILLIS, ed. *William Carlos Williams: A Collection of Critical Essays.* Englewood Cliffs, NJ: Prentice-Hall, 1966.

MILLER, LUREE. *Literary Hills of San Francisco.* Washington, DC: Starrhill Press, 1992.

UNGER, LEONARD, ed. *Seven Modern American Poets.* Minneapolis: University of Minnesota Press, 1967.

"William Carlos Williams." info.kent.edu/speccoll/poetry/williams.html

"William Carlos Williams' Writing Periods." gps.lhric.org/middle/ems/wcw.htm

EZRA POUND (1885-1972)

A technical genius and pivotal figure in world poetry, Ezra Loomis Pound was the iconoclast of his day. A restless seeker and experimenter, he disdained his American roots, kept a ménage à trois with his wife and a mistress, and cultivated a bohemian image by dressing in scruffy, romantic splendor—cane, billowing cape, and tunic topped by rumpled hair and a saucy Van Dyke beard. On Paris's fabled Left Bank, he kept company with expatriates Ernest Hemingway, James Joyce, and Gertrude Stein and counseled emerging writers of such stature and promise as Robert Frost, D. H. Lawrence, T. S. Eliot, H. D., e. e. cummings, William Carlos Williams, and Amy Lowell. In addition to producing a formidable canon of verse, essay, criticism, biography, and translation, Pound stirred international controversy and led a re-evaluation of language and meaning in modern verse.

Pound was born in a cabin in the frontier town of Hailey, Idaho, on October 30, 1885. He lived for a year in Jenkintown, Pennsylvania, and came of age in Wyncote outside Philadelphia, where his father was an assistant assayer for the U.S. Mint. Pound's public schooling ended with enrollment at Cheltenham Military Academy. After entering the University of Pennsylvania at age 15, he knew that his life would consist of mastering all there was to know about poetry. He focused on Latin, Medieval, and Renaissance studies and formed a close friendship with fellow student William Carlos Williams, who lived for a time with the Pound family.

Pound completed a B.A. in philosophy from Hamilton College; he then taught romance languages at the University of Pennsylvania, where he earned an M.A. in Spanish. After a year on the faculty of Wabash College in Crawfordsville, Indiana, in 1905, he was fired for befriending a transsexual. Fleeing provincialism and artistic sterility, he toured southern Europe and researched a doctoral thesis on the plays of Lope de Vega. He earned what he could from reviewing and tutoring and worked as secretary for poet William Butler Yeats while championing "imagism," his term for modern poetry.

In 1908, Pound published his first volumes, *A Lume Spento* [*With Tapers Quenched*], *A Quinzaine for This Yule*, and *Personae*

[*Masks*]. Content to live outside his native land, in September 1909, he settled in a sparse front room in London's Kensington section; five years later, he married Dorothy Shakespear. Under the influence of James Joyce and Ford Madox Ford, Pound rapidly produced *Exultations* in 1909 and *Provença* the following year. He covered new ground as poet-as-translator with *The Sonnets and Ballate of Guido Cavalcanti* (1912), which he set to music for opera, and the verse of French troubadour François Villon. Pound's translation of Li Po's poems in *Cathay* (1915) and *Certain Noble Plays of Japan* (1916) anticipated a demand for Asian literature. A greater predictor of change was "In a Station of the Metro" (1916), Pound's nineteen-syllable haiku that captures with impressionistic clarity the direction in which the poet intended his art to go.

Pound achieved his most influential imagism in *Homage to Sextus Propertius* (1919) and *Hugh Selwyn Mauberley: Life and Contacts* (1920), a collection of incisive poetic snapshots. During the post–World War I spiritual malaise, he joined Paris café society, a clamorous coterie known as the "lost generation." In search of quiet, in 1922, he dropped his literary friends and migrated to Rapallo, Italy, his home for twenty years. He pored over medieval manuscripts and became Paris correspondent for *The Dial*, which conferred a $2,000 prize on him in 1928. A mark of his achievement in language was publication of *Translations of Ezra Pound* (1933) and the political critiques in *ABC of Economics* (1933) and *Jefferson and/or Mussolini* (1935).

A racist, anti-Semite, and proponent of Hitler's butchery and Mussolini's Fascism, Pound supported the Italian government in short-wave broadcasts over Rome Radio that were addressed to the English-speaking world. In 1942, he repudiated democracy as "judeocracy" and declared American involvement in the war illegal. After the U.S. military arrested Pound in Genoa in May 1945, he was imprisoned outside Pisa for treason. After being returned to Washington, D.C., for trial, in February 1946, Pound escaped hard prison time by pleading insanity and senility. Critics accused him of perpetuating the pose of raving paranoic to avoid retrial and possible execution. Extolled as a modernist experimenter, he pursued an epic series, *The Pisan Cantos* (1948) and *The Cantos of Ezra Pound* (1948). In an atmosphere of jubilance and victory marred by virulent charges of fakery, he accepted the 1949 Bollingen Prize in

Poetry, which included a $1,000 purse awarded by the Fellows in American Letters of the Library of Congress.

In 1958, Pound, then aged 72, gained release from an asylum through the intervention of an impressive list of colleagues, including Robert Frost, Ernest Hemingway, Marianne Moore, W. H. Auden, Carl Sandburg, and T. S. Eliot. Freed of all charges, he returned to Italy. He continued writing and, without pausing to refine his work, published *Thrones: Cantos 96–109* (1959) and *Drafts and Fragments of Cantos CX–CXVII* (1968). When he died on November 1, 1972, he was laid among exiles on the island of San Michele beneath a stone that bears only "Ezra Pound."

CHIEF WORKS

"A Virginal," composed in 1912, is named for the diminutive keyboard instrument preferred by maidens during the late Renaissance. The poem reflects the early period of Pound's development and his skillful use of the fourteen-line Petrarchan sonnet. He rhymes the first eight lines abbaabba, closing with the rhyme scheme cdeecd. Opening with a burst of emotion, he introduces his rejection with two strong beats, "No, no!" Speaking in the guise of a lover rejecting a lady, he cloaks his commentary on poetry in dashing romanticism, brandishing the female image of the Latin vagina or scabbard, which he will not soil with a dull blade. His rejection of classicism turns on an amusing overstatement of departure from the arms that "have bound me straitly," a pun suggesting a straightjacket.

At the break between opening octave and concluding sestet, Pound returns to the original spondee and chops the line into three segments—another "No, no," a dismissal of his castoff love, and the beginning of his reason for abandoning the allure of traditional verse. Intent on experimentation, he prefers the green shoots that signal a new thrust through earth's crust. He alliterates the past as a "winter wound" and looks beyond to April's white-barked trees, a color symbolic of an emerging purity.

Much of *Hugh Selwyn Mauberley: Life and Contacts*, written eight years after "A Virginal," expresses Pound's exasperation with predictable American artistry and with poets who refuse to let go of the past. In "Ode pour l'Election de Son Sepulchre" ["Ode on the

Selection of His Tomb"], Pound draws on a work by Pierre de Ronsard, reclaimed by the initials E. P., to comfort the artist who is "out of key with his time." The second quatrain follows the pattern of iambic tetrameter rhyming abab, but refuses to be tamed into stiff old-style measures. In zesty rhetoric, the poet leaps from one allusion to another, linking Ronsard with Capaneus, a Greek hero in ancient times who was halted in mid-rebellion by a bolt of lightning from the god Zeus. Rapidly covering ground with a line in Greek from Homer's *Odyssey*, Pound extols another toiler, the sailor Odysseus, who had his men tie him to the mast so that he could experience the sirens' song. The fourth stanza reaches toward Gustave Flaubert, a nineteenth-century novelist who persisted in stylistic growth, even though obstinacy cost him the admiration of his contemporaries.

Gradually relinquishing dependence on a tightly formed quatrain, Parts II and III of the stanza speak clearly about Pound's annoyance with poetry that fails to acknowledge the "accelerated grimace" of the post–World War I era. To the poet, an artistic theft of the "classics in paraphrase" is preferable to a self-indulgent "inward gaze," his term for confessional verse that obsesses over personal feelings and sentimentality. In his estimation, no rigid plaster can suffice in an era that demands agile, up-to-date language. In a rage at commercialism, Part III surges back into the allusive mode with cryptic poetic shards contrasting Edwardian niceties and Sappho's spirited verses. Segueing into religion, Pound makes a similar comparison of the erotic Dionysians and breast-beating Christians.

By Parts IV and V, Pound has shucked off the constraints of pre-modern verse forms to embrace an expression free of rhyme and meter. The tone resorts to a free-ranging bitterness toward the literary status quo. His cunning rhythms, more attuned to pulpit delivery, depict the emotional drive of naive warriors marching to war. With bold pause, in line 71 he halts the parallel flow of complex motives—adventure, fear of weakness, fear of censure, love of slaughter, and outright terror—to note that some died, casualties for patriotism.

To Pound's thinking, the so-called Great War violated Horace's idealization of sweet and fitting martyrdom. Part IV concludes with a ghoulish belly laugh from the hapless dead as the stanza assails post–war distress. Disillusioned by leaders' lies in the 1910s, which pour from the foul jaws of an aged bitch dog, in Part V, the poet lambastes tricksters for luring fine young men to slaughter. For refusing to recognize the threat, a decaying world sent them "under earth's lid," an evocative image of finality—closed eyes and coffins covered with soil.

"A Pact," Pound's forthright confrontation with Walt Whitman, allows the poet to come to terms with a debt to his American fore-bear, the father of free verse expressionism. Flaunting hatred of a dismally self-limiting poet, Pound depicts himself as the petulant child of an obstinate father, but stops short of a meaningless tantrum. By reining himself in in the fifth line, he gives over peevish vengeance to acknowledge the development of modernism from its foundations. From this "new wood" that Whitman exposed, Pound intends to carve the future of poetry, thus achieving a "commerce" between himself and his predecessor.

Pound's lifetime of carving resulted in a masterwork of 116 stanzas that spanned the four decades of his mature and declining years. In "Canto I," from *The Cantos*, he imitates the style and diction of Homer, whose Odyssey follows the fate-hounded Greek sailor all over the Mediterranean. Capturing the music of keel over waves and wind on sail, Pound envisions a "swart ship," the boat that the Circe helped Odysseus build to make his final leg of the journey home. It is painted black, Greek fashion; the color prefigures description of that dark nether world that Odysseus must traverse and the murky rites he must perform to acquire the prophet Tiresias' direction. To stress the grimness of the underworld, the poet relies on a heavy sibilance of repeated sounds in "sterile bulls," "best for sacrifice," and the double alliteration of "flowed in the fosse."

In lush phrases, Pound enacts the scene at the trench, where Odysseus must feed the thronging ghosts on fresh-spilled blood to give them voice. After hearing Elpenor's sex-charged explanation of sleeping in "Circe's ingle" and descending the ladder of doom, Odysseus moves on to the next spirit—the sage Tiresias, who warns that return will cost him all his sailors. Following a two-line digression to acknowledge past translations of Homer, Pound venerates Aphrodite, the ancestor of Aeneas, whose subsequent voyage in Virgil's *Aeneid* parallels the wanderings of Odysseus.

Without warning, Pound breaks off the text, as though indicating that the chain of poetic renderings will keep epic alive in version after version.

"Canto XLV," subtitled "With Usura," displays flickering impressionism molded from splendid fragments, a mentally challenging style that Pound contributed to modernism. The haunting, exotic passage builds into fugue with melodic names of Renaissance artists and successors, none of whom paid the penalty of artistic usury. As though composing an oratorio of creative fragments, Pound pictures French churches and tools of the sculptor and weaver. A delicious verbal lyricism in "azure" and "cramoisi" (pronounced krah mwah **zee**) precedes a revelation: The publisher's financial dealings are the source of declining artistic vigor and the era's compromise of its artists. He suppresses the initial exuberance with a somber reminder that greed kills the artistic "child in the womb." With a pontiff's majesty, he thunders that usury— like whores replacing priestesses and corpses seated at banquets— is unnatural, that is, a violation of world order.

DISCUSSION AND RESEARCH TOPICS

(1) Typify Pound's violation of English grammar and syntax by analyzing the grammar of some of his cantos.

(2) Summarize the force of several of the more daring modern poets, including Wallace Stevens, Hart Crane, and Ezra Pound. Determine how subtle poetic controls channel verse energy into emergent image and theme. Consider, for example, Pound's re-creation of Odysseus' voyage or the dramatic monologue "The River-Merchant's Wife: A Letter."

(3) Characterize elements of parody in "Envoi," which Pound wrote as a reply to Edmund Waller's romantic "Go, Lovely Rose," a tribute to beauty.

(4) Contrast the emotion in Wilfred Owen's "Dulce et Decorum Est," T. S. Eliot's *The Waste Land*, W. H. Auden's "The Unknown Citizen," Robinson Jeffers's "Shine, Perishing Republic," or William Butler Yeats's "The Second Coming" with Pound's first canto of *Hugh Selwyn Mauberley: Life and Contacts*. Express the post war generation's fear of disintegration and decay.

(5) Is any of Pound's poetry confessional? If so, discuss those poetic lines that are. What makes them confessional?

SELECTED BIBLIOGRAPHY

"Ezra Pound." *Contemporary Authors*. Gale Research. galenet.gale.com

"Ezra Loomis Pound." www.qds.com/people/apope/Poetry/ap_elp.html

"Ezra Pound." www.lit.kobe-u.ac.jp/~hishika/pound.htm

HEYMANN, C. DAVID. *Ezra Pound: The Last Rower*. New York: Citadel Press, 1976.

MONTGOMERY, MARION. *Ezra Pound: A Critical Essay*. Grand Rapids, MI: William B. Eerdmans, 1970.

O'CONNOR, WILLIAM VAN, ed. *A Casebook on Ezra Pound*. New York: Thomas Y. Crowell, 1959.

RECK, MICHAEL. *Ezra Pound: A Close-up*. New York: McGraw-Hill, 1967.

"The Trials of Ezra Pound." home.earthlink.net/~centurion88/jewish_question/no1021

UNGER, LEONARD, ed. *Seven Modern American Poets*. Minneapolis: University of Minnesota Press, 1967.

H. D. (1886–1961)

A critic, novelist, translator, mystic, and poet, Hilda Doolittle, familiarly known by the pen name H. D., overthrew traditional male domination of myth to voice the female perspective. She produced the "signet," her term for an evocative, many-layered verse that influenced a generation of writers, including Allen Ginsberg and Denise Levertov. At heart a flamboyant narcissist, rambler, friend-maker, and creator, she toured much of the world and more of the self. The poems that record her search of the self epitomize imagism, the tight, precise construction of verse that calls up multiple meanings and implications through sound, rhythm, word etymology, and free-form syntax.

H. D. was born on September 10, 1886, in Bethlehem, a Moravian community in Pennsylvania. Her family moved to Philadelphia in 1895, when her father took charge of the Flower Observatory of the University of Pennsylvania. After excelling at classical and modern foreign language at Miss Gordon's School and the Friends' Central School in Philadelphia, she studied astronomy at Bryn Mawr for three semesters, from 1904 to 1906, before quitting. A three-sided romantic fling with poets Ezra Pound and Josepha Frances Gregg and the draw of London's literary circles superceded her interest in formal education. Her parents despaired of H. D.'s rebellion against home, school, and society, but allowed her to sail to Europe with the Greggs.

Before Ezra Pound introduced her to free verse, H. D. published children's stories in a Presbyterian magazine. At age 25, she resettled in London, cultivated literary friendships, and traveled before entering a twenty-three-year marriage to imagist poet and biographer Richard Aldington, editor of the *Egoist*, in October 1913. The couple collaborated on translations of Greek lyric verse until his departure with the British Army for France.

In 1913, Pound fostered H. D.'s career by issuing her verse in *Poetry Magazine*, under the pseudonym "H. D., Imagiste," and exhibiting her work in his anthology, *Des Imagistes* (1914). On her own, H. D. published *Sea Garden* (1916). When her husband went to war, she joined T. S. Eliot in editing the *Egoist*. The post–World War I period tried her stamina with grief over her brother Gilbert's death in combat, a miscarriage, her father's death, an affair with music critic Cecil Grey, and, in 1919, the painful birth of their daughter, Frances Perdita. About the time H. D. ended her marriage, she met a wealthy traveling companion, Annie Winnifred Ellerman, who named herself Bryher after one of the Scilly Islands. In 1920, H. D. and Bryher moved to Lake Geneva, which remained their home.

Mature verse colors H. D.'s collections: the life-affirming meditations in *Hymen* (1921), *Heliodora and Other Poems* (1924), and *Collected Poems of H. D.* (1925), the beginning of the poet's critical and popular success and literary independence. Subsequent publications display self-confidence and growing feminism: an experimental autobiography, *HERmione* (1927), a verse tragedy dramatically entitled *Hippolytus Temporizes: A Play in Three Acts* (1927), *Red Roses for Bronze* (1932), and a translation of Euripides's tragedy *Ion* (1937). Following *Collected Poems* (1940), she issued a pro-matriarchal trilogy—*The Walls Do Not Fall* (1944), *Tribute to the Angels* (1945), and *Flowering of the Rod* (1946)—and her last verse collection, *Helen in Egypt* (1961), an examination of necromancy through blended prose and epic poetry.

In addition to submissions to *Life and Letters Today*, H. D. flourished in long fiction, including an experimental three-part novel entitled *Palimpsest* (1926), the psycho-biographical comedy *Hedylus* (1928), *The Hedgehog* (1936), the Elizabethan-style *By Avon River* (1949), and *Bid Me to Live* (1960), which recaps her relationship with D. H. Lawrence and Aldington. Her tenuous mental state, worsened by her ambivalence toward bisexualism, required additional fine-tuning and shock therapy. In token of her treatment by the Viennese psychoanalyst Dr. Sigmund Freud in 1933–1934, a collection of personal essays, *Tribute to Freud* (1954), explored occultism and Freudian analysis.

H. D. was more content in her last years following treatment for nervous exhaustion, and she maintained a satisfying relationship with Bryher. Later, she was paralyzed and aphasic for three months from a paralytic stroke and died on September 27, 1961, at the Klinik Hirslanden in Zurich. To the end, Bryher supervised her care. The poet's ashes repose under a simple, flat gravestone among the Doolittles at Nisky Hill Cemetery in Bethlehem, Pennsylvania.

H. D.'s influence extends to both sides of the Atlantic. She was the first female poet to earn the American Academy of Arts and Letters gold medal. The subjects of three posthumous titles—the power of feminine love in *Hermetic Definition* (1972), her ambivalence toward D. H. Lawrence and Ezra Pound in *End to Torment: A Memoir of Ezra Pound by H. D.* (1979), and *The Gift* (1969), a collection of Freudian self-analysis and remembrances of her grandmother—have deepened understanding of H. D.'s place in modern poetry. A more detailed work, *Notes on Thought and Vision* (1982), is an articulate statement of her aesthetic credo.

CHIEF WORKS

In 1924, H. D. ventured into minimalism with "Oread," a six-line practice piece that profits from compulsive word associations. The poem overlays a description of an evergreen forest with the shapes, color, sound, and motion of the sea. In giving life to the Greek nymph of mountains and forests, the poet draws on geometric shapes of points, whorls, and rounded pools to end on a pun, "fir," which suggests a furry pelt covering the land. The skillful blending of glimpses, like impressionist art, relies on minute sense impressions to dazzle the eye and mind with potent connections.

By 1916, H. D. was wrestling with issues of feminism and artistic worth that dominated her later writings. In "Sea Rose," she contrasts the stereotypical long-stemmed beauty, emblem of idealized womanhood, with its homelier alter ego, the stunted blossom flung onto the shore. Having weathered the buffeting of tide and wind, it travels at the whim of nature. In the last of the sixteen-line poem, the poet proposes a paradox: how the spicy scent of the stereotyped rose fails in comparison with the bitter aroma of a blossom hardened by experience.

In 1924, a more mature poet produced "Helen." In three five-line stanzas (cinquains) linked by pure rhyme (stands, hands), sight rhyme (words that share elements of spelling but not pronunciation, such as unmoved and love), and assonance (feet, knees), she epitomizes the love-hate relationship between the famed Spartan queen and Greece, the nation she betrayed by eloping with a Trojan prince and triggering a twenty-year war. To move beneath historical details, the poet first characterizes the impeccable complexion with two evocative sight images—lustrous olives and whiteness, a suggestion of opposites—meant to symbolize blood-less cruelty and innocence.

The second cinquain replaces "white" from stanza 1 with "wan." The poet-speaker contrasts Helen's smiles with the revulsion of Greeks, who hated her charm and loathed even more the fallen queen's bold actions. The choice of "enchantments" suggests both a winsome female and the tradition that Helen worked magic through a knowledge of healing herbs and poisons. The severity of personal, political, and financial loss from the Helen-centered war worked a lasting hardship on Greece, which Homer and Virgil reconstructed in epic verse.

In the concluding cinquain, the poet defends Helen, a singular figure who bore the human qualities of her mother, Leda, and the divine elegance and grace of her father, Zeus. Implicit in her lineage is a conception that resulted from Zeus's trickery and rape of Leda by appearing to her as a male swan. H. D. acknowledges that such a dangerous beauty can't be appreciated in life. Only in death—reduced to "white ash amid funereal cypresses" like the burned city of Troy—does the goddess-like Helen acquire the nation's adoration.

The Walls Do Not Fall, which was written in seclusion during the closing months of World War II as the first installment of her war trilogy, highlighted the poet's final creative period. The verse cycle, which is a belated thank-you to Bryher for their 1923 trip to Karnak, Egypt, exults in the cyclic nature of writing, research, and self-study. The first canto explores the paradox of human effort, which survives the ravages of war and ruin to emerge in another incarnation, like Luxor's temple, centuries after its fall from greatness. A former patient of Freud, who characterized intelligence as a fusion of conscious and subconscious energy, H. D. depicts the subconscious workings of the mind, which, "unaware," draws meaning from the spirit.

Like the Pythia, one of a series of Apollo's priestesses who prophesied to seekers in obscure and rambling visions, the artist creates from fragments, which H. D. describes as the slow out-pouring of lava from the split surface of a volcano. She exalts inspiration as "Apocryphal fire" and links it to the vicissitudes of history, the dipping floor and swaying earth that bewilder and bedevil the individual. Bemused by creativity, she questions why she survived the challenge of purification to become a spokesperson for the arts. Cantos 2 and 3 continue the poet's immersion in mythic figures with a contemplation of the duality of inspiration. By "[searching] the old highways," the seeker contrives "the rightspell" and retrieves the good from history that "brings life to the living."

The intricacy of the self-limiting shell—a metaphor for H. D.'s periods of seclusion—leads to an assumption that, however self-contained, it must draw nourishment from the greater environment. In overt confession, she admits, "I sense my own limit," but relishes a sustaining inwardness, which ultimately creates "that pearl-of-great-price," a reference to the reward mentioned in Matthew 13:46. In Canto 5, she notes that recent self-discoveries outdistance her years "in the company of the gods," an allusion to an impressive circle of literary friends. The cultivation of an inner muse has rewarded her much as the Magi brought myrrh to the Christ child. Both precious gifts and foreshadowing of death, myrrh, a burial ointment, reminds the poet of her mortality.

Canto 6 enlarges on the notion of mortality as the poet rejoices in a fearless exploration of time and place. Undeterred by the calamities of two world wars, she learns from both nature and history, symbolized in the ravelings of gem-encrusted banners. Fed on good and bad, the leaf and the worm, the poet-speaker boldly profits from artistic opportunism while simultaneously "[spinning] my own shroud." The italicized finale, Canto 43, opens with the title image, "Still the walls do not fall." The final reach for excellence is a luminous paradox—a collapse into death as the floor and walls crumble and the air thins to a tenuous state too insubstantial for wings to ply. In a courageous statement of purpose, she acknowledges, "we are voyagers, discoverers / of the not-known." The daring of the artist's quest reaches toward the ultimate "haven, / heaven," a mystical, redemptive reward for fearless perseverance.

DISCUSSION AND RESEARCH TOPICS

(1) Contrast H. D.'s "Leda" with William Butler Yeats's "Leda and the Swan." Note images of dominance and fruition, which preface the birth of Helen of Troy, a dominant subject of H. D.'s poetry.

(2) Summarize H. D.'s concept of infectious ecstasy and fulfillment in *The Walls Do Not Fall*, "Pear Tree," "Sea Poppies," and
"Heat."

(3) Characterize the longing for personal and artistic freedom in
H. D.'s "Sheltered Garden" and similar works by Sylvia Plath
and Anne Sexton.

(4) Discuss H. D.'s view of World War II in *The Walls Do Not Fall*.
Is the war a major force in the poem? Why or why not? What
does the phrase "The walls do not fall" mean?

SELECTED BIBLIOGRAPHY

BLAIN, VIRGINIA, PATRICIA CLEMENTS, and ISOBEL GRUNDY. *The Feminist Companion to Literature in English*. New Haven, CT: Yale University Press, 1990.

BLOOM, HAROLD, ed. *H. D.* New York: Chelsea House, 1989.

DAVIDSON, CATHY N., and LINDA WAGNER-MARTIN. *The Oxford Companion to Women's Writing in the United States*. New York: Oxford University Press, 1995.

GUEST, BARBARA. *Herself Defined: The Poet H. D. and Her World*. Garden City, NY: 1984.

HAWKINS, HEATHER. "A Brief Biography of H. D." www.well.com/user/heddy/hdbio.html

"H. D." *Contemporary Authors*. Gale Research. galenet.gale.com

"Hilda H. D." www.cwrl.utexas.edu/~slatin/20c_poetry/projects/lives/hd.html

ROBINSON JEFFERS
(1887–1962)

John Robinson Jeffers, a master of cadenced verse in short lyric and long narrative, stands out from his contemporaries for earnest craftsmanship and tragic, doomed battles between nature and technology. Amid the constant cycles of earth, sea, and sky, his harsh voice strove in vain for a lyrical contentment in nature. In a poetic struggle unmatched by his contemporaries, Jeffers' solitary strife sets him apart from literary movements in a poetic world order of his own making.

Jeffers was born January 10, 1887, in Allegheny near Pittsburgh, Pennsylvania, and grew up in Sewickley and Edgeworth, Pennsylvania, and various parts of Europe. He was tutored and educated at private schools in Zurich, Lucerne, Vevey, Lausanne, and Geneva. In 1902, his family settled in California, where his lyric consciousness took shape. When he was 17 years old, he published "The Condor" in *Youth's Companion.*

Jeffers attended the University of Pittsburgh and Occidental College, where he edited a school journal, *The Occidental.* His only satisfying achievements in college were swim meets and running the mile. Unfocused graduate work at the universities of Southern California, Zurich, and Washington proved that his future lay in verse, not medicine or forestry.

After publishing a tentative volume, *Flagons and Apples* (1912), Jeffers came into a legacy that allowed him leisure to produce a steady flow of rough-hewn, idiosyncratic poems. In 1916, Jeffers published *Californians*, then achieved critical and popular fame with *Tamar and Other Poems* (1924). Subsequent collections—*Roan Stallion, Tamar, and Other Poems* (1925), set in Monterey, California, and *The Women at Point Sur* (1927), a well-received narrative poem—cinched his reputation for tragic lyricism and austere themes and backgrounds. His mature work—*Cawdor and Other Poems* (1928) and *Dear Judas and Other Poems* (1929)—reached toward a hopeful humanism. In the 1930s, Jeffers developed primitive passion in *Descent to the Dead* (1931), *Thurso's Landing and Other Poems* (1932), *Give Your Heart to the Hawks* (1933), *Solstice and Other Poems* (1935), *The Beaks of Eagles* (1936), and *Such*

Counsels You Gave to Me (1937), all imbued with moodiness and naturalistic creativity. In *Two Consolidations* (1940), *Be Angry at the Sun* (1941), *Medea* (1946), *The Double Axe* (1948), and *Hungerfield and Other Poems* (1953), he revealed a complex world view comprised of bleak introversion and inept reaches for the sublime through myth.

In 1941, John Gassner adapted Jeffers' *Tower Beyond Tragedy* for the stage at an outdoor theater in Carmel, where Dame Judith Anderson played the lead. In 1947, two more works—*Dear Judas* and *Medea*—were staged. Jeffers died in his sleep at home on January 20, 1962.

CHIEF WORKS

"Shine, Perishing Republic" (1925), Jeffers' most anthologized piece, contemplates the natural attrition of nations, which follow the flower in a three-stage development: fruit, decay, and absorption into earth. Characterizing the fall to earth as "home to the mother," the poet urges, "You making haste haste on decay," a deliberate repetition through a double beat to illuminate the rhythm of the process. With heavy irony, he impels the republic to emulate a meteor in hurrying toward a bright-hued demise.

At the beginning of the fourth stanza, the poet steps aside from personal wish to ponder his children, who risk corruption at "the thickening center," a viscid image that calls up visions of volcanic lava. Encouraging his sons to rise above fallen cities into moral mountains, like a god-driven Moses, he exhorts, "be in nothing so moderate as in love of man." The crux of the poem lies in the source of evil. Reflecting on classic myth, he envisions the natural lure to temptation, which even God did not elude "when he walked on earth."

"Apology for Bad Dreams" (1925) perpetuates the poet's placement of events at the extremes of good and evil. The four-part meditation expands from a view of seaside grandeur to a theatrical view of human savagery below as a woman and her son torment a horse chained by its tongue to a tree. Section II opens on bold strokes of red and black as the poet makes a choice between personal and invented suffering. Opting for literature, he justifies his choice with a warning: "It is not good to forget over what gulfs the spring / Of the beauty of humanity . . . floats to its quietness."

Following strong alliterated *b* sounds in Boulder/blunted/beds/break/below, section III looks into the past, when Indians "Paid something for the future / Luck of the country." The irony of luck prefaces another burst of *b*s as the poet-speaker asks that the "Beautiful country burn again." In the final segment, the poet identifies the work of the poet, "to bring the savor / From the bruised root." The characterization accounts for the troubled dreamer, who tortures himself to perform "the ways of my love."

Jeffers' identification with nature in a narrative, "Hurt Hawks" (1928), creates a palpable tragedy as a wing-damaged bird hobbles about, dragging one wing while contemplating slow starvation. As though honoring a fallen titan, the poet-speaker anticipates death as a form of divine blessing. With a stern Old Testament misanthropy, the poet comments that, in contrast with the humble bird, humanity has grown too arrogant for such grace. Distanced from God by choice, human sufferers deserve a graceless fate.

In the second half, the poet looks candidly at the choice between euthanizing a bird or a man. After six weeks of feeding the crippled hawk, he chooses to honor its unspoken request for release. With a "lead gift in the twilight," he frees the redtail. Its once-noble frame crumples into "Owl-downy, soft feminine feathers" as the spirit flies upward, "quite unsheathed from reality."

From a later period, "Carmel Point" (1951) speaks the poet's annoyance in urban sprawl as "the spoiler," a personification of all interlopers, arrives in his seaside neighborhood. The meditation, like a sonnet, breaks at line ten with the separation of human subjectivity and nature's objectivity. Human settlers mimic the ocean in their tide, which dissolves earthly works. Although dispersed into fragments of ancient beauty, nature's loveliness survives in minute glimpses of "the very grain of the granite." With a gesture to his contemporaries, the poet urges that we "uncenter our minds from ourselves," the "unhumanizing" effort that Jeffers committed himself to at his seaside hermitage.

"Vulture" (1954), one of Jeffers' clearest statements of merging with nature, is a first-person experience composed in a less gloomy and sorrow-laden period. The unnerving, up-close examination by a flesh-eater gladdens the observer, who lies as still as a corpse to follow the sweep of the vulture's circles. The surprising element of the poem is the notion that human beings die and become "part of him, to share those wings and those eyes." In celebration of such a rebirth, Jeffers looks forward to a sublime "enskyment," his personal notion of "life after death."

DISCUSSION AND RESEARCH TOPICS

(1) Contrast Jeffers' heart-weary imagery in "Hurt Hawks" with the reflective phrases of Ted Hughes' "Hawk Roosting" and the haunting cries in Edward Thomas' "The Owl."

(2) Compare the nationalistic theme of Jeffers' "Shine, Perishing Republic" with that of Allen Ginsberg's "A Supermarket in California."

(3) Characterize the grim fatalism in Jeffers' "Credo."

(4) Discuss Jeffers' use of the repeated "haste haste" in "Shine, Perishing Republic." Why does Jeffers repeat this word?

SELECTED BIBLIOGRAPHY

BROPHY, ROBERT, ed. *Robinson Jeffers: Dimensions of a Poet.* New York: Fordham University Press, 1995.

"Jeffers Studies." www.jeffers.org

KARMAN, JAMES. *Robinson Jeffers, Poet of California.* Brownsville, Ore.: Story Pine Press, 1994.

"Poet Robinson Jeffers." www.monterey.edu/other-sites/history/jeffers

"Robinson Jeffers, a Bibliography and Sources." www.fix.net/~boon/jeffers

"Robinson Jeffers Chronology." www.torhouse.org/tdfchron.htm

"The Robinson Jeffers Association." www-acc.scu.edu

MARIANNE MOORE
(1887–1972)

Marianne Craig Moore, a notable figure who liked to dress in a black tricorn hat and cape, became one of mid-twentieth-century America's most recognized poets. Readers identified with her rigorous portrayal of ordinary themes, which included baseball, street scenes, common animals, and public issues, notably in "Carnegie Hall: Rescued." Her friendships with poets made her a force in directing modern poetry away from the rigid verse forms of the Victorian era. For her generous mentoring, William Carlos Williams referred to Moore as a female stele supporting the efforts of her peers.

Moore was born November 15, 1887, in Kirkwood, Missouri, near St. Louis to Mary Warner, a teacher, and John Milton Moore, who died in 1894. Moore and her brother, John, grew up in Carlisle, Pennsylvania. Her mother taught English at the Metzger Institute to support the trio. In 1909, Moore completed her education in biology and history at Bryn Mawr, where she edited and published fiction and verse in the college literary journal, *Tipyn o'Bob*.

A tour of England and France provided Moore with inspiration from art and architecture she found at museums and Victor Hugo's residence. To support a publishing career, she completed a year's business training at Carlisle Commercial College. She taught math, typing, commercial law, and shorthand at Carlisle's U.S. Industrial Indian School for four and a half years while publishing "Pouters and Fantails" in *Poetry*, "To a Man Working His Way Through the Crowd" and "Poetry" in *Others*, and "To the Soul of Progress" in *The Egoist*. Her tentative literary beginnings earned the support of poets H. D., Ezra Pound, and William Carlos Williams.

After moving with her mother to Chatham, New Jersey, then to Greenwich Village, New York, Moore tutored privately while working part-time as assistant librarian at the Hudson Park Public Library from 1918 to 1925. During this era, she established literary friendships with Robert McAlmon and Winifred Ellerman, who published a Moore collection, *Poems* (1921), in London without her knowledge. A well-received beginning, *Poems* was issued in the

United States as *Observations* (1924), winning an award from *The Dial*, which Moore edited from 1925 to 1929. Additional submissions to *The Egoist* established her reputation for imagist modern poetry. She ceased writing for three years, then earned the 1932 Helen Haire Levinson Prize and the 1935 Ernest Hartsock Memorial Prize for *Selected Poems* (1935).

Moore's friendships with poets Elizabeth Bishop and Wallace Stevens placed her at the heart of the era's literary achievement, which color her essays later collected in *Pedilections* (1955), an examination of the artistry of poets Ezra Pound and Louise Bogan and dancer Anna Pavlova. In the introduction to *Selected Poems*, T. S. Eliot epitomized Moore's writing as durable and continued to laud and promote her verse for thirty years. She maintained a steady output with *The Pangolin and Other Verse* (1936), *What Are Years* (1941), and *Nevertheless* (1944), her most emotionally charged anthology.

Following the death of her mother in 1947, Moore worked for seven years translating the fables of Jean de La Fontaine. A significant addition in her canon, *Collected Poems* (1951), won a National Book award, Bollingen Prize, and Pulitzer Prize for poetry. She issued five more volumes—*Like a Bulwark* (1956), *O To Be a Dragon* (1959), *The Arctic Ox* (1964), *Tell Me, Tell Me: Granite Steel, and Other Topics* (1966), and *A Marianne Moore Reader* (1961), a compendium of poetry, prose, and an interview—and concluded her verse contributions at age 81 with *The Complete Poems* (1967). In addition, in 1962, she produced a stage version of Maria Edgeworth's *The Absentee* and revised Charles Perrault's fairy tales (1963).

Moore died on February 5, 1972, at her Brooklyn home, and was memorialized at the nearby Lafayette Avenue Presbyterian Church.

CHIEF WORKS

Moore's critical essay in verse, "Poetry" (1921), plays the devil's advocate by forcing the art to prove itself. Composed in her fastidious "if . . . then" style, the poem names types of response: "Hands that can grasp, eyes / that can dilate, hair that can rise / if it must . . ."

In line 18, she reaches a pivotal point in the discrimination between poetry and prose with the declaration that "One must make a distinction." Like a punctilious grammar teacher, she calls for "imaginary gardens with real toads in them," an image freighted with her expectations of "raw material" that she labels "genuine."

With the graceless pedantry of a schoolmarm, Moore pursues a clear definition of nationality in "England" (1921). In line 26, she halts differentiation between English and French style or Greek from American to pose a rhetorical question: "Why should continents of misapprehension / have to be accounted for by the fact?" As though chastising the slipshod student, she concludes, "To have misapprehended the matter is to have confessed that one has not looked far enough." With crisp geometric finality, she winds down her argument against comparisons with incontrovertibility of logic: "It has never been confined to one locality."

Curiously devoid of humanity, "A Grave" (1924) offers a naturalistic view of the sea as a repository of lost objects and the dead. Moore pictures the "well excavated grave" flanked by firs standing appropriately at attention, "reserved in their contours, saying nothing," like well-disciplined ushers. She pictures the drowned corpse as unheeding to scavenging fish and unintrusive on sailors, who row on the surface with no thought to the skeletal remains below.

The second half of the poem plays with a flexible analogy—the water-spider shape of a boat propelled by oars as seen from under water. The seriality of motion parallels waves rustling the seaweed, but in no way inhibits the sea bird overhead that scouts the scene at water level. The advance of the tide is significant to the combined movement of shore life "as usual," sweeping over the restless turnings of objects below. Moore enlarges meaning in the choice of "breathlessly," a reminder of drowning, and "rustle," a suggestion that the sea carries off its conquests like a rustler stealing livestock.

"The Mind Is an Enchanted Thing" (1944), a masterwork of deliberation and diction, pursues a similarly minute definition by following human sense perceptions over explicit stimuli—a "katydid-wing," kiwi, piano performance, and gyroscope. Mimicking a question in line 1, the poem moves over examples of meticulous mental analysis to arrive at a conclusion in line 13: "It has memory's ear / that can hear without / having to hear."

The ability of the brain to replicate stored sounds, smells, and images bemuses the poet-speaker, who describes the power as "strong enchantment." In the last three stanzas, the puzzle of intricate patterns leads Moore to conclude that memory delights in "conscientious inconsistency." Unlike the heart, which veils itself in self-willed mist, the mind dismantles dejection, the eye-to-the-ground state introduced in line 12. By accepting variant patterns as "unconfusion," the mind opens itself to an unlimited number of interpretations.

DISCUSSION AND RESEARCH TOPICS

(1) Summarize the milieu of Mountain Rainier as depicted in Moore's ode "An Octopus."

(2) Analyze several of Moore's verse fables—for example, "His Shield," "The Fish," and translations from la Fontaine.

(3) Using "To a Snail," "Silence," "No Swan So Fine," "The Jerboa," "O To Be a Dragon," or "The Paper Nautilus," locate examples of what Moore calls "the genuine."

(4) Contrast Moore's scientific eye for detail with that of poet A. R. Ammons.

(5) Discuss the role of memory in Moore's poetry.

SELECTED BIBLIOGRAPHY

DAVIDSON, CATHY N., and LINDA WAGNER-MARTIN. *The Oxford Companion to Women's Writing in the United States*. New York: Oxford University Press, 1995.

"Marianne Moore." *Contemporary Authors*. Gale Research. galenet.gale.com

UNALI, LINA. "Taoist Concepts and Chinese Imagery in the Poetry of Marianne Moore." dbweb.agore.stm.it/market/sml/moore.htm

T. S. ELIOT (1888-1965)

Thomas Stearns Eliot, an American-born scholar, sophisticated eclectic, and poetic genius claimed by both the United States and England, is the twentieth century's touchstone author and critic. His monumental verse, written during a period of emotional turmoil and personal re-evaluation, gave voice to the post–World War I trauma that left a generation in doubt about the future of civilization. His style transcended previous literary movements with a surprising sense of humor. Both frustratingly obtuse and dazzlingly memorable, his masterworks redirect attention from the collapse of Edwardian respectability to the birth of modernism.

It seems inconceivable that so British a poet could be an American Midwesterner. The seventh son of brick maker Henry Ware Eliot and poet and biographer Charlotte Stearns, Tom Eliot was born in St. Louis, Missouri, on September 26, 1888. His distinguished intellectual family derived from immigrants from East Coker, Somersetshire, a setting that Eliot returns to in his poetry. After completing studies at Smith Academy and a year at Milton Academy, he turned his back on America and cultivated the air, grace, and mannerisms of a London dandy.

Heavily influenced by Irving Babbitt at Harvard, Eliot earned a B.A. in literature and an M.A. in philosophy and Sanskrit, all in four years. To increase his fluency in French, he studied for a year at the Sorbonne in Paris, then returned to Harvard for doctoral work in philosophy. Eliot had traveled in Germany and begun a doctoral dissertation at Merton College, Oxford, when he married Vivienne Haigh-Wood. As World War I engulfed Europe, health problems kept him out of the army.

After Eliot's father altered his will to underscore disappointment in his son's marriage, Ezra Pound influenced Eliot to remain in the British Isles and join the Bloomsbury Circle, a powerful intellectual force in England in the 1920s and 1930s. Following brief teaching stints at High Wycombe and Highgate Junior School, from 1919 to 1922, he worked for Lloyds Bank and began submitting verse of subtle brilliance to magazines. His poems departed from the modish romantics to concentrate on the mystic outlook of the metaphysics and the Christian divines.

Forever done with teaching and money handling, Eliot entered the book world for life as director of publisher Faber & Faber. He distinguished himself with a remarkable first collection, *Prufrock and Other Observations* (1917), followed by *Ara vos prec* (1920) and *The Sacred Wood* (1922). Immediately, he began composing two controversial works, *The Waste Land* (1922), winner of *The Dial* award, and *The Hollow Men* (1925), a profound verse of postwar malaise and a prime influence on the "lost generation." Among scholarly successes were *Three Critical Essays* (1920), *Andrew Marvell* (1922), and *The Criterion*, a literary quarterly he published and edited from 1923 to 1939. He received British citizenship in 1927 and sought baptism and confirmation in the Church of England. In 1932, he returned temporarily to the United States as Harvard's Charles Eliot Norton poetry professor and undertook a series of lectures on U.S. campuses.

A period of Anglo-Catholic thought influenced Eliot's *The Journey of the Magi* (1927), *Ash Wednesday* (1930), and *The Four Quartets* (1943), a war commentary begun in 1935. He exercised versatility in a melodrama, *Sweeney Agonistes* (1932), and two stage works: *The Rock* (1934), a pageant with choruses, and *Murder in the Cathedral* (1935). The latter, a poetic drama commemorating a significant act of violence perpetrated by Henry II, was performed on the site of the assassination of Bishop Thomas à Becket at Canterbury Cathedral's Chapter House.

Subsequent works displaying Eliot's piety and religious philosophy include *The Family Reunion* (1939), *The Idea of a Christian Society* (1940), and *The Cocktail Party* (1950), the most successful of his stage dramas. A lighter work, *Old Possum's Book of Practical Cats* (1940), is the basis for *Cats*, the longest-running production in stage musical history. Less noteworthy are *The Confidential Clerk* (1954) and *The Elder Statesman* (1958), both more suited to reading than to acting. Lauded as English literature's most incisive critic, Eliot surveyed a range of interests with *Homage to Dryden* (1924), *The Use of Poetry and the Use of Criticism* (1933), *Elizabeth Essays* (1934), and *On Poetry and Poets* (1957).

In 1948, Eliot received the Nobel Prize for literature for his erudite treatment of modern sterility. He died in 1965; his ashes were interred in the village church of East Coker, the ancestral home of the Eliot family.

CHIEF WORKS

The dramatic monologue "The Love Song of J. Alfred Prufrock" (1915), an artistically fresh, visually inventive work, is a landmark of emerging modernism. Composed during the poet's period of casting about for a career and lifestyle, it blends the Victorian forms and rhythms of Alfred, Lord Tennyson, and Robert Browning with the disdain and self-doubt of Charles Baudelaire. Eliot prefaces the poem with an epitaph in Italian from *Inferno*, Dante's epic journey into hell. The 131-line main text opens in a seedy part of London, a modern parallel of hell in its joylessness and perpetual torment. Propelled by the walk of the speaker and an unidentified "you," the action moves over doubts and questions neatly unified by rhymed couplets, interspersed in lines 3 and 10 with the odd incidents of unrhymed endings. Surreal and menacing, the skewering of the protagonist Prufrock on a surgical table terrorizes at the same time that it draws the viewer to a subject pinned down for study like an insect in the lab.

The theme is an overt admission of weakness: The speaker confesses an inability to commit to sexual love. Prufrock has become a twentieth-century cliché for the prissy, conflicted bachelor obsessed with a balding head and prim wardrobe and mannerisms, not unlike Eliot himself. Like the sinuous fog, his gaze glides indoors, then outdoors, from surgery to street, social gathering, storm drains, terrace, and back into the "soft October night," another reference to his flaccid character. The juxtaposition of trivialities with life-disturbing doubts stretches out the tedium of modern life over "a hundred visions and revisions," an internal rhyme with "decisions." Unlike the outward control of selecting a tie pin or creasing his slacks, Prufrock's inner turmoil threatens to "disturb the universe." The pathetic hyperbole frames his chaotic thoughts, which swirl around the unexpressed question that dogs him.

Prufrock is not alone in courting disaster through uninvolvement. Passing acquaintances who discuss the arts, take tea and coffee, but take no action, are typical of the modern quandary. Still transfixed in line 57, Prufrock, choking on "the butt-ends of my days and ways," once more wriggles away from a decision. Aware of the fear of intimacy, he envisions himself as "a pair of ragged claws / Scuttling across the floors of silent seas," a starkly sibilant, crablike image that echoes Macbeth's terror of scorpions in his mind. Well past his prime, Prufrock the shirker ironically envisions himself beheaded like John the Baptist, the prophet of Christ. More realistic is the companion image of the sissy gentleman stretching his arm for death, "the eternal Footman," to dress in burial shroud.

Returning to biblical allusion, Prufrock sees himself as Lazarus, a character in hell, proposed in Luke 16 as a messenger warning mortals to change their ways. Fearful of rejection, of being misunderstood, Prufrock lies splayed on a screen, his nervous system illumined by a magic lantern. Unable to claim the tragic significance of Hamlet, Prufrock settles for Polonius, the fuddy-duddy court adviser who gets himself killed by lurking at the edge of the action. Dismayed by the effects of age, Prufrock imagines women on the beach tittering to each other, but not summoning him with their songs. In the greater scope, the overripe bachelor is merely a symptom. Too long enthralled by fancy, the modern world, like Prufrock, has lingered in romanticism and self-indulgent frolic until the realities of the modern world threaten to consume it.

Also from Eliot's initial burst of brilliance, "Sweeney Among the Nightingales" (1919) features the opposite of Eliot's refined Englishman in a laughable, working-class buffoon. The poem, a sharp, cold satire that Stephen Spender labels "a violent cartoon," pictures its characters in animal images of an ape, zebra, giraffe, and Rachel Rabinovitch's "murderous paws."

Eliot loads the poem with mounting menace. End words are predominantly monosyllabic, producing a stabbing series of moon/place/above/gate and wood/aloud/fall/shroud. Through enjambment, the ten stanzas present a running account of Sweeney threatened by a "gambit," the trickery of bar girls. The poet shifts to dark humor by depicting Orion and his dog, the prophetic constellation that takes the shape of the stalking hunter. The point of the plotting is unclear. Like Agamemnon, the Greek king whose murder is recounted in the epigraph, Sweeney is sappily drunk and unaware of any sinister intent, whether to rob him or do bodily harm. Amid the omens of Death and the raven, he merits no pity from nature, as depicted by wisteria vines trailing around the framed face of an observer and the songs of nightingales, or from divine intervention, as implied by "The Convent of the Sacred Heart."

"Gerontion" (1920) is more universal in meaning as a bleak meditation prefiguring the symbols of dry sterility that dominate Eliot's later work. The poem was intended as a preface to *The Waste Land*. The title means "little old man" in Greek and introduces the text with a suitable epigraph from Shakespeare's *Measure for Measure*. In the action, a lifeless, uncommitted old man lives out his declining years and ponders the erratic gifts of history. In a series of dense, interrelated images, the speaker regrets the worldwide decline of Christian faith. The images are the "hot gates" of Thermopylae, "Christ the tiger," and a slate of fictional characters, Mr. Silvero, Hakagawa, Madame de Tornquist, and Fräulein von Kulp, followed in line 68 with De Bailhache, Fresca, Mrs. Cammel. The names imply human faults: Silvero (money), Hakagawa (violent hacking), Tornquist (torn by quest), von Kulp (from the Latin culpa for fault). Like Gerontion's elderly body, exercising the remains of his withered "sight, smell, hearing, taste, and touch," current generations seek escape in crass pleasures. Driven by nature—that is, the Trade winds—they age toward "a sleepy corner," their final resting place.

The Waste Land, a plotless elegy set among realistic images of London, is the most analyzed poem from modern times. It is the work of Eliot, concluded during his retreat to a Swiss sanitarium for rest and recuperation, and of Ezra Pound, the poet's adviser who supervised extreme cuts in the original text. In disjointed scenes and truncated dialogues, the poem, labeled an anti-epic, details an ongoing nightmare, the spiritual and emotional breakdown of Western civilization. Through interwoven allusions to myth, scripture, and document, the poem acts out the disorientation and collapse of modern humanity, which turned from religion but found nothing to replace it. Beginning at life's end, the poem, prefaced by a death urge, opens on a burial scene in April, when the stirrings of spring force buried roots back to life. Against a sterile, lifeless desert, the poet juxtaposes an erotic scene of "the hyacinth girl" and the cynical Madame Sosostris, the fakir who claims to tell fortunes with tarot cards.

Eliot brings the setting closer to home in line 60 with direct reference to London. Caught up in a daily cycle of meaninglessness, victims repeat actions that perpetually deny humanity and rob life of hope. In stave II, a wealthy couple go through the motions of a depleted relationship, their sexual malaise symbolized by the mechanics of a chess game. Like death-in-life skulls, their lidless eyes look toward the door as though awaiting the personified death to knock. With lines 128–130, Eliot shifts from the gravity of former lines with an abrupt "O O O O that Shakespeherian Rag," a vaudevillian tagline that epitomizes the ardent striving, goallessness, and banality of contemporary amusements.

A quick change to a dragged-down woman with rotted teeth and a body sapped at age 31 from a chemically induced abortion reprises the notion of hovering death. As she listens to a chastising friend, the insistent voice of the barkeep warns that time is running out. The reminder, in capital letters, is an alarm to a generation of couples whose physical union has lost significance. The image parallels a breakdown of communication in Eliot's own marriage, which ended with separation in 1932 and his first wife's mental disintegration and retreat to an asylum for the rest of her life.

Stave III, "The Fire Sermon," echoes Psalm 137, a biblical lament for the fallen realm of Babylon. Eliot updates the poem with ironic images of the Thames polluted with the trash of a summer night's entertainment. The couplings of lovers degenerate to the rape of Philomel, a pervasive Greek myth that results in the transformation of sisters into birds. The urbane Eugenides sets up a weekend of carnal pleasures. Viewed by the Greek seer Tiresias, the androgynous messiah figure condemned to abandon maleness for a period of life as a woman, the uninspired seduction scene of a clerical worker on her divan-bed wearies and bores. The surreal connection with Elizabeth I, seduced in a canoe, heightens the poet's dismay at unloving, uninspiring human actions, the "broken fingernails of dirty hands."

Staves IV and V, the most marked by literary curiosities, modulate to abject figures of a waterless desert. Longing overwhelms the dominant pentameter lines with pulsing dimeter calling for "water / A spring." The dry rot that destroyed a mélange of ruling cities—"Jerusalem Athens Alexandria"—moves into the modern era to devour "Vienna London." Remorse for the death of Christianity takes the form of a cockcrow, an allusion to Peter, the disciple who denied the Messiah. The allusion is pertinent to Eliot's personal philosophy, for he was the sole Christian holdout among lapsed believers, atheists, and agnostics of his literary circle.

The final voice is that of the ill-fated Fisher King, a vegetating authority figure who reigns over a sterile land. He suffers physical wounds that symbolize the impotence and fruitlessness of his kingdom, now reduced to a valley of dry bones. Only a worthy warrior can lift the curse through a dual initiation rite—by entering the castle and explaining a series of obscure symbols, which the poet depicts as the Buddhist triad "Datta. Dayadhvam. Damyata" [give, sympathize, control]. Eliot ends the poem with the ritual call to peace, repeated three times in pattern with the Buddha's three-part command.

Written over two decades after his early masterpieces, "Burnt Norton" (1936) is the first of *The Four Quartets*. Eliot observes his typical stylistic patterning with an erudite epigraph drawn from Heraclitus and a division into five staves, a parallel of the movements of a musical composition. Lulling the reader with repetition in "Time present and time past," "time future," and "all time," the poet-speaker mimics a Buddhist chant, a compelling intonation that, like self-hypnosis, draws the reader into a veiled, mystic consciousness. The mesmerizing effect of these time-oriented phrases embodies his philosophic consideration of history, which is comprised of time and action. With exaggerated simplicity, in line 42, the poet speaks through a bird, which commands, "Go, go, go . . . human kind / Cannot bear very much reality."

Stave II intensifies Eliot's contemplation of time and his contemporaries' inability to escape from a "bedded axle-tree," which brings action to a halt. Toying with the conjunctions "neither . . . nor," he looks beyond to "the still point," life's end, which concludes "the dance." The bewildered human mind attempts to make sense of life, but acquires only "a little consciousness." The agony of confusion over purpose creates the "place of disaffection" in stave III, a characterization of a world of distractions and fancies, of "bits of paper, whirled by the cold wind," an allusion to the Cumaean sybil's leaves on which she wrote prophecies. The spirit, overwhelmed by sterility, emptiness, and malaise, sinks into torpor. Staves IV and V find hope in eternity. As Eliot describes it, "the end and the beginning were always there." Words fail to capture the purpose of creation, which Eliot epitomizes as "unmoving" love, the conclusion to his formal deliberation on meaning.

DISCUSSION AND RESEARCH TOPICS

(1) Account for critics who reject abstruse, densely referential poetry like Eliot's *The Four Quartets* and *The Waste Land* as self-consciously pedantic and too obscure for most readers. Summarize contrasting opinion that lauds the intricate allusions, exacting logic, and multiple meanings of Eliot's work.

(2) List significant lines from *The Waste Land* along with their literary influences. Account for the fruitlessness of human strivings and potential for chaos that Eliot stresses in his vignettes of failed love.

(3) Compose an extended definition of mock-heroic with elements drawn from Eliot's "Sweeney Among the Nightingales."

(4) Compare "Gerontion" to the cynical old Roman in Joseph Heller's novel *Catch-22*. Determine why the characters neglect virtue and embrace a slow drift toward oblivion.

(5) Discuss religious images in "The Love Song of J. Alfred Prufrock." How do such images function in the poem? Does Eliot treat religion seriously?

SELECTED BIBLIOGRAPHY

ACKROYD, PETER. *T. S. Eliot: A Life*. New York: Simon & Schuster, 1984.

EBLE, KENNETH, ed. *T. S. Eliot*. Revised edition. Boston: Twayne, 1982.

GISH, NANCY K. *The Waste Land: A Poem of Memory and Desire*. Boston: Twayne, 1988.

SPENDER, STEPHEN. *T. S. Eliot*. New York: Viking Press, 1975.

UNGER, LEONARD, ed. *Seven Modern American Poets*. Minneapolis: University of Minnesota Press, 1967.

JOHN CROWE RANSOM (1888-1974)

Poet John Crowe Ransom accepted the challenge of correlating empirical fact with the shadowy world of feeling. Grouped with Robert Penn Warren, Merrill Moore, Allen Tate, and Donald Davidson as one of the original Fugitive Agrarians, an influential circle of Southern scholars, critics, and poets, he was the most distinguished critic and editor of his age. His verse, composed during a complex period of phenomenal scientific and technological advancement, registered a modern paradox—the intellectual delight in progress set against the spirit's ambivalence, a tortuous state that the poet described as a "[walk] in hell." His literary fervor precipitated a rebirth of Southern literature and resultant awards and honors to the era's foremost proponent of modern verse.

Ransom, a native of Tennessee and the third of four children, was born in Pulaski on April 30, 1888, to Sara Ella Crowe and the Reverend John James Ransom, a Methodist minister. He studied at home with his father during his childhood, when the family moved among four parishes. In 1899, he profited at a Nashville boys' academy from the teachings of its principal, Angus Gordon Bowen. Ransom was tops in his high school class, completed two years at Vanderbilt University, then left to teach middle grades in Taylorsville, Mississippi, and Latin and Greek at Haynes-McLean School in Lewisburg, Tennessee.

Ransom was eager to get back to scholarship and completed a B.A. at Vanderbilt, again graduating valedictorian with membership in Phi Beta Kappa. He was selected Rhodes scholar in 1910 after a year as principal in Lewisburg, and he earned an M.A. with honors in the classics from Christ Church College, Oxford, before traveling Europe and the British Isles. After a year of teaching Latin in Lakeville, Connecticut, he returned to Vanderbilt in 1914 to teach English literature, numbering among his pupils Cleanth Brooks, Donald Davidson, Randall Jarrell, Robert Lowell, Allen Tate, and Robert Penn Warren.

Before serving as first lieutenant in the field artillery in France during World War I, Ransom had already begun submitting poems to *Contemporary Verse* and *Independent*. With the help of essayist

Christopher Morley and poet Robert Frost, he published *Poems About God* (1919) in England before returning to the United States. About the time that his conservative discussion group, the Fugitives, was meeting to debate the future of Southern literature, he married Robb Reavill and began a family of three—daughters Helen and Reavill and son John James. Ransom developed into a skilled, restrained wordsmith and a master of clarity who admired dense texts enhanced by precise diction and technical skill.

Ransom continued to issue poems and essays in *American Review*, *Southern Review*, and *The Fugitive*, Vanderbilt's literary-social journal that professed agrarian values and rejected modern technology, big business, and human displacement. In support of his coterie's strongly earth-based, anti-industrial philosophy, he joined eleven regional writers in two literary debates: *I'll Take My Stand: The South and the Agrarian Tradition* (1930), for which he supplied an opening essay, "Statement of Principles," and *Who Owns America?* (1936). He published a stand-alone volume of essays, *God Without Thunder* (1930), which criticized insipid religion, and in 1938 publicly debated the essence of agrarianism.

Ransom established himself among America's finest poets while at the same time growing as a teacher, critic, and philosopher. He produced two volumes in 1924: *Chills and Fever* and *Grace after Meat*. The latter was shortlisted for a Pulitzer Prize. He followed with the critically successful *Two Gentlemen in Bonds* (1927), additional submissions to *Virginia Quarterly Review* and *Southern Review*, and *Selected Poems* (1945), a solid contribution to his canon that was twice reissued.

In 1937, Ransom founded and edited *Kenyon Review*, a leading literary journal for twenty-two years. He decided that he was finished with poetry, but issued revisions in subsequent collections in 1945, 1963, and 1969. Ransom then concentrated on essays, which he published in *The World's Body* (1938) and *The New Criticism* (1941), a call for literary analysis that focuses on the work alone, excluding considerations of movement, age, and the author's life. He received a Guggenheim Fellowship to the University of the Southwest, Exeter, a Bollingen Prize in Poetry, Russell Loines Memorial award from the American Institute of Arts and Letters, and honorary consultancy in American literature at the Library of Congress.

Ransom remained active, publishing critical essays on poetry and a collection, *Beating the Bushes: Selected Essays, 1941-1970,* and serving as visiting professor at Northwest University and Vanderbilt. Despite his shift from pure creative art, by the end of his long life, his reputation had already begun to revert to master poet rather than mentor or critic. He died in his sleep in Gambier, Ohio, on July 3, 1974; his ashes were interred at the Kenyon College Cemetery. Posthumous works include *Selected Essays of John Crowe Ransom* (1984) and a compendium of letters in 1985.

CHIEF WORKS

"Here Lies a Lady" (1924), a piquant commentary on the clash of reason and sensibility, displays Ransom's early vigor and the focal themes of his later works. The speaker, as though reciting an old English ballad, speaks in four-line stanzas composed of five beats per line and rhyming abab, cdcd, efef, ghgh. In line 16, the peculiarities of the lady's demise are neatly summarized: Her last days were marked by twelve episodes, six of depression and six of manic passion. Speaking through the mask of a courtly gentleman, the poet remains involved and yet detached by ordering the four verses with mathematical precision: one to begin the eulogy for the fallen aristocrat, a beloved family-centered woman; two to describe alternating fever and chills; and a fourth addressed to survivors. In mock antique language, the speaker wishes for all "sweet ladies" a balance of bloom and languor. With self-serving irony, he demands, "was she not lucky?" a moot point in the greater question of a promising life plagued by troubles and prematurely snuffed out.

From the same period, "Philomela" is charmingly set in traditional iambic pentameter (five-beat lines) rhymed abbaa and falling away on the last line of each stanza to three beats. Its text draws on a disturbingly tragic pair of myths that Ovid, a major classic poet from the early days of the Roman Empire, states in Book 6 of his *Metamorphoses.* Unlike most of Ransom's verse, the eight-stanza narrative is a personal statement that recalls his graduate days at Oxford and subsequent return to the United States to write in classical mode. His doubts about American readers appears in line 37,

"I am in despair if we may make us worthy," a true question of the nation's capacity for traditions that date to Greek mythology. For all its ponderous diction and mock-serious tone, the poem sets in verse one of the concerns of the Fugitives, who doubted that a bustling country absorbed in industrial and commercial progress was capable of a parallel development of the arts.

"Bells for John Whiteside's Daughter" (1924), one of modern poetry's unflinching perusals of hard-edged reality, sets out with a courteous, subdued tone and veiled dismay to observe traditional rituals honoring a little girl's passing. The syntax is precise, the imagery lighthearted, yet compelling as the poet surveys the unnatural reserve of a formerly boisterous child. Speaking as a mourner reconciling the perversely mannered stillness of a corpse laid out for burial, the poet can't resist visions of past rascality as she "bruited" backyard wars and, in a pastoral setting, shadow-fenced against her own image. As though unable to allay the grief, the poet hears the honk of the tricky, sleepy-eyed geese calling "alas," an archaism and stylistic connection to chivalric romance.

Deeply respectful of custom, Ransom, speaking from the point of view of a Southern gentleman, controls his probing paradox, carefully rhyming abab and guiding line lengths to four beats. Even the title resists harsher diction, substituting "bells for" as an indicator of death. As though tipping his hat to the inevitable, he lops off the fourth line of each stanza to dimeter or trimeter. Allusions to death are numerous, but restrained—the shadowed adversary, the whitening of grass with snowy feathers, and the irony of a "tireless heart" and "noon apple-dreams," now permanently frozen in time.

Like an overly fastidious adult, the speaker searches for the appropriate terms to fix on the child's unusual torpor. The incongruity of her pose vexes a mind that once demanded ladylike behavior in place of willful caprice. Now, the swift-footed Miss Whitesides is forever forced into a "prim [propping]," another euphemism for death. The formerly durable "little body"—a phrase that allies the double meaning of human frame and corpse—takes on an unnatural reverie, a rigid "brown study" that astonishes with its finality.

"Piazza Piece" (1925), a model of quiet formality, demonstrates Ransom's mastery of the fourteen-line Petrarchan sonnet. The poet follows a tight pattern of rhyme, meter, and thought development. He transcends these mechanics by judicious enjambment, which carries over from line to line significant statements, in particular, the focus of the lady's dalliance, "waiting / Until my truelove comes." His rhymes vary masculine and feminine forms, the monosyllabic small/all, moon/soon and the less importunate falling away of trying/sighing/dying. By repeating end words at the beginning and closing of the octave and sestet, he effectively separates the paired statements as though sculpting two figures in confrontation.

Heavily emphasizing the differences in age, the speaker, Ransom's famous "gentleman in a dustcoat," bears the civility and demeanor of a courtly male forced into the role of traducer of beautiful young womanhood. Soon to turn to dust, the lady, idealized in speech and intent, refuses to listen to insistent warnings of mortality from the "grey man." Her vaudevillian reply is the standard line of the stalked virgin. Beneath a frail trellis, symbol of a human effort to shape nature, she stands at the height of loveliness and fools herself into believing that human hands can stay death's menace.

Published in 1927, "Janet Waking," a frequent companion piece to "Bells for John Whiteside's Daughter," conveys in seven stanzas the poet's ironic commentary on a child's initiation into the finality of death. The title indicates a duality: The main character awakens to search for her hen and is unceremoniously awakened to loss. Like Little Miss Muffet or Goldilocks, Janet appears one-dimensional in her goodness as she kisses mother and daddy, then displays another side of her personality, a childish orneriness toward a brother, an obvious rival. Summoning her pet, she learns the particulars of its death, killed by a bee enhanced to mock epic proportions by the fearful adjective "transmogrifying." The crucial fourth stanza spills over into the fifth as enjambment continues the details of a purple rising and the pseudo-humorous conclusion that the topknot rose, "But Chucky did not."

In imitation of fable, the crux of the poem turns on "So" at the beginning of stanza six as the poet guides the dramatic situation to a jarring moral. Baffled that Chucky no longer can "rise and walk," Janet overtaxes her breathing with a flow of tears. With typical girlish petulance, she begs for adults to revive Chucky and rejects the obvious conclusion that there are laws of nature that humans cannot override. As though tiptoeing past a poignant and private scene, the poet softens his rhymes to breath/death, sleep/deep, an acknowledgement of Janet's painful turning away from babyhood.

A contemporary of "Janet Waking," Ransom's "The Equilibrists," a 56-line mock chivalric narrative, moves back in time with Tennysonian archaisms and Arthurian characters drawn from the tragic love of Tristan and Isolde. In a peculiarly sanitized study of lovers' obsessions, the poet relies on syntactic inversions—"traveled he," "mouth he remembered," and "came I descanting"—and the high-sounding diction of "jacinth," "stuprate," "orifice," "saeculum," and "beseeching" to distance viewer from object. Like an accounting of feminine anatomy in the erotic verse of the Song of Solomon, the speaker inventories the white-armed beauty's loveliness in metaphors: "grey doves" for eyes, "officious tower" for mind, and "lilies," a quaint substitute for breasts.

As the compelling iambic pentameter couplets press on, the crux arises in line 21—"Predicament indeed, which thus discovers / Honor among thieves, Honor between lovers"—as though man, woman, and the personified abstraction Honor were elements of a stylized love triangle. The speaker toys with the lovers' choices. He muses on the precarious balance of physical attraction held off by high ideals and enhances the standoff with a metaphysical conceit—the farfetched notion of binary stars held in a twirling dual orbit, at once locked in near-embrace and forever imprisoned out of reach by centrifugal force. Like stars, they burn with unrequited love.

Ransom makes a clear break with myth in line 33 to ponder the Christian overtones of the lovers' quandary. Like St. Augustine, they must decide whether to burn or burn in hell—to suffer thwarted passion or be damned eternally for consummating it. From the Christian point of view, the poet acknowledges that eternity lacks the combustible "tinder" (a pun on "tender") and inflaming lechery. After death, flesh is "sublimed away" as heaven refines the liberated spirit. Those "great lovers" who acquiesce to their desires spend the afterlife in tormented embrace. Like predators, their disintegrating bodies forever tear at each other.

Out of awe and reverence for the "equilibrists," the speaker is unable to retreat from their cosmic dance—forever untouching, but linked in a fiery, yet decorous attraction. In a final gesture to their exquisite torment, the speaker offers an epitaph typical of ancient Roman tombstones in its apostrophe to the passing stranger. Although decayed to mold and ash, the lovers remain inextricably locked in a virginal mockery of coupling, their chastity preserved by obedience to purity. For the speaker, their supine splendor is both "perilous and beautiful." For the modern reader, however, their contretemps suggests a cosmic puzzle, an academic paradox that forever teases without hope of solution.

DISCUSSION AND RESEARCH TOPICS

(1) Analyze Ransom's consternation in "Bells for John Whiteside's Daughter" or "Dead Boy" alongside that of Dylan Thomas's "A Refusal to Mourn the Death, by Fire, of a Child in London." Determine which poet makes the more universal statement about premature death.

(2) Apply the dramatic situations in Andrew Marvell's "To His Coy Mistress" and John Keats' "Ode on a Grecian Urn" to the perpetual separation of lovers in Ransom's "The Equilibrists," "Piazza Piece," and "Winter Remembered."

(3) Account for Ransom's use of antique syntax, pronouns (ye, thy), and diction and his penchant for metaphysical conceits or farfetched comparisons. Contrast poses in art works by the Pre-Raphaelite painters William Morris and Dante Gabriel Rossetti to Ransom's traditional male/female encounters set in stylized verse.

(4) Trace the theme of evanescence through Ransom's poems in *Chills and Fever* and *Two Gentlemen in Bonds*. Account for his persistent lament for endangered art and beauty in the rapidly changing South. Determine whether such preservation of Western tradition is a worthy endeavor or a symptom of a retreat from reality.

(5) Discuss the speaker's tone in "Here Lies a Lady." Does the speaker come to terms with the woman's death? Does the poem end on a tragic or accepting tone? How does the poet evoke this tone?

SELECTED BIBLIOGRAPHY

"John Crowe Ransom." *Contemporary Authors*. Gale Research. galenet.gale.com

"John Crowe Ransom Papers." www.library.vanderbilt.edu/speccol/jcrbiog.html

MALVASI, MARK G. *The Unregenerate South: The Agrarian Thought of John Crowe Ransom, Allen Tate, and Donald Davidson*. Baton Rouge: Louisiana State University Press, 1997.

RUBIN, LOUIS D., Jr., comp. and ed. *The Literary South*. Baton Rouge: Louisiana State University Press, 1979.

UNGER, LEONARD, ed. *Seven Modern American Poets*. Minneapolis: University of Minnesota Press, 1967.

YOUNG, THOMAS DANIEL. *Gentleman in a Dustcoat: A Biography of John Crowe Ransom*. Baton Rouge: Louisiana State University Press, 1976.

EDNA ST. VINCENT MILLAY (1892-1950)

A precocious Jazz Age feminist, social rebel, and popular literary figure, Edna St. Vincent Millay is arguably America's finest sonneteer. She earned a reputation for mastering verse drama and intricate, emotional poetry free of Victorian cant. With fluent, sensuous grace, she contained her passions in traditional poetic forms. Her poems espouse an intimate and, at times, detached knowledge of love, but she long put off suitors who threatened her free-spirited individuality and determination to write. Her mature talent retained a sensitivity and bravado that balance heartbreak with humor.

Millay was born on February 22, 1892, in Rockland, near Maine's Penobscot Bay, a setting for her naturalistic poems as well as such localized sonnets as "I Shall Go Back" and "The Cameo." The eldest and favorite of three girls, "Vincent" grew up in Camden under the loving hand of her mother, who reared three girls alone after her husband's abrupt departure in 1900. Encouraged to study piano and literature, Millay graduated from Camden High. Disliked for intellectual snobbery, she failed to win the post of class poet because spiteful classmates refused to vote for her.

At age 14, Millay published "The Land of Romance" in *Current Literature*. At age 19, and already the recipient of the Intercollegiate Poetry Society prize, she achieved a rare maturity with "Renascence," chosen from 10,000 entries for the anthology *The Lyric Year* (1912). The most enduring of her lines, "O world, I cannot hold thee close enough," introduces "God's World," an inventive self-revelation that earned lasting critical acclaim.

Public reception brought Millay a patron, Caroline B. Dow, who heard her read "Renascence" at the Whitehall Inn. Dow paid Millay's college tuition to Vassar, where language study and feminist ferment infused her socialist bent. Energized by a romantic attachment to poet Arthur Davison Ficke, she began a sonnet cycle while completing a degree, which was momentarily threatened when she was suspended for disobedience. In 1917, she published a first volume, *Renascence and Other Poems*, comprised of lyrics and both Elizabethan and Shakespearian sonnets.

Intent on an acting career, Millay settled in Greenwich Village, New York, where she helped found the Cherry Lane Theater. To earn a living, she served as a personal secretary and freelanced short stories for *Ainslee* and *Metropolitan* under the pen name Nancy Boyd. Her dreams of acting faded, but her one-act experimental drama, *Aria da Capo*, a stylized piece protesting World War I, flourished at the Provincetown Playhouse in 1919. Influenced by Village radicals, she expressed social consciousness, pacifism, and sexual freedom in *A Few Figs from Thistles* (1920), which showcased euphoric love in "Recuerdo" and a notorious cynicism in "My candle burns at both ends," a wholehearted declaration of the unconventional life.

The release of *Second April* (1921) cinched Millay's reputation as the leading female poet of the age and the spokeswoman for the independent female, whom she championed for setting personal standards of love and sexuality. She completed two more plays, *Two Slatterns and a King* (1921) and *The Lamp and the Bell* (1921).

Millay further substantiated her place in American literature with tour de force sonneteering in *The Ballad of the Harp Weaver and Other Poems* (1923), which netted her a Pulitzer Prize for poetry, the first given to a female writer. After her marriage to Dutch-American importer Eugen Jan Boissevain, her health failed. The couple settled in the Berkshires at Steepletop, a secluded 700-acre farm in Austerlitz, New York, in 1925. Collaborating with Deems Taylor, she supplied a blank verse libretto written solely in one-sylable words for the wildly popular *The King's Henchman* (1927), which the Metropolitan Opera produced on stage and in a popular book form.

Still dedicated to radical issues despite her compromised energies, Millay crusaded for clemency for anarchists Nicola Sacco and Bartolomeo Vanzetti, a cause célèbre of the period commemorated in "Justice Denied in Massachusetts" and "Fear," a vehement diatribe published in *Outlook*. She kept vigil at the Boston Court House the night in 1927 when the pair were executed for payroll robbery and murder, and she dedicated proceeds from *The Buck in the Snow and Other Poems* (1928) to their posthumous defense. Lacking her youthful verve, she battled headaches, visual distortion, and undiagnosed abdominal pain while writing spirited, intensely personal verse laced with contemporary themes, collected in *Fatal Interview* (1931) and *Wine from These Grapes* (1934), which features a superb sonnet sequence, *Epitaph for the Race of Man*. In addition, she honored her friend and colleague, poet Elinor Wylie, with six elegies in *Huntsman, What Quarry?* (1939).

As the world rushed toward a second global war, Millay issued *Make Bright the Arrows: 1940 Notebook* (1940), *There Are No Islands Any More* (1940), *Collected Sonnets* (1941), the Writers' War Board radio play *The Murder of Lidice* (1942), which details Nazi atrocities, and *Collected Lyrics* (1943), which influenced the style of poets Sylvia Plath and Anne Sexton. Intense radical propaganda and political activism weakened her further in 1944, when she published *Poem and Prayer for an Invading Army*. While in seclusion in the months following her husband's death, she drank heavily. On October 19, 1950, she died of heart failure at the head of the stairs in her home. Steepletop, the country estate where her ashes are interred, was the setting for a private funeral. Her last volume, *Mine the Harvest*, issued in 1954, contains works from the last decade of her life and features her salute to the sonnet, "I Will Put Chaos into Fourteen Lines."

CHIEF WORKS

Edna St. Vincent Millay had been erroneously categorized as just another woman writing about love until feminist critics revived her canon with fresh insights into her stark images and commentary on humanist themes. A sizable portion of her early works displays a hard, intellectual edge and harsher determinism. One of the early sonnets, "Euclid Alone Has Looked on Beauty Bare" (1923), lauds structure. To demonstrate logic, the text further constrains the fourteen-line Petrarchan form by reducing the number of rhymes from five to four. The rhyme scheme of abbaabbacddccd admits only one feminine foot with "nowhere," which ends on an off beat. The subject is also tightly controlled, focusing on geometry as the only pure beauty.

In contrast, "The Return" (1934), a less idealized study of transience, pictures nature as a constant, a dispassionate entity apart from the romanticism, escapism, religion, and philosophy that humans invest in it. The text develops a lyric approach with four-beat lines rhyming abab. In five quatrains, she again objectifies nature by describing the earth mother receiving dead beings—a man and a lynx—who "Come trailing blood unto her door." Devoid of outward grief, the divine goddess offers shelter, but no pity, because sentiment is inconsistent with nature. The detachment suggests a departure from suffering that writers of the post–World War I era found difficult to achieve.

In 1928, Millay produced "Dirge Without Music," a disturbingly clear-eyed, bittersweet love plaint. The twelfth line offers only a glimpse at the bright-eyed person the poet-speaker has lost. Opening on a petulant, wordy argument for private grief, the poet-speaker stops herself in line 2 with a firmly resigned four-stage pause: "So it is, and so it will be, for so it has been, time out of mind." Battling impermanence all the way to the grave, she bears resentment like an Olympic baton in a prim assertion, "I know. But I do not approve." The final stanza, returned to the previous tight-lipped self-absorption, winds down to repetition of the speaker's earlier disapproval, as though her mind is unable to compromise on the subject of losing a loved one.

After two decades of focusing on technically precise verse, Millay wrote "On Thought in Harness." With its emotional free-style verse in three rhymed stanzas, the poet overturned criticisms that she was a purist rightfully placed among the Edwardian traditionalists. As a testimony to her versatility, the poem is a suitable antithesis to "I Will Put Chaos into Fourteen Lines." With varying line lengths, she demonstrates hesitancy at letting her mind free of an unnatural containment.

The poem's chief delight is a controlling metaphor of the falconer with hooded bird. It is significant that the bird is female, a symbol of inhibited womanhood. A jarring detail in line 9 notes, "Her head stinks of its hood, her feathers reek / Of me, that quake at the thunder." The candor of the poet's introspection produces a remarkable list of commands to the falcon, which she bids to "Soar, eat ether, see what has never been seen; depart, be lost. / But climb." The departure from stricter metrical forms complements earlier works with deliberate pacing that concludes on a resolute double beat.

A similar urge to flee stifling convention dominates "Wild Swans," an earnest, complex, eight-line stanza rhyming abbccbbc. The reversal of positions, bird with woman, places the poet-speaker indoors and the migrating flock overhead. Again, Millay punches out her determination with a double beat and supportive pause when she calls, "Wild swans, come over the town, come over / The town again, trailing your legs and crying." As does the hood in the previous poem, the house stifles with its implications of dreary domesticity, but the poet blames not housewifery, but her "tiresome heart, forever living and dying." Identification with the wild flight transfers the crying to the speaker, who feels compelled to depart and lock the door behind her.

DISCUSSION AND RESEARCH TOPICS

(1) Summarize the tone and personal values of "I Shall Go Back," "Pity Me Not," "Sonnet xli," and "Sonnet xcv" in light of feminist progress toward political and economic equality in the early 1920s.

(2) Contrast the refined protest of Millay's "Justice Denied in Massachusetts" with the more strident outbursts of Allen Ginsberg and the Beat movement.

(3) Analyze the everyday details and psychological realism of Millay's *Sonnets from an Ungrafted Tree*. Account for her sympathy with the mismatched farm couple.

(4) Determine the value of literature and music to Millay in the fervid apostrophe "On Hearing a Symphony of Beethoven."

(5) Discuss how Millay characterizes nature in "The Return."

SELECTED BIBLIOGRAPHY

DAVIDSON, CATHY N., and Linda Wagner-Martin. *The Oxford Companion to Women's Writing in the United States*. New York: Oxford University Press, 1995.

"Edna St. Vincent Millay." *Contemporary Authors*. Gale Research. galenet.gale.com

"Edna St. Vincent Millay." www.millaycolony.org/ednabio.html

GURKO, MIRIAM. *Restless Spirit: The Life of Edna St. Vincent Millay.* New York: Thomas Y. Crowell, 1962.

NIERMAN, JUDITH, and JOHN J. PATTON. "An Introduction to Edna St. Vincent Millay." www.inform.umd.edu/EdRes/Topic/ WomensStudies/Bibliographies/Millay/intro.html

UNTERMEYER, LOUIS. "The Poet and Her Book: The Life and Work of Edna St. Vincent Millay." *Saturday Review,* 7 June 1969, 30–31.

JEAN TOOMER (1894–1967)

Virtuoso, mystic, and modernist author of the first mature work of the post–World War I Southern Renaissance, Nathan Eugene "Jean" Toomer was an alienated seeker, a forerunner of the racial neutrality of 1990s multiculturalism. A steadfast humanist, he was uncertain of his ethnic makeup yet identified solidly with black themes. He once said, "I am of no particular race. I am of the human race, a man at large in the human world, preparing a new race." A metrical whiz, he assimilated social themes into a varied canon; like his friends, poets Langston Hughes and Hart Crane, he attempted to transform jazz into verse. Along with Richard Wright's *Native Son* and Ralph Ellison's *The Invisible Man*, publication of Toomer's creative montage *Cane* (1923) was a defining moment in Harlem's era of artistic experimentation.

Toomer was born on December 26, 1894, in Washington, D.C. Following his parents' divorce, he faced social and financial ruin after his mother married an irresponsible man and settled in New Rochelle, New York. At her death in 1909, he moved in with his grandfather, Pinckney Benton Stewart Pinchback, son of a slave woman and a Louisiana lieutenant governor during Reconstruction. He enrolled at six institutions and studied law at the University of Wisconsin and history at City College of New York but gave up on scholastics and returned to Washington to manage the Howard Theater. In 1922, he took his first job in education, a four-month stint as principal of an agricultural and industrial academy in Sparta, Georgia. The experience—his only direct contact with the South—generated a rhapsodic love of Negro spirituals and folklore.

Toomer was influenced by poets William Blake and Walt Whitman and the artistic genius of novelist James Joyce. He associated with other black writers at the stylish salons hosted by Ethel Ray Nance and Georgia Douglas Johnson. The support of editor Jessie Redmon Fauset encouraged Toomer to publish poems, excerpts, sketches of Southern life, and short fiction. His stark picture of Southern segregation powered *Cane*, an experimental three-part study of black identity and citizenship in the United States. The work, set in Georgia, enlarges on Afro-centrism and prefigures the vast black migration to Chicago, Washington, D.C., and other northeastern urban centers and the "black is beautiful" movement of the 1960s and 1970s. The mixed-genre text contains verse, sketches, commentary, and drama. Its inventiveness earned him a place at the Harlem symposium of young artists in March 1924, when he, Langston Hughes, and Countée Cullen received accolades from W. E. B. Du Bois, James Weldon Johnson, and Alain Locke, the revered elder statesmen of the Harlem Renaissance.

In 1923, the Howard University Players performed Toomer's poorly conceived play, *Balo, A Sketch of Negro Life*, a study of black Georgian peasant life. That same year, he failed to find a producer for *Kabnis* (1923), a modern drama based on his experiences while teaching in Georgia. Restless and dissatisfied, he moved from New York to Chicago and then to France. In Fontainebleau, France, he came under the influence of Russian mystic Georges Ivanovitch Gurdjieff's Institute for the Harmonious Development of Man, a utopist gathering intent on founding an ideal society based on mutual understanding. After returning to the United States, Toomer lost his readership while sponsoring a Gurdjieff colony on Chicago's Gold Coast.

Toomer's on-again, off-again literary drive bemused his circle. They questioned why he seldom published and how he could afford to reject James Weldon Johnson's offer to publish his poems in *Book of American Negro Poetry*, which Toomer disdained because of its insistence on blacks only. Although Toomer persevered with a wealth of writing, including poems, novels, nonfiction, and short fiction, his career stalled. He produced only two works, the self-published book of sayings, *Essentials* (1931), influenced by Pennsylvania Quakers, and *Portage Potential* (1932). He went into a depression after his wife, novelist Marjorie Latimer, died giving birth to a daughter in August 1932. The publication of a rhapsodic long narrative poem, *The Blue Meridian* (1936), ended his role in the Harlem Renaissance.

At loose ends, Toomer was an artistic dropout turned Quaker. He withdrew into religious mysticism; his work passed out of print. He died on March 30, 1967, at a rest home in Bucks County, Pennsylvania, leaving unpublished a sizable sheaf of stories, drama, novels, and an autobiography. In 1974, Darwin Turner issued *The Wayward and the Seeking: a Collection of Writings by Jean Toomer*. Editors Robert B. Jones and the poet's second wife produced a subsequent verse anthology, *The Collected Poems of Jean Toomer* (1988). The boldness of Toomer's racial neutrality influenced subsequent students of the black experience, notably novelist Alice Walker.

CHIEF WORKS

"Karintha," a focused vision, opens the seminal work *Cane*. The tribute to her beauty brims with the earthy eroticism of a male speaker overwhelmed by the dusky allure of a twenty-year-old. She has possessed eye-catching beauty since childhood, when the old men riding her "hobby-horse upon their knees" prefaced the prowl of lustful boys. Toomer breaks this entry into four lyric and three prose segments. Redolent with sexuality in the spring of rabbits on pine straw, the vignette depicts Karintha through potential tragedy—the failed hopes of a lush Venus "ripened too soon." By extension, the black race, hurrying to urban industrial centers, fling easy money at their goddess of pleasure without recognizing how quickly their energizing, rejuvenating "sun goes down." To stress his pessimism, the poet can't resist a second "goes down."

Prefacing a vignette called "Fern," Toomer's "Georgia Dusk" immerses the reader in seven stanzas extolling an idyllic black South. Sensuous and languid, the sawmill halts and people mingle at sunset in anticipation of a folk celebration—the "night's barbecue." A mélange of sense impressions summons "blood-hot eyes," sweet cane, and improvised folk airs. The poet saturates the lines with alliteration ("soft settling pollen," "pyramidal sawdust pile"), simile ("pine-needles fall like sheets of rain"), and metaphor ("blue ghosts of trees"). The poet identifies the graceful passage of celebrants down a swamp footpath with the pomp of African royalty, including king, high priests, and juju-man, or shaman. To Toomer, the import of this caroling assembly of singers and "cornfield concubines" is both erotic and holy.

"Seventh Street," an epigraph to a prose section of *Cane* describing Chicago and Washington, D.C., reduces to a single quatrain a rhythmic, imagistic glimpse of city high life. He describes the good-timer spending money, bootlegger in gaudy finery, fast-moving Cadillacs, and trams as examples of living fast and grabbing as much enjoyment as possible. The depiction suits its historical setting, which Toomer lists as "Prohibition and the War," meaning World War I. The impersonal speaker, who relishes alliteration and onomatopeia, passes no judgment on urban entertainments. Only the pain in the pocket suggests a physical need to escape through tactile, visceral pleasure.

DISCUSSION AND RESEARCH TOPICS

(1) Assess realistic details in the stylized portraiture of "Fern" in Toomer's *Cane*, Edgar Lee Masters's *Spoon River Anthology*, and Sherwood Anderson's *Winesburg, Ohio*.

(2) Express Toomer's vision in "Blue Meridian." Determine the practical means by which he hoped to "uncase the races," "open the classes," and "free man from his shrinkage."

(3) Determine the purpose of the tightly controlling parallelism and fearful imagery in Toomer's "Portrait in Georgia."

(4) Contrast the focus on light imagery in "Karintha" and "Song of the Son." Express Toomer's concern that the "New Negro" is fated to lose the sensuality, grace, and loveliness of a simpler, less frenetic time.

(5) Discuss how World War I serves as a backdrop to "Seventh Street." How does the war influence the poem?

SELECTED BIBLIOGRAPHY

CAMPBELL, MARY SCHMIDT. Introduction. *Harlem Renaissance Art of Black America*. New York: Harry N. Abrams, 1987.

CHAPMAN, ABRAHAM, ed. *Black Voices: An Anthology of Afro-American Literature*. New York: New American Library, 1968.

HASKINS, JIM. *The Harlem Renaissance*. Brookfield, CT: Millbrook Press, 1996.

JACQUES, GEOFFREY. *Free Within Ourselves: The Harlem Renaissance*. New York: Franklin Watts, 1996.

LEWIS, DAVID LEVERING. *When Harlem Was in Vogue*. New York: Alfred A. Knopf, 1981.

PLOSKI, HARRY A., and JAMES WILLIAMS, eds. *The Negro Almanac*. Detroit: Gale Research, 1989.

RUBIN, LOUIS D., JR., comp. and ed. *The Literary South*. Baton Rouge: Louisiana State University Press, 1979.

LOUISE BOGAN (1897–1970)

Acclaimed as reviewer, autobiographer, and poet, Louise Bogan earned a place among the female voices of the mid-twentieth century. As a distinct loner living in a clannish New York circle, she produced an idiosyncratic style marked by epigram, dreamy landscapes, terse phrasing, and incisive images of sexual betrayal and patriarchal constraints on women. Of her 105 published titles, the majority are brief, but pungent and darkly truthladen. She was much admired by Ford Madox Ford and Allen Tate. Her accomplished lyrics, conflicted subjects, and powerful physicality anticipated the themes and subjects of May Sarton and Sylvia Plath.

Bogan was born in Livermore Falls, Maine, on August 11, 1897. She attended Mount St. Mary's Academy before entering Boston's Girls' Latin School. In her mid-teens, she turned from fantasies of the operatic stage to poetry, which she published in the school journal, *The Jabberwork*, and in the *Boston Evening Transcript*. She patterned her writings after the late Victorians Christina and Dante Gabriel Rossetti and Algernon Swinburne, as well as the works of William Butler Yeats, W. H. Auden, and Rainer Maria Rilke.

While at Boston University, Bogan published in the *Boston University Beacon*. To her mother's dismay, before her sophomore year, she chose marriage to Silesian army officer Curt Alexander over a scholarship to Radcliffe. During World War I, the couple settled first in New York, then in Ancon, Panama, where she gave birth to a daughter, Mathilde, affectionately called "Maidie." Bogan returned to New York to contemplate the emotional upheavals of motherhood and marriage to a demanding, self-centered mate. Shortly after Bogan's older brother Charles died in combat, the marriage frayed. In 1920, Alexander died of pneumonia following ulcer surgery. A widow's pension freed her to study piano in Vienna. In 1925, she married poet and bank researcher Raymond Holden, a charming, romantic wit. She remained with him until their divorce in 1937.

A private person, Bogan settled in New York and sent Maidie to live with her parents in Massachusetts. She supported herself by clerking in a bookshop and working in a public library, and she made a new home among Greenwich Village radicals Louise

Bryant and John Reed and notable literati William Carlos Williams, Malcolm Cowley, Edmund Wilson, and Conrad Aiken. Writing in the style of metaphysical poet John Donne, she submitted highly compressed, personal poems to various publications before issuing *Body of This Death* (1923) and *Dark Summer* (1929). She richly detailed both volumes with erotic fantasy and disdain for male-centered marriage. Subsequent contributions appeared in *The Nation, The New Yorker, Scribner's,* and *Atlantic Monthly* and won her *Poetry* magazine's 1930 John Reed Memorial Prize. In 1931, she joined *The New Yorker* staff as poetry critic, a post she held until 1969.

Bogan's work suffered from disruptions, first by a fire in 1929, which destroyed her manuscripts, then by loss of Holden's inheritance in the stock market crash, and finally by depression, which required hospitalization at the New York Neurological Institute. Illness and her pathologic jealousy ended her second marriage. Vivid self-revelation energizes *The Sleeping Fury* (1937), published the year she was divorced. She followed with *Poems and New Poems* (1941) and two works of criticism: the highly successful *Achievement in American Poetry, 1900–1950* (1951) and *Selected Criticism: Poetry and Prose* (1955). Her *Collected Poems* (1954) won the Bollingen Prize.

Bogan's accomplishments include a $10,000 National Endowment for the Arts award; publication of her entire canon in *The Blue Estuaries: Poems 1923–1968* (1968), and her election to the American Academy of Arts and Letters, which honored her most enduring verse. In 1964, she published *The Journal of Jules Renard,* co-translated by Elizabeth Roget. After a fatal heart attack in her New York apartment on February 4, 1970, a posthumous collection, *A Poet's Alphabet* (1970), amassed her critical reviews of the influential poets of the age. It was followed by three more posthumous publications: a translation of Goethe's *The Sorrows of Young Werther; Novella* (1971), collected letters to female friends in *What the Woman Lived* (1973); and a painfully honest, witty autobiography, *Journey Around My Room* (1980).

CHIEF WORKS

In her first collection, Bogan epitomized the faults of her sex in "Women" (1923), a stiff, pinched accusation devoid of sympathy.

Composed in five quatrains rhyming abcb, the work belies the speaker, who advises her sex to suppress the feminine passions that bind them to diminished expectations. Sharp jabs strike out in nine lines beginning with "they" and a verb, each characterizing some flaw or fault. As though dissociating herself from membership in womanhood, she belittles women for circumscribing their lives and for reining in curiosity and emotion. Through misjudgment and limited horizons, they invest too much of self in "every whisper that speaks to them." Parallel to a lack of "wilderness" in the opening line, in the conclusion she disparages the self-defeat of far-ranging altruism and counsels women to "let . . . go by."

In 1941, Bogan published "Evening in the Sanitarium," which contained a more flowing line and generous compassion than she employed in "Women." The title introduces an elegy on desolation, the sunset of hope for institutionalized women. Dour and dispirited, the gentle voice quells belief that inmates can achieve a complete cure. Against their "half-healed hearts" batter insuperable odds—a return to childbirth, rejection, and the monotony of middle-class domesticity, which she characterizes as "[meeting] forever Jim home on the 5:35."

Bogan blames society for killing off the asylum's survivors. At the climax, she notes with an alliterative double beat, "There is life left." Pasted-on smiles, suicide, and habitual drinking compromise full recovery. Of her own burden, she speaks of "the obscene nightmare" of wretched childhoods. The poem closes on the seemingly endless corridor that leads to perpetual aquatherapy as Mrs. C and Miss R return to the unresolved conflicts that imprison them.

A change in Bogan's outlook is evident in "The Roman Fountain" (1968). In imagistic style, it blooms at the time of her December/June affair with Theodore Roethke. Written in an overlong pseudo-sonnet, its joyous lyricism, mirroring a baroque piazza centerpiece, takes shape around assonance (man-made/Shaping), consonance (flaw/fall), and an arrhythmic rhyme scheme of aabcddbbefgefgf. With light-edged trimeter lines, she exults in the beauty of water gushing from black bronze that lifts "clear gouts of water in air." Breaking at the end of the second stanza in the style of a fourteen-line Petrarchan sonnet, she introduces deductions about sculpture with "O," an emotional embrace of the human touch and an acknowledgment of her own works of imagination.

From this same period, "The Dragonfly," commissioned by the Corning Glass Company, links to "Roman Fountain" by a concluding reference to summer. Unlike her more compact verse, the poem builds on the nothingness of insect wings and their seeming halt in midair. Composed in second person, the praise poem balances the harshness of "grappling love" and "beyond calculation or capture" with delight in iridescent colors and a weightlessness that seems to defy gravity. The buoyancy stalls in line 18 and outlines an unsentimental glimpse of mutability, the demise of the insect among the other seasonal "husks."

"Night" (1968), unlike the heavier sound patterns of "The Dragonfly," shimmers with s's and repeated breathy w sounds. Encompassed in a single sentence, the four-stanza verse gradually diminishes from six lines per stanza to five, then four as it affirms the timeless grandeur of nature. Set in the balance of life forms that inhabit the mating of salt water with fresh water, the estuary becomes the coastal pulse point, forever renewing itself with a steady, reassuring beat. The abrupt contrast of tidal rhythm with human circulation emerges from a direct address to the reader. Beginning with "O" as she did in "The Roman Fountain," Bogan pulls back from the shoreline to "narrowing dark hours," when the spirit is too obsessed with dwindling mortality to take comfort in communion with nature.

DISCUSSION AND RESEARCH TOPICS

(1) Contrast Bogan's "Evening in the Sanitarium" with Sylvia Plath's autobiographical recall in *The Bell Jar* or Anne Sexton's self-study in *The Death Notebooks*.

(2) Compare the naturalism of Bogan's "Night" with that of Robert Frost's "Come In" or Stave V of Hart Crane's *Voyages*.

(3) Explain how Bogan's "Women" implies that the more "provident" woman should reach out for "wilderness" and widened horizons. Contrast the poem's impetus with that of "The Sleeping Fury," which blames "false love" and "the kissed-out lie" for robbing women of contentment.

(4) Compare the stunted women in Bogan's "Evening in the Sanitarium" with the futureless athlete in John Updike's "The Ex-Basketball Player."

(5) Discuss water imagery in "The Roman Fountain." What does water symbolize in the poem?

SELECTED BIBLIOGRAPHY

DAVIDSON, CATHY N., and LINDA WAGNER-MARTIN. *The Oxford Companion to Women's Writing in the United States*. New York: Oxford University Press, 1995.

FRANK, ELIZABETH. *Louise Bogan: A Portrait*. New York: Columbia University Press, 1985.

"Louise Bogan." *Contemporary Authors*. Gale Research. galenet.gale.com

"Louise Bogan Biography." shrike.depaul.edu/~cfoster1/bogan.html

HART CRANE (1899–1933)

An ecstatic, visionary jazz lover and verse talent eclipsed by self-induced angst and silenced by suicide, Harold Hart Crane is a literary enigma. His brief show of vitality raises conjecture about his true artistic promise, which flickered to extinction in the last months of his life. Obviously adept at imagery, yet willfully obscure, he allowed profusion to mount into a hopeless tangle, thus ruining his verse. In the evaluation of critic Allen Tate, Crane was a flawed genius, a lyric poet who reached too far for epic grandeur.

Crane was born in Garrettsville, Ohio, on July 21, 1899. He was an only child whose father, Life Saver candy inventor Clarence Arthur Crane, was too fond of business to nurture art in a precocious son. His parents' marriage ended when his mother, Grace Hart, suffered a breakdown in 1908. Family tensions and outbursts presaged Crane's complex battles with manic depression, psychosomatic seizures, and insecurity. In boyhood, he shut out the uproar by retreating to a tower room in the family home and cranking up his Victrola. In his teens, he made two suicide attempts.

Crane began writing in his teens while living with his grandparents in Cleveland and attending East High School; but later he dropped out of school. His first experience with the sea had set him off in his mid-teens to roam the streets in search of spiritual solace outdoors. In New York, he steamrolled friends with a manic gregariousness that approached hysteria. He played the role of poet in an effort to escape his troubled past.

Crane admired sea verse, the metrics of Edgar Allan Poe, Oscar Wilde's exotic diction, and Walt Whitman's urban romanticism, but he lacked the control of his first idol and the richness and forthright expression of the other two. He published "C-33" in *Bruno's Weekly* and "October–November" in *The Pagan* by age 18. Because he was dependent on handouts from family members, he returned to Ohio in despair to work as a riveter, advertising copywriter, candy store clerk, reporter for the *Cleveland Plain Dealer*, and laborer in a munitions plant while he edited *The Pagan*. Following his first homosexual affair, he alternated between flights of joy and confrontations with blackmailers.

At age 21, Crane made his first cash sale ($10) with "My Grandmother's Love Letters." Artistically, he distanced his writing from the precise logic of T. S. Eliot to emulate the ecstatic symbolism of Wallace Stevens. In the postwar era, he rejected his father's attempts to force him into business. He was his own man at last; he began writing copy for New York's J. Walter Thompson Agency and continued submitting to *Dial*. In 1922, he first described the wonders of technology in "For the Marriage of Faustus and Helen," a preface to the themes of his loftiest poems. Editor Marianne Moore brought him back to earth by rejecting "Passage" and suggesting improvements in "The Wine Menagerie." Her criticism hurt his feelings and precipitated an infantile tantrum.

In 1925, Crane was still unable to support himself and lived at the New York farm of poet Allen Tate and novelist Caroline Gordon while he worked on *The Bridge*. With their help, he acquired a patron who advanced $1,000 so that Crane could travel and compose in leisurely fashion. Because he lacked self-discipline and mismanaged money, he drank himself into the gutter, brawled with sailors, and was arrested for fighting.

From 1927 to 1928, Crane lived in Pasadena, California, where he worked as a personal secretary. His advancement suffered from self-indulgence in alcohol and sex followed by bouts of self-pity and abusive language. He changed his residence frequently, which took him all over Manhattan, particularly Greenwich Village and along the East River overlooking the Brooklyn Bridge. Crane completed two symbolic poetry suites: *White Buildings* (1926), introduced by admirer Allen Tate, and *The Bridge* (1930), a mystical American epic. These works earned Crane *Poetry* magazine's Helen Haire Levinson Prize, a 1931 Guggenheim Fellowship, and lasting tribute as a major American poet.

Crane's surge of critical acclaim came too late to rescue him from ruinous debauchery and fistfights, exacerbated by the disapproval of his family and friends. A failed love affair with Peggy Baird Cowley ended Crane's illusion of a heterosexual lifestyle. With the collapse of his plans for an Indian epic, *Montezuma*, he sank into exaggerated paranoia and made a show of suicide by drinking iodine and mercurochrome. Released from jail for disturbing the peace, he returned from a sojourn in Mexico in low spirits, the result of a quickening of intermittent manias.

With a loan of $200 from his uncle for a subsequent journey, Crane set sail for New York with Cowley on the steamboat *Orizaba* in April 1932. He leaped into the Gulf of Mexico 300 miles north of Havana at noon on April 27. Whether he was frenzied or truly suicidal, no one could determine. His body was not recovered. A comprehensive anthology, *Collected Poems*, was issued in 1933, followed in 1972 by *Ten Unpublished Poems* and in 1986 by *The Poems of Hart Crane*.

CHIEF WORKS

From his youthful surge of the early 1920s, Crane composed "Black Tambourine," an outgrowth of a warehouse job he obtained after a black worker was fired. The twelve-line verse, similar in style and tone to works of the Harlem Renaissance, criticizes society's degradation of blacks and, by extension, of poets. The outcast, who resides in a physical and emotional cellar, sits amid the squalor of gnats and roaches. In the middle stanza, the poet moves back in time to Aesop, the Greek fable writer who earned "mingling incantations" by writing about lowly beasts. With much regret, Crane envisions the wandering tambourine player in "some mid-kingdom," his art "stuck on the wall," and his heart far from the ancient world that echoes in his soul.

Written in 1921, the optimistic "Chaplinesque," composed in five five-line stanzas, reprises the exuberance of comic Charlie Chaplin's film *The Kid*. Like "Black Tambourine," the poem studies the lowly state of the poet, this time from a "we"-centered point of view. To honor the silent screen's "little tramp," Crane's poetic devices turn young writers into fragile kittens and encode with a pun on his first name a promise that "the heart [lives] on." The poet's intent is obvious in line 7, which seeks rescue "from the fury of the street."

The poet's overstated slap at critics depicts them as smirking while thumbing a "puckered index" before turning a "dull squint" on the naive writer. With the beginner's idealism, he declares, "We can evade you." In the concluding lines, an emotional upsweep lifts his sights to the moon and transforms the ash can to a holy goblet brimming with laughter. Truly appreciative of Charlie Chaplin, Crane sent him a copy of the poem and delighted in a thank-you note from the comic.

With *Voyages* (1926), Crane reached a lyric maturity, inspired by his passionate love for sailor Emil Opffer. A six-part adoration of the sea, the complex suite mirrors, in the restless, resplendent wave and tide, the shifts in the poet's life. In five-line stanzas composed in classic iambic pentameter, he mimics turbulence. Moving lightly in stave I, he begins with a child's sensations—the feel of surf, sand, and shell—before proposing a paradox in line 16: "The bottom of the sea is cruel." This tension between the power to delight and the power to kill relieves the poem of mere nature worship and invests it with a mystic synthesis of positive and negative energies.

In stave II, Crane bathes his five stanzas in generous sibilance, as in "bells off San Salvador / Salute the crocus lustres of the stars." His choice of "rimless" and "unfettered" captures a tyrannic force that refuses to be contained or tamed. He balances the sea's willfulness with a divinity enhanced by "processioned," "diapason knells," and "scrolls of silver," which set a liturgical scene of advancing worshippers, organ swells, and scriptural readings. He takes heart in the timeless motion of the deep, which he equates with paradise. The third stave whirls images in a technique peculiar to Crane. With a brief nod to Shakespeare's "sea change," a phrase from *The Tempest*, the poet, like a suppliant before majesty, makes his formal request, "Permit me voyage."

The notion of the petitioner persists in the sixth stave, a prayer to Aphrodite, the Greek goddess of love and beauty born of sea foam. The poet depicts his limitation as sightlessness, which contrasts the dazzling sun. As though feeding on nature, he awaits, "afire" for inspiration. Resonating *oh* sounds [unspoke/rose/repose/holds/glow/know] enhance a deep reverence. Implicit in the artist's voyage is the potential for death on the mighty waves, which may give back "Some splintered garland for the seer." In the sixth stanza, the goddess herself arises on the surf. Like an empress, she "[concedes] dialogue" and offers "the imaged Word," a gift only to those willing to challenge the sea.

Water stabilizes the remainder of Crane's canon as a mystic symbol of steady motion and permanence. Written primarily in one summer, *The Bridge* (1930), a fifteen-part epic, thrives on a tangible man-made structure, a symbol of the American myth. Less rhapsodic than *Voyages*, the panoramic suite is equally dependent on kaleidoscopic impressions, notably sight, sound, and touch. Multiple references to American history create a grand procession dotted with familiar faces. The totality owes much to T. S. Eliot's *The Waste Land*, which Crane studied with a critical eye and determined to outdistance by producing a more esthetic whole. Vast in scope and noble of purpose, like Virgil's *Aeneid*, the epic survives in a tenuous, unrefined state, having been published before the poet had made final adjustments.

Looking out from the very room that served bridge-builder Washington Roebling as an observation post, the poet opens with an introduction, "Proem: To Brooklyn Bridge," a symbol of permanence set against an unpredictable world. For structure, he chooses a blank verse apostrophe and admits occasional rhymed couplets and alternate rhymes [clear/year] as well as assonance [parapets/caravan, stars/arms]. Throughout, meter and rhyme shepherd an urgency that threatens to break into chaos. To maintain contact with land, Crane stresses a subjective response to the visual glory of the bay, where sea birds wheel above the Statue of Liberty. The pageantry of people crossing the bridge halts momentarily as a mocker ridicules a potential suicide clinging to the parapets. The ever-shifting human scene yields an "anonymity time cannot raise." With mythic splendor, the bridge, a triumph of human artistry, dwarfs the cityscape below and prevails like great arms supporting the night sky.

Through sections celebrating Christopher Columbus, the Cutty Sark, Pocahontas, and the legendary Rip Van Winkle, Crane allies the bridge with landmarks of American history. In stave I, "Ave Maria," he elevates the tone to an anthem. The epic invocation "Be with me, Luis de San Angel, now" initiates the traditions of the post-Homeric literary epic. Allusions to Columbus's ship on the way to the New World discoveries inject a first-person immediacy. With a piety appropriate to the era, he concludes with the resonant cathedral hymn, "Te Deum laudamus" (We praise thee, God).

In "The River," glimpses of human figures juxtapose "hobo-trekkers" alongside trains and "redskin dynasties." The rhythm, overtly jazzy, settles into what Crane called "a steady pedestrian gait" as the poet moves back in time to plodding pioneers. Awed by the power of "iron, iron—always the iron," the poet reveres technology and forgives it for robbing nature of its quiet grace. The speeding Pullman bears "pilgrims" across the Mississippi, which the poet depicts as a gulping giant outlasting transient human life. Crane's ecstasy in the passionate tide swells into a hymn to the mingling of fresh water with the Gulf of Mexico.

Subsequent passages traverse the United States in a poetic tour. The least polished segment, "Cape Hatteras," places the reader at the threshold of discovery. In view of the flashing horizon, the poet addresses his ode to Walt Whitman, New York's famed poet and mythmaker. As though consumed by the thrum of a dynamo, Crane states new truths derived from the industrial age. Revisiting the concept of blindness, he exalts sensation over sight in an exaltation of flight, which the Wright brothers pioneered on North Carolina's outer banks at Kitty Hawk in sight of the Hatteras lighthouse.

The staves "Three Songs," "Quaker Hill," "The Tunnel," and "Atlantis" are the weakest elements of *The Bridge*. Crane's reliance on verbal music has forced critics to use such Italian terms as *agitato*, *lento*, and *crescendo* to describe the pure sounds that gush from his ecstacy. In "Southern Cross," he puns on the name of a constellation and the blazing symbol of the Ku Klux Klan. With "Virginia," he draws on street slang from a Bleecker Street crap game. The three-stanza praise hymn transposes Mary into a secular figure, a blue-eyed woman marked by "claret scarf." In the final refrain, Mary rises once more to the cathedral tower to beam a holy light.

Stave VI balances an ebullient divinity with the earth-bound acts of dancer Isadora Duncan and poet Emily Dickinson. Composed in octaves formed of iambic pentameter couplets, the rhythm slows as the eye drops from heaven to earthly heroines. Still church-centered, the whippoorwill's solo echoes from "dim elm-chancels," a liturgical call that "Breaks us and saves, yes, breaks the heart" before crumbling into an autumn of descending leaves and mortal despair.

The remainder of *The Bridge* epitomizes the unbridled mental gymnastics that turned readers away from imagism. Set on New York streets, stave VII breaks free once more from classic stanza forms with irregularly rhymed iambic pentameter interspersed with free verse and conversational style. Modern figures seek guidance, calling "IS THIS / FOURTEENTH?" A flip miss retorts, "if / you don't like my gate why did you / swing on it, why didja."

The tunnel becomes a pulsing underworld inchoate in active verbs, yet still vital, "Unceasing with some Word that will not die." In the eighteenth stanza, the poet reins in his ecstatic musings with the toot of a tugboat horn. The echoes search the harbor and "the oily tympanum of waters." Freed from the tunnel, the poet cries "O my City" in rapture to commune once more with the East River. Like a worshipper bathing in sanctified waters, he anticipates the finale.

The conclusion, "Atlantis," returns to the bridge with a tactile adoration of wires, granite, steel, and mesh. In steady iambic pentameter, ships at sea call to the massive bridge, "Make thy love sure." Crane links the quest to Jason, the Greek sailor, "Still wrapping harness to the swarming air." Sibilant lines extend the classic allusions to Aeolus, the god who provided winds to return the wandering Odysseus to Ithaca. Swelling to an oratorio, Crane declares that his verse "chimes from deathless strings." With orphic majesty, he sweeps the focus upward once more to the bridge, an "Everpresence" that anchors Columbus's New World to eternity.

DISCUSSION AND RESEARCH TOPICS

(1) Compare how poets are treated in "The Black Tambourine" and "Chaplinesque." How are outcasts treated in each poem?

(2) Analyze evidence of emotional discordance in the congested images of Crane's "Lachrymae Christi."

(3) Assess the interplay of euphony and cacophony that dominates Crane's "At Melville's Tomb," "The Dance," and "The Tunnel."

(4) How does Crane create pageantry in *The Bridge*? What role does this grand parade serve in the work?

SELECTED BIBLIOGRAPHY

"Bridges and Towers." *Time,* 18 July 1969, 80.

"Hart Crane." *Contemporary Authors.* Gale Research. galenet. gale.com

JACQUES, GEOFFREY. *Free Within Ourselves: The Harlem Renaissance.* New York: Franklin Watts, 1996.

QUINN, VINCENT. *Hart Crane.* New York: Twayne, 1963.

SCHWARTZ, JOSEPH. *Hart Crane: An Annotated Critical Bibliography.* New York: David Lewis, 1970.

SIMPSON, EILEEN. *Poets in Their Youth, A Memoir.* New York: Vintage Books, 1982.

TROTTER, WILLIAM. "Hart Crane: 'Afire with Love of Life.'" *Charlotte Observer*, 3 August 1969, 5F.

UNTERECKER, JOHN. *Voyager: A Life of Hart Crane.* New York: Farrar, Straus & Giroux, 1969.

UNTERMEYER, LOUIS. "Poet Stranded on a Bridge." *Saturday Review*, 19 July 1969, 27, 39.

ALLEN TATE (1899-1979)

A teacher, biographer, poet, and leader of the New Criticism movement, John Orley Allen Tate joined his peers at Vanderbilt University in defaming modernity and encroaching technology, which he feared compromised humanity. He was born on December 19, 1899, in Winchester, Kentucky, and he sparked wonder and speculation in his parents. Visitors examined his oddly bulging head, which they identified as a sign of mental retardation. Tate studied at Tarbox School in Nashville for one year before entering Cross School in Louisville; he then completed pre-college courses at Georgetown University Preparatory School.

Tate, one of John Crowe Ransom's gifted freshmen, entered the English program at Vanderbilt with a considerable reading background and familiarity with metaphysical poetry and the French symbolists. He made good on his early promise by publishing in *The Fugitive* and *The Double-Dealer* and composing "The Chaste Land," an irreverent parody of T. S. Eliot's *The Waste Land*. The onset of tuberculosis temporarily interrupted his graduating *magna cum laude* with the class of 1922. He taught high school in Lumberport, West Virginia, and worked briefly in his brother's coal office. Incapable of commercial thinking, he put his mind to literature, his life's work.

After moving to New York to edit *Telling Tales*, Tate married fiction writer Caroline Gordon in 1924 and resettled at a farmstead in Clarksville, Tennessee. The couple had a daughter, Nancy Meriwether. Late in their marriage, the Tates collaborated on *The House of Fiction* (1950), a standard composition text for English majors. Tate worked at various editorial posts while publishing increasingly mature verse. The recipient of two Guggenheim Fellowships, he returned from a sojourn in Paris to contribute to *Literary Review*, *Minnesota Review*, *Shenandoah*, *Partisan Review*, *Yale Review*, *Criterion*, and *Le Figaro Litteraire*. He showcased his poetry in *Mr. Pope and Other Poems* (1928) and demonstrated Southern loyalties in biographies of two notable nineteenth-century Confederates, *Stonewall Jackson: The Good Soldier* (1928) and *Jefferson Davis: His Rise and Fall* (1929).

Tate was a consummate versifier and supporter of the Vanderbilt coterie known as the Fugitive Agrarians who sought a return to earth-based life and values; Tate was the group's only undergraduate member. He participated with Donald Davidson, John

Crowe Ransom, Robert Penn Warren, and eight others in the symposium *I'll Take My Stand: The South and the Agrarian Tradition* (1930). At the height of his literary career, he published *Poems: 1928–1931* (1932), *The Mediterranean and Other Poems* (1935), and *Selected Poems* (1937), and co-edited *Who Owns America* (1936) with Herbert Agar. *The Fathers* (1938), a self-revelatory historical novel, detailed his family's role in American and Southern history. As a literary theorist, Tate issued criticism in *Reactionary Essays in Poetry and Ideas* (1936); *Reason in Madness* (1941), co-authored by H. Cairns and Mark Van Doren; *The Language of Poetry* (1942); *On the Limits of Poetry: Selected Essays* (1948); *The Forlorn Demon: Didactic and Critical Essays* (1953); and a compilation, *Essays of Four Decades* (1969).

Tate's major contribution to classroom teaching took him to Southwestern College, the Woman's College of the University of North Carolina (now UNC Greensboro), and Columbia. In 1939, he was named Princeton's first fellow in creative writing. Parallel to classroom brilliance, he served the Library of Congress as its 1943 poetry consultant. Before retirement, he edited and taught at the universities of Chicago and Minnesota, where he published *Collected Essays* (1959) and *Poems* (1960). After a divorce from Gordon, he was married to Isabella Gardner for eleven years and then for thirteen years to Helen Heinz, mother of his sons John Allen, Michael Paul, and Benjamin Lewis.

Tate's last titles include *Memoirs and Opinions* (1975) and two verse compendia, *The Swimmers and Other Poems* (1971) and *Collected Poems 1919–1976* (1977), compiled two years before his death on February 9, 1979, in Nashville. His honoraria brought him numerous awards, including the Bollingen Prize and the National Medal for Literature.

CHIEF WORKS

Begun in the mid-1920s and completed in 1936, Tate's "Ode to the Confederate Dead," his most anthologized work, questions whether his contemporaries are capable of true honor to the past. The poem, a free-flowing, private meditation, opens on irony by employing the Pindaric ode, a lyric, metrically precise form intended for public reading to honor a single hero. Instead of narrowing his focus on one person, the poet broadens his scope to the unified body of war dead and to the spiritually dead community that suffers eroded ties with history. The unidentified cemetery visitor envies military casualties for their sense of purpose at "Shiloh, Antietam, Malvern Hill, Bull Run," in part because he lacks their understanding of myth. His dislocation stems from a modern narcissism, expressed by the headlong self-destructive leap of the jaguar toward "his own image in a jungle pool, his victim." The physical separation symbolized by the cemetery gate shuts the timeless dead away from "The gentle serpent," an Edenic metaphor for time, which interlaces past and present, the dead and the living who are marked for the grave.

The text blends Greek form with Southern themes as the modern viewer attempts to empathize with the Civil War dead. Crucial to loose iambic lines are frequent interweavings of one-syllable rhyme (there/stare, plot/rot), slant rhyme (there/year), harsh sounds (hound bitch), repetition (Stonewall, Stonewall), alliteration (sagging gate), and assonance, as with the various *oh* and *oo* sounds of "you know the rage, / The cold pool left by the mounting flood, / Of muted Zeno and Parmenides." The flow of dense rhetoric reaches dramatic stopping points with the plunge of leaves in lines 25 and 26 and again in lines 41and 42.

Anchored to a passage of autumns, the poem focuses on physical decay, both in buried corpses and the chipped slabs that mark each plot. At the emotional height, the poet asks, "What shall we say of the bones, unclean, / Whose verdurous anonymity will grow?" The question makes its demand on the South as a whole, which must choose whether to carry its history in the heart or bury it along with the era's diminished sensibilities.

DISCUSSION AND RESEARCH TOPICS

(1) Determine from Tate's verse his concept of the Southerner and the South's purpose in retaining traditions, rituals, and customs dating to days of glory.

(2) Compare Tate's "Ode to the Confederate Dead" with other modern verse rich in fragmentary chaos, particularly that of Hart Crane.

(3) Discuss the imagery of branches and leaves in "Ode to the Confederate Dead." What do the branches and leaves symbolize?

(4) Contrast Tate's regional images in "The Swimmers" with similarly localized word pictures in the verse of Joy Harjo and James A. Wright.

SELECTED BIBLIOGRAPHY

"Allen Tate." *Current Biography*. New York: H. W. Wilson Co., 1994.

RUBIN, LOUIS D., JR., comp. and ed. *The Literary South*. Baton Rouge: Louisiana State University Press, 1979.

———, et al., eds. *The History of Southern Literature*. Baton Rouge: Louisiana State University Press, 1985.

SIMPSON, EILEEN. *Poets in Their Youth, A Memoir*. New York: Vintage Books, 1982.

TATE, ALLEN. *Collected Poems, 1919–1976*. New York: Farrar, Straus & Giroux, 1977.

UNGER, LEONARD, ed. *Seven Modern American Poets*. Minneapolis: University of Minnesota Press, 1967.

STERLING BROWN (1901-1989)

Immersed in the ballads and lore of African-Americans, Sterling Allen Brown devoted his life to surmounting black stereotypes. He was a master teacher as well as a master poet of the ballad, sonnet, free verse, and blues form in the years following the urban-centered Harlem Renaissance. Brown elevated rural themes and championed black heroes like Stagolee, Big Boy, John Henry, and Casey Jones. Both an author and literary historian, Brown preserved natural black dialect and religious and secular folk culture, as demonstrated by Slim Greer, his ballad hero, and by essays on the jazz of Earl "Fatha" Hines, Fats Waller, and Louis Armstrong. For his Afro-centrism, Brown earned the praise of his peers, in particular, James Weldon Johnson.

Brown was born on May 1, 1901, in Washington, D.C., the son of a former slave, the Reverend Sterling Nelson Brown, who was a religion professor at Howard University's divinity school. His mother, Fisk graduate Adelaide Allen, encouraged him to love classic verse, as well as the writings of Paul Laurence Dunbar.

By 1922, Brown had become a Phi Beta Kappa graduate of Williams College in Williamstown, Massachusetts. During graduate studies at Harvard on a Clark fellowship, he spurned the scholarly elitism of T. S. Eliot and emulated the populism of Edwin Arlington Robinson, Robert Frost, Edgar Lee Masters, and Carl Sandburg, as well as the folk inspiration of Afro-American work songs, blues, and spirituals.

After marrying Daisy Turnbull, Brown made the most of the Harlem scene by hobnobbing with black artists. Poet/editor Countée Cullen included him in the anthology *Caroling Dusk: An Anthology of Verse by Negro Poets* (1927); James Weldon Johnson did likewise in *The Book of American Negro Poetry* (1930), as did Benjamin A. Botkin, editor of *Folk–Say* (1930). Brown initiated "The Literary Scene: Chronicle and Comment," a column for *Opportunity*, which helped steer audiences to authentic black literature.

An exacting writer, editor, and critic, Brown thought of himself primarily as a professor of English. He taught at Virginia Seminary and College and at Lincoln, Fisk, and Howard universities. Among his most promising students were actor/playwright Ossie Davis, activist Stokely Carmichael, and Nobel Prize-winning Toni Morrison; similarly, Brown's Afro-centrism influenced poet Amiri Baraka and folklorist Zora Neale Hurston.

Brown took serious interest in black representation in the arts, as demonstrated by his eloquent artistic commentary and film reviews in *Opportunity* and by a notable first collection, *Southern Road* (1932). An energized first-person collection, it took its title from the richly humorous, compassionate material he acquired while teaching in the Jim Crow South. To Brown's dismay, a second collection, *No Hiding Place*, found no publisher because the Depression ended easy access to white publishing houses, which had once courted black poets.

Brown, a pragmatist above all, turned from poetry to prose. Simultaneous with a Guggenheim Fellowship, he served the Federal Writers' Project for three years as editor of Negro affairs and contributor to *American Stuff: An Anthology of Prose and Verse* (1937) and *Washington City and Capital* (1937), both published by the U.S. Government Printing Office. In 1939, he joined the staff of the Carnegie-Myrdal Study of the Negro in American Life. In addition to issuing literary criticism, he collaborated with Arthur P. Davis and Ulysses Lee on a comprehensive Afro-centric anthology, *The Negro Caravan* (1941).

The poet's writings added to the wealth of post–Harlem Renaissance fervor in numerous anthologies and journals. Four prose masterworks—*Negro Poetry and Drama* and *The Negro in American Fiction*, published in 1937 and reissued in 1969, and *The Negro Newcomers in Detroit* and *The Negro in Washington*, written with George E. Haynes in 1970—display his scholarship and articulate analyses. In 1973, Folkway Records released *Sixteen Poems* by Sterling Brown, a disc recording. Late volumes of verse include *The Last Ride of Wild Bill* and *Eleven Narrative Poems* (1975) and *The Collected Poems of Sterling A. Brown* (1980), winner of the Lenore Marshall Poetry prize.

Brown earned a reputation for refinement, pedagogical skill, an easy, unpretentious manner, and commitment to his race. In his scholarly essays, he defied the Fugitive Agrarian set at Vanderbilt and warned of a trend toward glorifying the slave-era South. To combat false memories that glossed over slavery, he urged black authors to discredit short-sightedness and to create literature from a stringently truth-seeking perspective. Shortly before his death in 1989, he was named Poet Laureate of the District of Columbia.

CHIEF WORKS

"Ma Rainey," a four-part literary portrait published in 1932, characterizes the delight of fans who flock to hear vaudeville singer Gertrude Malissa Rainey, mistress of "Backwater Blues." One of the rural and small-town South's favorites, she pours out bright humor to the beat of Long Boy's piano accompaniment. Her engaging humor dispels the audience's "aches an' miseries." The poem opens on two-beat lines of irregular iambics rhyming alternate lines with town/aroun', Bluff/stuff, and mules/fools. Section II slows the pace with seven-beat lines as the viewers take seats and focus on her "gold-toofed smiles." Revving up short lines in Part III, the speaker appreciates the singer's ability to strengthen spots "way inside us" and to assuage the hurt of "hard luck" on "de lonesome road." Candidly stage-struck at Ma's emotive power, the final segment cites one of her songs and an anonymous listener's gratitude that "she jes' gits hold of us dataway."

From the same collection, "Slim in Hell" captures another memorable character from the black experience. A folk figure who escapes death, Slim Greer roams outside heaven to spy on hell. The freedom goes to his head. Like a rambunctious "Lucky Lindy," the nickname of pilot hero Charles Lindbergh, Slim sails back to earth. In part two, no longer winged, he receives the devil's permission to observe the wicked doings in hell. Amid Memphis gamblers and New Orleans high-timers, Slim recognizes sinful ministers, booze runners, and white imps who stoke hell's furnace with their black counterparts. The devil, transformed into a redneck sheriff, terrorizes Slim, who clips on his wings and flees back to heaven.

A blatant satire overwhelms the finale. On reporting to St. Peter, Slim is confused by the state of hell, which is a ringer for Dixie. Annoyed with Slim's naïveté, St. Peter returns him to earth because he's "a leetle too dumb" for heaven. The poet's control of tone, pacing, and humor allies the folksy ballad stanza with the fool tale, a popular form dating to ancient times. Composed in jouncy sermon rhythms, vivid scenes of the afterlife epitomize earth-bound evils to prove that human misbehavior condemns the racist, drinker, gambler, and womanizer.

In 1939, Brown made a turnabout from his light hearted narratives with a spiteful vendetta entitled "Bitter Fruit of the Tree." Speaking of family suffering borne by grandmother, grandfather, and father, the central voice recites the familiar injunction to avoid bitterness. Carefully couched in pseudo-courtesy, the admonition rings hollow when balanced against hateful hardships: loss of relatives to slavery, violence, and oppression and the ongoing exploitation of sharecroppers. No longer the jaunty composer of ballad stanzas, Brown grinds deep the black resentment with explosive *p* sounds and hurtful *b* sounds.

DISCUSSION AND RESEARCH TOPICS

(1) Characterize Brown's "Sister Lou" in terms of the humanism displayed in "Ma Rainey," "Break of Day," "Puttin' on Dog," and "Slim in Hell." Determine how the poet blends graciousness and delight in individuals with realism.

(2) Contrast Brown's command of idiom and piquant humor in "Mister Samuel and Sam," "Break of Day," and "Master and Man" with the poetic vignettes of Edwin Arlington Robinson, Mari Evans, Maya Angelou, Sonya Sanchez, Edgar Lee Masters, and Langston Hughes.

(3) Discuss how Brown evokes the speaker's bitterness in "Bitter Fruit of the Tree." What does the "tree" in the poem's title symbolize?

SELECTED BIBLIOGRAPHY

CAMPBELL, MARY SCHMIDT. Introduction. *Harlem Renaissance Art of Black America*. New York: Harry N. Abrams, 1987.

CHAPMAN, ABRAHAM, ed. *Black Voices: An Anthology of Afro-American Literature*. New York: New American Library, 1968.

JACQUES, GEOFFREY. *Free Within Ourselves: The Harlem Renaissance.* New York: Franklin Watts, 1996.

LEWIS, DAVID LEVERING. *When Harlem Was in Vogue.* New York: Alfred A. Knopf, 1981.

"A Literary Tribute to Sterling A. Brown." www.founders.howard. edu/event1.html

PLOSKI, HARRY A., and JAMES WILLIAMS, eds. *The Negro Almanac.* Detroit: Gale Research, 1989.

SMITH, JESSIE CARNEY, ed. *Notable Black American Women.* Detroit: Gale Research, 1992.

"Sterling Brown." *Contemporary Authors* (CD-ROM). Detroit: Gale Research, 1994.

"Sterling A. Brown." Dictionary of Literary Biography. galenet.gale.com

THOMAS, LORENZO. "Authenticity and Elevation: Sterling Brown's Theory of the Blues." *African American Review* (Fall 1997): 409–417.

LANGSTON HUGHES
(1902–1967)

The master poet of the Harlem Renaissance and one of America's most translated authors, James Mercer Langston Hughes captured the blues stanza and the dialect music of mainstream black America. The rare professional poet and playwright who earned a living from publication, at the height of the Harlem Renaissance, he became America's first internationally known black writer. He attempted most literary venues, including short and long fiction, songs, history, humor, journalism, travelogue, juvenile literature, stage comedy, and screenplay. Hughes was an inveterate collector of bits of Afro-Americana gleaned from chance encounters, sonorous sermons, jingles and advertisements, and snatches of jazz tunes.

Hughes was born on February 1, 1902, in Joplin, Missouri. He grew up in Lawrence, Kansas, on a literary diet of the Bible and *Crisis*, the NAACP magazine. When his parents divorced in 1913 and his mother married a white man, he lived in her ramshackle apartment in Lincoln, Illinois. He served as class poet of his elementary school.

Hughes attended Central High School in Cleveland. After graduation, he lived in Mexico for fifteen months with his father, from whom he wheedled tuition to Columbia University. On the dismal train ride to Mexico, he displayed his literary promise with "The Negro Speaks of Rivers," which he wrote while crossing the Mississippi River near St. Louis. On his return north in 1921, he published it in *Crisis*.

Hughes left college after two semesters and worked as a truck farm laborer, waiter, and valet before accepting a berth as seaman aboard the *S. S. Malone* on a transatlantic haul to west Africa. This was his first trip abroad, and he anchored his optimism on the support of Joel Spingarn and Jessie Fauset and letters from Countée Cullen and Alain Locke. He became the only member of the Harlem Renaissance artists to sample the atmosphere of Nigeria and Angola. He reveled in the exotic fragrances and sights of the Canary Islands, Dakar, Timbuktu, and Lagos, source of his anti-European manifesto, "Liars."

In 1924, Hughes cooked and washed dishes at Le Grand Duc, a chi-chi cabaret in the fashionable Montmartre section of Paris. After capturing dawn hours on the Rue Pigalle in "The Breath of a Rose," he welcomed the tutelage of Locke, who escorted him to the city's landmarks and the Piazza San Marco of Venice. Hughes returned to New York and published eleven poems in Locke's anthology, *The New Negro* (1925).

While busing dishes at the Wardman Park Hotel, Hughes left a few sheets of verse for the perusal of a diner, poet Vachal Lindsay. The next morning, the newspapers reported that Lindsay had discovered a prodigy among the kitchen help. By age 23, Hughes netted a poetry prize from *Opportunity* magazine for "The Weary Blues," a masterwork about a pianist he had heard at the Cotton Club. Hughes gained the ear of critic Carl van Vechten, who passed him on to publisher Alfred A. Knopf and encouraged the editors of *Vanity Fair* and *American Mercury* to publish a glittering new talent. On a Southern tour, he won the admiration of playwright Eugene O'Neill and poet James Weldon Johnson but met with smug, eloquent racism at Vanderbilt University, where Allen Tate declined to meet the celebrated Harlemite.

In 1926, Hughes completed the groundbreaking Afro-American manifesto "The Negro Artist and the Racial Mountain." He asserted that blacks must free themselves from a pervasive self-loathing for being black and from the styles and topics indigenous to white literature. To express his individuality, a first stand-alone title, *The Weary Blues* (1926), assimilated black music and verse. He completed a B.A. in literature at Lincoln University and worked at the Association for the Study of Negro Life in Washington, D.C. While living in Westfield, Pennsylvania, at the beginning of the Depression, he published a novel, *Not Without Laughter* (1930), a depiction of small-town life in the Midwest that earned enough royalties to free him from patrons.

In the spring of 1931, Hughes collaborated with folklorist Zora Neale Hurston on *Mule Bone*, a three-act folk comedy. After a quarrel over how to pay a typist, the duo ended their friendship. The play remained unperformed until its debut in February 1991 at New York's Lincoln Center.

As the Harlem Renaissance slowly fizzled, Hughes, influenced by the verse of Paul Laurence Dunbar, Carl Sandburg, and Walt

Whitman, absorbed the essence of Harlem street life and characterized the Negro's plight in America in *Fine Clothes to the Jew* (1927) and *Dear Lovely Death* (1931). In addition, he wrote *The Dream Keeper* (1932) and *Popo and Fifina* (1932) for young readers and translated socially conscious verse by black poets from Cuba, Haiti, and Mexico. He wrote for *New Masses*, a Communist journal, and, in 1932, toured Russia, China, and Japan, a journey that brought FBI scrutiny during the paranoid McCarthy era. He collaborated with musician James Price Johnson on a stage work, *De Organizer* (1932), and crafted *Scottsboro Limited* (1932) for the stage, a propaganda piece that hammered out the message that the South still denied justice to blacks. In 1935, he composed "To Negro Writers," an essay demanding a world free of Jim Crow laws, lynchings, and handouts.

In 1939, Hughes established Los Angeles's New Negro Theater, which produced his plays *Trouble Island, Angela Herndon Jones,* and *Don't You Want to Be Free?* Resituated at Chicago's Grand Hotel, he wrote an autobiography, *The Big Sea* (1940), that mourned the decline of interest in black culture, as did the essay "When the Negro Was in Vogue." In addition to adult literature, Hughes assembled four volumes of children's stories about the adventures of a doughty, Harlem-based scamp, Jesse B. Semple, called "Simple." The adventures of the optimistic, street-smart youngster ran in the *Chicago Defender* and *New York Post* and dominates *Simple Speaks His Mind* (1950), *Simple Takes a Wife* (1952), *Simple Stakes a Claim* (1957), *The Best of Simple* (1961), *Simple's Uncle Sam* (1965), and a Broadway musical, *Simply Heavenly* (1957). Favorites of poetry anthologizers are "Dream Variations," "Harlem," and "Theme for English B" from his Harlem cycle, *Montage of a Dream Deferred* (1951).

Into the 1960s, Hughes continued to make headlines. He published a poetry anthology, *Ask Your Mama: Twelve Moods for Jazz* (1961), and his play *Tambourines to Glory* (1965) ran on Broadway. He died of cancer on May 22, 1967; a posthumous title, *The Panther and the Lash* (1967), rounded out his twelve published volumes.

CHIEF WORKS

In a burst of youthful genius, Hughes wrote "The Negro Speaks of Rivers" when he was only 20 years old, at the height of Marcus Garvey's "Back to Africa" movement. It mimics Sandburg in its omnipresent first-person speaker. The persistent parallel observations—for example, "I bathed," "I built," "I looked," "I heard"—survey Asian, African, and North American scenes over millennia as though a single long-lived observer relished the beauties of each. Rich with a distilled wisdom, the poem turns on an image in lines 2 and 3 that merges flowing waters with the human circulatory system. The muddy depths are the primal source of rebirth, both for the speaker and the budding poet.

Without naming the hardships of the black race, Hughes epitomizes the speaker's peaceful, life-affirming experiences as a parallel of the sun's daily cycle. Life as a black has benefited the speaker, who claims "My soul has grown deep like the rivers." The image suggests that historical events and the cyclical rise of civilizations have amassed an invaluable heritage. The speaker's depth of soul is the strength that stabilizes black people, who survive weather shifts in world power as easily as water flows to the sea.

In 1926, the poet wrote one of his most compressed, lyrically self-expressive poems, "Dream Variation." An intensely physical image of spontaneous, joyful whirling and dancing in sunlight gives place to a symbolic night, which brings rest, cool, and a subtly powerful reminder that darkness and blackness are his birthright and the source of his creativity. A three-syllable beat buoys the speaker into a second verse. In rhapsodic mode, the dancer again gyrates in sunlight and into the shady darkness, which tenderly enfolds the body at rest into a reassuring blackness. Hughes's final line, "Black like me," was an awakening to people hungry for a reason to take pride in self. The phrase served as the title of Richard Wright's autobiography.

At the crest of his poetic powers, Hughes crafted "The Weary Blues," a deliberately winsome, vernacular hymn to a Lenox Avenue jazz pianist. Like a Scott Joplin rag, the poem melds African rhythms and themes with European verse traditions. Lightly, almost fondly, it illuminates old-style complacence. Like a dismal dog, the player sounds out old woes and thumps the floor with his foot as heavenly lights wink out. By early morning, the pianist, dreaming his bluesy theme song, lies moribund, as lifeless as a rock or corpse.

The controlled artistry of the poem summons blues syncopation and repetitions, linking lines with a loose rhyme scheme comprised of simple monosyllables—for example, tune/croon, play/sway, and night/light. At high points in the development, the poet moves to a dominance of *oo* and *ooh* sounds. The subdued sound, like a jazz lament, overwhelms the text with a self-induced inertia that condemns the singer for his soul-paralyzing melancholy, the result of a lifelong indulgence in self-pity.

In 1927, Hughes perpetuated his music-based verse in "Song for a Dark Girl," a twelve-line ditty that develops a keen-edged irony through repetitions of "Way Down South in Dixie," the closing line of the Confederacy's unofficial national anthem. Stoutly rhythmic, the three-beat lines alternate feminine and masculine rhymes of Dixie/me to land firm-footed on the monosyllabic "tree," a fusion of the lover's lynching site with a symbol—"wood"—which stands for the device on which Christ was executed. The intense wordplay links "cross roads" with the Christian cross; alliteration unifies "gnarled and naked" for a stark picture of Southern injustice in an area also famed as the Bible Belt, center of fundamentalist religion.

An example of Hughes's easy conversational mode and lithe tone, "Madam's Calling Cards" (1949), depicts a woman in conference with a printer about an order for personal cards. Her surname, Johnson, is common among black Americans; Alberta is a favorite female given name. Both appear alongside an honorific, "Madam," which the printer approves. Misunderstanding his question about which font to use, Old English or Roman, she asserts that she is completely American and wants nothing foreign appended to her heritage. Beyond the lighthearted exchange, Hughes implies that the speaker, presumably a strong black woman, has paid dearly for her nationality, which derives from enslaved African forebears.

Late in Hughes's poetic growth, he composed "Harlem," a crisp, bleak succession of rhetorical questions about oppression. Opening on a series of alliterated *d* sounds, he inquires about the effects of suppressed artistry and self-expression. His deceptively simple parallelism begins with an image of a crinkling raisin, a putrescent sore, and reeking rotted meat, then retreats to a less loathsome vision of a sweet, a symbol of black behaviors that mask mounting discontent with sugary manners. Abruptly, Hughes shifts the rhythm and rhyme of his brief ten lines to a vision of a sagging burden. He concludes with a single question in italics—an ominous warning that Harlemites are capable of postponing dreams, but may someday lose control to erupt in riot and rebellion.

DISCUSSION AND RESEARCH TOPICS

(1) Characterize Langston Hughes' disdain for Jim Crow mannerisms in "Harlem" and "Merry-Go-Round." Apply his warning to prose predictions in Richard Wright's *Black Like Me* and Ralph Ellison's *Invisible Man*.

(2) Contrast Hughes' ear for native dialects with Countée Cullen's preference for polished literary lines and Mari Evans's standard English.

(3) Determine the source of rage in Hughes's poems "Notes on Commercial Theater" and "Harlem," August Wilson's play *Fences*, and Toni Cade Bambara's short story "Blues Ain't No Mockin' Bird."

(4) What does the image of night symbolize in "Dream Variation"?

SELECTED BIBLIOGRAPHY

CAMPBELL, MARY SCHMIDT. Introduction. *Harlem Renaissance Art of Black America*. New York: Harry N. Abrams, 1987.

CANTOR, GEORGE. *Historic Landmarks of Black America*. Detroit: Gale Research, 1991.

CHAPMAN, ABRAHAM, ed. *Black Voices: An Anthology of Afro-American Literature*. New York: New American Library, 1968.

HASKINS, JIM. *The Harlem Renaissance*. Brookfield, CT: Millbrook Press, 1996.

HUGHES, LANGSTON. *The Dream Keeper and Other Poems*. New York: Alfred A. Knopf, 1994.

JACQUES, GEOFFREY. *Free Within Ourselves: The Harlem Renaissance*. New York: Franklin Watts, 1996.

LEWIS, DAVID LEVERING. *When Harlem Was in Vogue*. New York: Alfred A. Knopf, 1981.

RAMPERSAD, ARNOLD. *The Life of Langston Hughes, Volume I: 1902–1941, I, Too, Sing America*. New York: Oxford University Press, 1986.

COUNTÉE CULLEN (1903–1946)

Countée Louis Porter Cullen, a metrical genius and star of the Harlem Renaissance, wrote less out of racial consciousness than for the joy of poetic music. He profited from readings in the works of John Keats, A. E. Housman, Edna St. Vincent Millay, and Edwin Arlington Robinson. He stood apart from his milieu in a split self that W. E. B. DuBois referred to as "two unreconciled strivings, two warring ideals in one dark body." In place of a prevalent heavy-handed social criticism, he integrated contemplation of négritude and white dominance with graceful phrasing, traditional British forms, and universal themes. He and colleague Langston Hughes became the era's most sought-after, most published poets.

Cullen was born under obscure circumstances on May 30, 1903, in Louisville, Kentucky. His mother transported him to Baltimore to the care of his paternal grandmother, who moved with him to Harlem in 1912. At her death in 1918, a friend implored her minister to take the orphaned youth. No longer linked to living family members, Cullen's last name changed after he entered the family of Carolyn Belle Mitchell and the Reverend Dr. Frederick Asbury Cullen.

Cullen, the only poet of the black renaissance to come of age in Harlem, attended DeWitt Clinton High School. His first submission to national journals was "To a Brown Boy" (1923), dedicated to Langston Hughes and published in *Bookman*. That same year, editor Jessie Redmon Fauset lauded his verse in *Crisis*, the NAACP magazine.

A self-confident go-getter during the heady days of Harlem's creative surge, Cullen asserted his voice in the Harlem Writers Guild, a significant Harlem symposium of young artists. A Phi Beta Kappan with a B.A. in literature from New York University, he completed his studies with a thesis on the verse of Edna St. Vincent Millay. He launched his literary career as an undergraduate with *Color* (1925), a youthful triumph based on classical forms and introduced by "Yet Do I Marvel," one of his most anthologized titles. "Heritage" remains a masterpiece of the era's joy in a long-subdued African past.

Cullen earned an M.A. in English literature from Harvard in 1926 and married Nina Yolande, the daughter of W. E. B. DuBois, in 1928. A post as assistant editor for *Opportunity* (1926–1928) was significant to Cullen's literary ripening. In addition, he flourished with the column "The Dark Tower," which far outlasted a marriage doomed by Yolande's frivolity and his covert homosexuality.

While teaching French and creative writing at Frederick Douglass High School in New York City, Cullen published two volumes of conventional poetry: *Copper Sun* (1927), which he dedicated to wife Yolande, and *The Ballad of the Brown Girl* (1927). The second black to win a Guggenheim Fellowship, he spent a year in Paris at the Sorbonne and wrote *The Black Christ and Other Poems* (1929), a mediocre, self-conscious volume unworthy of his better efforts.

Cullen turned to prose by reworking Euripides' tragedy *Medea*. The staging never materialized, but Cullen published the text in *The Medea and Some Other Poems* (1935). He edited *Caroling Dusk: An Anthology of Verse by Negro Poets* (1927) and produced the clumsy, stilted novel *One Way to Heaven* (1932), a blend of vigorous characterization and leaden satire. As his health deteriorated from hypertension, he composed light verse, including *The Lost Zoo* (1940), about the animals that Noah failed to load, and *My Lives and How I Lost Them* (1942), based on the activities of his pet, Christopher Cat.

Following a lecture engagement at Fisk University in 1940, Cullen returned to Harlem to collaborate on an adaptation of Arna Bontemps' novel *God Sends Sunday* (1931). Titled *St. Louis Woman* (1946), the play is the basis for the Broadway musical for which Vernon Duke provided music. Rehearsals were in progress at the time of Cullen's death on January 9, 1946, at Sydenham Hospital in the Bronx. He was eulogized at his father's church and buried at Woodlawn Cemetery. A posthumous collection, *On These I Stand* (1947), appeared two years after his death.

CHIEF WORKS

At the age of 21, Cullen employed the standard English ballad stanza for "Incident," an impromptu but sturdy memoir of meeting a vulgar, impudent boy his own age. Set in Baltimore, the three-stanza recollection focuses on a youthful anticipation spoiled by an adversary's out-thrust tongue, which is both childish and ominous of future encounters with racism. The inevitable epithet "Nigger" reminds the speaker of the invisible boundary between blacks and whites. Composed in the raw stages of the poet's development, "Incident" minimizes action and states poetry's aims—to clarify and enlarge on human behaviors and attitudes in a single image.

That same year, Cullen produced a more polished effort, "From the Dark Tower," a fourteen-line Petrarchan sonnet that illustrates the form's division into octet and sestet for the purpose of presenting a problem and a solution. In the opening five-beat lines, he speaks generally about the eventual demise of servitude, which he pictures as reaping others' harvests and entertaining the master with soulful flute music. Majestically, the closing lines turn to two examples from nature—the star-pocked night and frail blossoms that flourish out of the sun—to express the beauties of darkness. He closes with anticipation of a better time, when the poet's heartfelt "seeds" will flourish.

Keatsian in tone, style, and imagery, the poem refrains from the bold thrust of "Incident" with a genteel, almost tender restraint. His choice of romantic terms like "beguile," "sable breast," and "no less lovely" disclose the poet's immersion in nineteenth-century romanticism and in the stylistic touches common to European masters. With consummate skill, he links monosyllables in a firm rhyme scheme of abbaabbaccddee. The rhymes focus on a pure *ee*, *oo*, and *ah* sounds. Nearly obscured by classic grace and technical perfection are the implications of the plantation's "bursting fruit," a foreboding of the former slave's own seeds, which produce a tortured mix of anguish and promise.

In 1925, Cullen crafted one of the most memorable works of the Harlem Renaissance, "Yet Do I Marvel," an Elizabethan sonnet showcasing a saucy, yet poignant retort that has become a prized epigram. In the opening octave, the speaker ponders the purpose of God's creation, which immures the blind mole underground just as it shrouds human spirits in mortal flesh. Turning to the standard Greek images of the underworld, where Tantalus forever snatches at a grape cluster out of range of his fingers and Sisyphus never pushes the boulder to the top of the hill, the speaker hesitates to accuse God of torment. In answer to the puzzle, he avoids militance or sacrilege to conclude that the human mind is incapable of judging God's actions. Still, the one question won't stop nagging at him: Why would God create a black poet and place him in a world where white domination suppresses the nonwhite writer's song?

At the height of his poetic power, Cullen wrote his masterpiece, "Heritage," a beguiling, lyric odyssey set in a hypnotic three-beat line. Evocative and moody, the rhapsodic journey takes the speaker on a mental tour of Africa's beauty. Along the coast on paths echoing bird voices, he enters jungle bowers. With careless ease, the speaker ponders beasts of the savannahs and the black lovers who couple freely in "tall defiant grass." Without specifying a fault, the speaker makes a pun on *lie,* meaning "recline" and "falsify," in token of his or her concealment of Negro heritage. By deliberately shutting out the jungle thrum, the speaker rejects the blackness that courses through the speaker's veins like a bloodtide that threatens to overwhelm human control.

Combining wry commentary with mysticism, the viewer, paging through a book on Africa, muses over the hidden snake sloughing its skin and the furtive lovers concealed in rainforest damp. The speaker questions a driving, elusively erotic impulse to slip back in time to Africa's former grandeur. He ignores self-doubt and proceeds along the imaginative path, alliterating *bough* with *blossom* and *flower* with *fruit* as the eye converges on the tentative nest-building of a jungle bird. The image returns the speaker to the initial question: Why yearn for a fragrant land that his ancestors left 300 years ago?

In the falling action of the speaker's anguish, he continues to conceal the internal throb of black heritage. Obsessed in mind and spirit, he enunciates "primal measures," a carnal music that impels the body to nakedness and the feet to tread forbidden measures out of keeping with a Christian upbringing. At the poem's high point, he must admit "a double part," a duplicity of behavior and identity that conceals love of blackness and primitivism. In the last twelve lines, the speaker acknowledges a poignant truth—that leading a double life is hazardous if it masks fierce yearnings.

DISCUSSION AND RESEARCH TOPICS

(1) Contrast the rhythms and tone of Cullen's "Life's Rendezvous" with Claude McKay's "If We Must Die" and "The Harlem Dancer" or Alan Seeger's "I Have a Rendezvous

with Death." Express the interplay of youthful optimism and pessimism in each work.

(2) Discuss Cullen's ethnic pride in "Heritage." Compare his spirit with that revealed in Carl Sandburg's Chicago poems, Isabel Allende's nationalism in *House of the Spirits*, Amy Tan's ambivalence toward China in *The Kitchen God's Wife*, or tribe-centered lines from N. Scott Momaday's *The Way to Rainy Mountain* or Derek Wolcott's Caribbean epic *Omeros*.

(3) Apply Keats's comment in "Ode on a Grecian Urn" that contemplation "doth tease us out of thought / As doth eternity" to the throbbing African cadence that distracts and consumes the speaker in Cullen's "Heritage." Determine how and why the two poets can experience a simultaneous ecstasy and misery and why Cullen earned the sobriquet of "the black Keats."

(4) What does the term "Dark" in the title "The Dark Tower" symbolize? Does this term change meanings throughout the poem? If so, what are the different meanings of the term?

SELECTED BIBLIOGRAPHY

ANDERSON, JERVIS. "Keats in Harlem." *New Republic,* April 8, 1991, 27–34.

CAMPBELL, MARY SCHMIDT. Introduction. *Harlem Renaissance Art of Black America.* New York: Harry N. Abrams, 1987.

CHAPMAN, ABRAHAM, ed. *Black Voices: An Anthology of Afro-American Literature.* New York: New American Library, 1968.

"Countée Cullen." www.csustann.edu/english/reuben/pal/chap9/cullen.html

Early, Gerald L., ed. *My Soul's High Song: The Collected Writings of Countee Cullen, Voice of the Harlem Renaissance.* New York: Doubleday, 1991.

HASKINS, JIM. *The Harlem Renaissance*. Brookfield, CT, Millbrook Press, 1996.

JACQUES, GEOFFREY. *Free Within Ourselves: The Harlem Renaissance*. New York: Franklin Watts, 1996.

LEWIS, DAVID LEVERING. *When Harlem Was in Vogue*. New York: Alfred A. Knopf, 1981.

SMITH, JESSIE CARNEY, ed. *Notable Black American Women*. Detroit: Gale Research, 1992.

ELIZABETH BISHOP
(1911–1979)

Treasured for spare elegance, imagery, and precise language, Elizabeth Bishop revealed her thoughts to readers through regular poetry submissions to *The New Yorker* magazine. She was skilled at dreamy fantasy and detachment as well as solid description, and she filled her work with the places and emotional states that marked a life much influenced by nomadic travel, lesbianism, depression, and alcohol. In addition to poetry collections, she produced a musical score, juvenile verse, and translations of the poems of Octavio Paz. She also introduced the English-speaking world to Brazilian poetry.

Bishop was born on February 8, 1911, in Worcester, Massachusetts. The instability of her childhood derived from the death of her father from kidney failure when she was eight months old and the permanent committal of her mother to an asylum five years later. From that point on, Bishop never saw her mother again. Deprived of interaction with her peers, she grew up among adult relatives.

Placed with maternal grandparents in Great Village, Nova Scotia, Bishop attended a one-room school at age six. Her elementary education was sporadic because of frequent attacks of asthma, bronchitis, and eczema. She then returned to Worcester and lived with an aunt while attending two Massachusetts boarding schools: North Shore Country Day School in Swampscott and Walnut Hill School in Nantick. At both schools, she published in student newspapers and composed poems and skits for class performance.

While attending Vassar, ostensibly to study piano, Bishop read Henry James and Joseph Conrad and discovered American poets H. D., Emily Dickinson, and Walt Whitman. She regretted that she did not study more Greek and Roman poets, whom she considered sources of mastery. When the editors of *The Vassar Miscellany* rejected a submission of modern verse, she joined with classmates Mary McCarthy, Eleanor Clark, and Muriel Rukeyser in founding a less conventional literary journal, *Con Spirito*. With the aid of the college librarian, in 1934, Bishop established a friendship with mentor Marianne Moore that lasted until Moore's death in 1972.

After graduating, Bishop produced evocative verse while living on an inherited income. Moore published a few of Bishop's poems in 1935 in *Trial Balances*, a collection of the works of beginning poets.

Bishop spent the next three years in Europe and North Africa, then settled in Key West, Florida, where the vigor of storms at sea and fishing trips empowered her verse. She then moved to Mexico. Her work appeared in *Partisan Review* and, in 1945, she won a $1,000 Houghton Mifflin Poetry Fellowship. In the late 1940s, friendships with Randall Jarrell and Robert Lowell sparked a new literary direction. From 1949 to 1950, she served the Library of Congress as poetry consultant, a prolific period that earned her the American Academy of Arts and Letters award and a Houghton Mifflin honor for *North and South* (1946).

In 1951, after a bout of gastitis sidelined her from a South-American cruise, Bishop remained behind in Brazil, where she established a satisfying relationship with Lota de Macedo Soares. She earned critical acclaim and a Pulitzer Prize for poetry for a collection set in Nova Scotia, *A Cold Spring* (1955). In her Brazilian period, she translated Alice Brant's *The Diary of "Helena Morley"* (1957) and composed *Brazil* (1962), an overedited volume stressing the struggle of South America under entrenched patriarchy. She followed with a National Book Award-winner, *Questions of Travel* (1965).

After the death of her mate in 1967, Bishop returned to the United States and wrote a volume of children's verse, *The Ballad of the Burglar of Babylon* (1968). In 1969, she began a satisfying teaching career as Harvard's poet-in-residence. During this period, she issued *Complete Poems* (1969), edited *An Anthology of Twentieth-Century Brazilian Poetry* (1972), and published *Geography III* (1976), which earned her an election to the American Academy of Arts and Letters and the National Book Critics' Circle award. Bishop died of a cerebral aneurysm in Boston on October 6, 1979. Posthumous works include *The Complete Poems* (1983) and *The Collected Prose* (1984).

CHIEF WORKS

A model of Bishop's tendency toward singular or isolated figures, "The Man-Moth" (1946) opens on an incisive description that was her trademark. The image of a man standing in moonlight depicts him as "an inverted pin, the point magnetized to the moon." With a deft twist, she envisions him like toothpaste in a tube "forced through . . . in black scrolls on the light." Unlike the man himself, the "man-moth" shadow attempts the unthinkable by climbing buildings and trailing along behind his source "like a photographer's cloth." The fourth and fifth stanzas imperil the shadow during a subway ride, where he "always seats himself facing the wrong way" and cowers from the dangers of the third rail. The poet merges the play of light on dark with fantasy in the sixth stanza, in which the shadow, like a mime, acquires humanity by squeezing out a tear, the pure substance of "underground springs."

Critics have characterized Bishop's detachment as the result of emotional inertia, the atmosphere of "The Fish" (1955). The vignette inventories physical parts, which she catalogs without dissection. The fish, sapped of fight, becomes an elder statesman who bears the marks of past challenges. The poet-speaker delights in his "medals with their ribbons/frayed and wavering"; then, in line 75, experiences an unforeseen surprise of "rainbow, rainbow, rainbow." Her victory over the fish gives place to admiration. In sympathy with the water world below, she exults, "I let the fish go."

Similarly immersed in minutiae, "At the Fishhouses" (1955) notes a paradox: the inflexible rule of change. The poem moves through crisp air beyond the net-mender's niche to seaside structures and equipment that wear has silvered with "creamy iridescent coats of mail." Similar in color imagery to "The Fish," the poem equates the shimmer of scales with a store of experience. Through a simple poet's trick, Bishop compares coastal glamour to the old man's "Lucky Strike," a cigarette logo rich in implications of sensory wealth.

Beginning at line 41, Bishop speculates on the net-mender's milieu. In an atmosphere "Cold dark deep and absolutely clear," the poet-speaker encounters a familiar companion, a seal "curious about me." The semi-serious bombardment with Martin Luther's hymn "A Mighty Fortress Is Our God" earns the seal's disinterest,

as though fundamentalist theology "were against his better judgment." In place of sectarian assurance, the poet-speaker turns to
experience—the swift plunge of hand and arm into icy depths. The
burning pain of freezing water and the bitter, briny taste of the sea
crystallizes an analogy: Knowledge is likewise "dark, salt, clear,
moving, utterly free." Unlike philosophy, the experience with cold
salt water is a paradox: a constant flux, "historical, flowing, and
flown."

"Filling Station" (1965), one of Bishop's more whimsical poems, offers a snoopy inventory of elements in the life of a working-
class family. Soiled with the grease inherent to their trade, they
exist in "a disturbing, over-all / black translucency," another example of illustrative paradox. In the third stanza, the poet-speaker
moves into the private realm of family life, including the oil-
stained family's dog. The fourth stanza introduces evidence of sensibility in comic books, a doily atop a drum-shaped table, and a
hairy begonia.

As though questioning the individual's right to examine a life,
the poet-speaker reaches a peak of interest with three parallel
questions: "Why the extraneous plant? / Why the taboret? / Why,
oh why, the doily?" The answer lies in the "somebody" who loves
the father and sons. Bishop extends domesticity to an image of
murmuring, a shelf of oil cans whispering "Esso-so-so-so," a play
on the original logo of the Eastern Standard Oil Company. With a
teasing twist, the poet-speaker concludes with the reassurance,
"Somebody loves us all."

Another of Bishop's poems is less assuring. Dedicated to
Robert Lowell, her lifelong friend and fellow poet, "The Armadillo"
(1965) is a naturalistic meditation on skepticism. The poem focuses
on an unforeseen clash between fire balloons and frail beings on
the ground below. Composed in a precise quatrain rhyming abab
with abcb, the poem follows a pattern of iambic trimeter in lines 1,
2, and 4 with line 3 expanding to five beats. The masculine rhymes
vary from exact patterns (year/appear, night/height) to approximate
rhyme (alone/down) and conclude with aaxa in the union of mim-
icry/cry/fist/sky.

Early on, the poet introduces hints of instability with "frail, illegal fire balloons" and the flicker of light like a beating—or possibly inconstant—heart. She compacts the action as the wind carries

shapes that "flare and falter, wobble and toss" toward the constellation known as the Southern Cross, a literal crux of the action. Repeated present participles (receding, dwindling, forsaking, turning) exaggerate the mobility of the image to a height in line 20, which concludes with a warning of danger.

In the final five stanzas, Bishop describes in detail the fall of a large balloon, which "splattered like an egg of fire," an introduction to the destructive power that looms above living creatures. The first, a pair of owls, shriek as they flee the combustion in their ancient nest. The lone armadillo departs like an exile, "head down, tail down," leaving the poet-speaker to marvel at an ashy-soft baby rabbit whose gaze carries the fire in "fixed, ignited eyes." The final italicized stanza reproves a scene that is "too pretty," turned hellish as "falling fire" injures and terrorizes unseen life-forms below. As the title directs, the poem focuses on the seemingly protected armadillo, an image of unsuspecting weakness. Like the armadillo, the poet implies that human beings make weak provisions for catastrophes that can fall from an unidentified source. Written at the height of the Cold War, when people built bomb shelters to protect them from atomic attack, the poem expresses a realistic doubt that any man-made shell can erase a pervasive unease.

One of Bishop's autobiographical commentaries, "In the Waiting Room" (1976), returns to the end of her sixth year with a serendipitous coming-to-knowledge. Set precisely on February 5, 1918, while her Aunt Consuelo keeps a dental appointment in Worcester, Massachusetts, the young speaker must entertain herself with a copy of *National Geographic*. A precocious reader, she examines articles in a revealing order—the inside of a volcano, the explorations of Osa and Martin Johnson, and photos of bare-breasted native women. In line 36, the poem's high point, an unsolicited burst of emotion, like a volcanic eruption, surprises the speaker, who at first believes the sound bursts from her "foolish, timid" aunt, who quails at dental treatment. Discovering that the cry came from her own mouth, the child experiences an emotional plunge.

At the climax of observation, Bishop notes that the child identifies with "them," the other people in the waiting area. Personalized as an "I," she wonders at the listing of human beings according to physical and cultural traits. The sensation of fainting "beneath a big black wave, / another, and another," precedes a return to reality through the immediacy of the room, the cold

142

outdoors, and World War I, which evidences the child's awareness of current history. The simplistic child's world picture exalts the flexibility of the imagination, which can catapult the mind into exotic locales, then reel it in to a fixed point. Like an aerial artist on a maiden leap, the speaker is surprised that she recovers so quickly from the first mental venture beyond self-imposed boundaries.

DISCUSSION AND RESEARCH TOPICS

(1) Explain James Merril's tribute to Elizabeth Bishop, whom he characterizes as "a Dream Boat / Among topheavy wrecks."

(2) What does the image of a man standing in moonlight in "The Man-Moth" symbolize? How does Bishop use light to create feeling in the poem?

(3) Ally images from "In the Waiting Room," "Sestina," and "In the Village" with situations and events in Bishop's childhood.

(4) Discuss the image of fire balloons in "The Armadillo." What do the balloons symbolize?

(5) Contrast realistic details in Bishop's "Filling Station" and John Updike's "The Ex-Basketball Player."

SELECTED BIBLIOGRAPHY

DAMMAN, SEBASTIAN. "Elizabeth Bishop." ikarus.pclab-phil. uni-kiel.de/daten/anglist/PoetryProject/Bishop.html

DAVIDSON, CATHY N., and LINDA WAGNER-MARTIN. *The Oxford Companion to Women's Writing in the United States.* New York: Oxford University Press, 1995.

"Elizabeth Bishop." iberia.vassar.edu/bishop/Biography.html

"Elizabeth Bishop." *Contemporary Authors.* Gale Research. galenet.gale.com

JOHN BERRYMAN (1914-1972)

John Berryman, a talented scholar driven to write poetry, is best known for transforming his personal suffering into verse. Like Robert Frost and Randall Jarrell, he loved teaching poetry and felt most at home with literature and the humanities. For his own composition, he was adept at the song and sonnet but preferred large dramatic roles that altered his identity. He was influenced by Gerard Manley Hopkins, W. H. Auden, William Butler Yeats, and e. e. cummings; his aberrant syntax and multilevel language produced a poetic exhibitionism consistent with a flawed past and troubled mind.

At his birth on October 25, 1914, in McAlester, Oklahoma, the poet bore the surname of his parents, teacher Martha Little and John Allyn Smith, a bank examiner. In 1924, bankrolled by Martha's mother, his family moved to Tampa, Florida. In 1926, his father sank into despair over unwise speculation in real estate. One morning, he shot himself in the head outside his elder son's bedroom window. Berryman later wrote, "A bullet on a concrete stoop / close by a smothering southern sea / spreadeagled on an island, by my knee." Berryman suffered insomnia as he relived his family's pain.

Within ten weeks of his father's death, Berryman and his mother and brother resettled in Queens, New York, where he took the surname of his stepfather, bond dealer John Angus Berryman. He attended South Kent, a boarding school in Gloucester, Massachusetts, in his early teens. He lapsed into fainting spells and faked epileptic seizures; his willful craziness set the pattern of his mature years.

Adult success brought Berryman fame and some degree of s elf-respect. At 21, he published his first poems in *The Columbia Review*. While completing a degree at Columbia University, he studied under Mark Van Doren. On a Kellett Fellowship, Berryman studied at Clare College, Cambridge, where he became the rare American to win the Oldham Shakespeare Scholarship. He launched a lengthy and distinguished teaching career, which took him to Wayne State, Harvard, Princeton, Brown, the universities of Washington and Connecticut, and the University of Iowa Writer's Workshop. During his classroom career, he completed a much-debated psychoanalytic biography, *Stephen Crane* (1950), which revived interest in Crane as a poet.

Dubbed a confessional poet, Berryman produced verse for thirty-five years, publishing *Poems* (1942), *The Dispossessed* (1948), and an early masterwork, *Homage to Mistress Bradstreet* (1956), a 57-stanza hymn to New England's Anne Bradstreet, which he wrote while living in Princeton, New Jersey. Inspired by Walt Whitman's *Song of Myself*, his lyric sequence, *77 Dream Songs* (1964), won the 1965 Pulitzer Prize for poetry; four years later, he earned a National Book Award for *His Toy, His Dream, His Rest: 308 Dream Songs* (1968), a second immersion in dream states. Intensely personal, the poems relive a child's attempt to establish order in a disintegrating family. The most hopeless stave, number 145, speaks of the imaginary character through which the poet projects misgivings about life and sanity. Narcissistic and self-serving, *Dream Songs* characterizes Berryman's debilitating need for a prop, whether grandstanding, alcohol, fantasy, or poetry.

Severely limited by faltering energy, nightmares, and hallucinations, Berryman rallied into manic overproduction in *Love and Fame* (1970) and an incomplete novel, *Recovery* (1973), ostensibly an autobiography about his defeat of the demons that stalked him. Repeatedly combating premonitions of death, convulsive rages, and addictive behavior, he committed suicide on January 7, 1972, in Minneapolis, by leaping from a bridge into the frozen Mississippi River. A posthumous work, *Henry's Fate,* was published in 1972. Four years later, Berryman's critical essays were issued as *The Freedom of the Poet* (1976).

CHIEF WORKS

Rated a distinguished American narrative by critic Edmund Wilson, *The Homage to Mistress Bradstreet* (1956) surprises the reader by its engaging conversation between people born more than three centuries apart. By dissociating into wrangling voices, he traces the character and history of a literary ancestor, Anne Bradstreet, a fellow anomaly stalked by loss and failure. Introduced in stanzas 1 through 4, the poet establishes his identification with the colonial poet, with whom he shares doubt, alienation, and hardship. Internalizing her barrenness alongside his literary and personal misgivings, he claims, "Both of our worlds unhanded us."

Stanza 17 opens on Bradstreet, who mourns, "no child stirs / under my withering heart." In straightforward diction suited to confession or journal, she continues her plaint, which swells to high drama in stanza 19 with an eerily erotic birthing scene. Wracked with staccato bursts of caesura, it demands, "No. No. Yes!" then bears down as the child is born. Her emotion outdistances syntax in the next stave, forcing her to admit, "I can *can* no longer." The mounting adversity of "Mistress Hutchinson [ringing] forth a call" in folk assembly stages the dangers to an intelligent woman within a male-dominated theocracy.

By stave 25, the poet is unable to suppress a call back in time. He mourns, "Bitter sister, victim! I miss you, / —I miss you, Anne, / day or night weak as a child, / tender & empty, doomed, quick to no tryst."

Her failure to "quicken" parallels an assessment of failure in his own start-stop literary career. The tossing rhythms, Berryman's trademark, give place to a verbal aria in stanza 31. Verb-heavy, the piece resonates from close placement of action words—for example, "heavy-footed, rapt, / make surge poor human hearts." Intricacies of language bandy layered implications as the speaker justifies why he can't be Anne's lover: "—I hear a madness. Harmless to you / am not, not I?—No." Unsteady in his grasp of divinity, the poet-speaker debates with Anne the likelihood of salvation. The duet concludes with the poet's form of salvation: keeping Anne's memory strong in his verse.

Ambivalence characterizes the remainder of Berryman's canon. The first of his *Dream Songs*, "Huffy Henry" (1964), modeled on the poet's dentist, represents through an imaginary character the incorrigible naughtiness in a standoff against other conscious states. Alternately solemn and overconfident, the childishly disruptive self acts out desires, fears, and fantasies in a befuddling series of revelations set to a razzing syncopated rhythm. Less courtly than *Homage to Anne Bradstreet*, a reckless momentum fuels a pungent black humor filled with self-destruction. As though glimpsing himself "pried / open for all the world to see," the poet marvels that Henry can survive betrayal. Atop a sycamore, the poet slips into Henry's impish point of view to look out to sea, a symbol of untamed menace. His conflicted song, an obscure blend of sexual pun with despair, wonders at the emptiness of life and love.

The fourteenth stave of *Dream Songs*, "Life, Friends," continues Berryman's surreal study of raw emotion. In this immersion in boredom, he regrets the manic-depressive states of flash followed by yearning. As though arguing with the mother's voice recorded in his mind, he counters her claim that bored people admit to a lack of "inner resources." His dissociation of the dog's tail from the act of wagging displays Berryman's elusive dream states, where unforeseen disconnections from reality produce startlingly exact images. In this case, he puns on wag, an implication of brashness. The leaden tone indicates that, for all his dark humor, the poet is unable to halt a crushing mood swing.

In Stave 29, "There Sat Down, Once," the poet ponders Henry's pervasive sense of guilt. Linking words with ampersands and varying tenses within the line, he unhinges the reverie from time constraints to allow him to ponder a century of "weeping, sleepless," a disordered state that Berryman knew well. The nun-like Sienese face, a still, yet cruelly accusing profile, reproaches Henry, whose inability to change impedes him from pardon. Lost in private thoughts, he is unable to locate any victims of his imagined sin.

DISCUSSION AND RESEARCH TOPICS

(1) Contrast the depth of confession in John Berryman's poems with those of Anne Sexton, Robert Lowell, and Sylvia Plath.

(2) Account for Berryman's interest in the writings of Anne Bradstreet.

(3) Analyze the play of halting rhetoric on rhythm in Berryman's characterizations of insanity.

(4) What does the image of the sea symbolize in Berryman's *Dream Songs*? Does the sea have more than one meaning in the cycle? If so, what are some of them?

SELECTED BIBLIOGRAPHY

HALL, DONALD. "Back to Berryman." *Sewanee Review* (Fall 1991): 652–659.

"John Berryman." *Contemporary Authors*. Gale Research. galenet.gale.com

KELLY, RICHARD J. "John Berryman: His Life, His Work, His Thought." www.metronet.lib.mn.us/lol/umn-ber1.htm

SIMPSON, EILEEN. *Poets in Their Youth, A Memoir*. New York: Vintage Books, 1982.

RANDALL JARRELL (1914–1965)

An intimidating perfectionist wedded to compassionate humanism, Randall Jarrell (pronounced juh **rehl**) combined the talents of author, translator, and strident critic. Like poet-critic T. S. Eliot, he earned the respect of his elders, including poets John Crowe Ransom, Allen Tate, and Marianne Moore. Essentially shy and soft-spoken before an audience, he gained a reputation for impassioned public readings, zippy sports cars, delight in fairy tales, and fierce public debates on the status of modern poetry, including that of Allen Ginsberg and the Beat generation.

Jarrell maintained his Tennessee mountaineer's decorum and naïveté by refusing alcohol, tobacco, gossip, and racy talk. He was born on May 6, 1914, in Nashville and spent his childhood in Hollywood, California. After the divorce of his parents, he returned to his hometown at age 12 to live with his grandparents. Although he majored in psychology in his undergraduate years at Vanderbilt University, he studied under Fugitive Agrarians John Crowe Ransom and Robert Penn Warren and demonstrated a remarkable intellectual range and gift for language and analysis. He completed an M.A. in English in 1938 and taught at Kenyon College until 1939, when he joined the faculty of the University of Texas and married his first wife, Mackie Langham.

Influenced by the plain-spoken truths of Robert Frost, Walt Whitman, and William Carlos Williams, Jarrell published verse in *Five American Poets* (1940) before producing his own collection, *Blood for a Stranger* (1942). Then World War II intervened in his career. He served for three years as an army flying instructor and tower operator. He regretted that he was too old for combat, but nevertheless turned his wartime experience to advantage in *Little Friend, Little Friend* (1945) and *Losses* (1948). From 1949 to 1951, he edited poetry for *Partisan Review*, establishing a reputation for truth-telling evaluations at whatever cost to fellow poets.

The mature stage of his career included publication of a series of pro-Frost, pro-Whitman critical essays in *Poetry and the Age* (1953). Less successful was a satirical novel, *Pictures from an Institution: A Comedy* (1954), a witty putdown of academic life. His most famous works appeared in *The Seven-League Crutches* (1951); *Selected Poems* (1955); *The Woman at the Washington Zoo: Poems and*

Translations (1960), winner of a National Book Award; and *The Lost World* (1966). He displayed the whimsical side of his nature in the playful children's works *The Gingerbread Rabbit* (1963), *The Bat-Poet* (1964), *The Animal Family* (1965), and *Fly by Night* (1976).

On October 14, 1965, while in Chapel Hill at UNC's Memorial Hospital undergoing a skin graft on his hand, Jarrell stepped in front of a car, leaving unsettled whether his death was accidental or self-inflicted. Complicating the coroner's task were Jarrell's hospitalization earlier that year for manic-depression and episodes of death wish. Issued posthumously were *The Complete Poems* (1969) and two essay collections, *The Third Book of Criticism* (1969) and *Kipling, Auden & Co.* (1980). Colleagues Robert Lowell, Peter Taylor, and Robert Penn Warren mourned Jarrell's abrupt death with a collection of tributes, *Randall Jarrell, 1914–1965* (1967). In 1985, his widow edited Jarrell's *Letters: An Autobiographical and Literary Selection*.

CHIEF WORKS

"The Death of the Ball Turret Gunner" (1955), a grim, brooding masterpiece, is the most quoted poem to come out of World War II. Enfolded in the plexiglass dome posed like a blister on the underside of a B-17 or B-24 bomber, the speaker is ripe for catastrophe. To intensify the image of doom, the poet robs the five-line poem of suspense by establishing in the title that the speaker does not survive the war. To enhance the stark terror of a gunner's task, Jarrell makes him soft and vulnerable, like a tender, unborn fetus. Swiveling like a latter-day watchman in the round, the gunner hunches in the turret to track the enemy below with .50-caliber machine-gun fire. The collar of his napped flight jacket freezes in the frigid air six miles up, where he meets the death-dealing black bursts that "loosed" him from a "dream of life," the poet's term for late-teen unsophistication and a forgivable idealism.

Jarrell's skill with imagery derives from incisive wordcraft. Within the brief poem are few rhymes: froze/hose as end links and "black flak" as an abrupt, cacophonous internal punch at the airman. The victim jolts awake from his youthful illusions to a "State" necessity—the waste of callow, expendable warriors. The unseen challengers are "nightmare fighters" who leave the shattered gunner in pitiable shape. The conclusion is sensational, ghoulish: Like a dismembered fetus, his remains are jet-washed from the turret with a steam hose. Without comment, the poet halts, leaving the reader with the inhuman remnants of air combat.

"Lady Bates," also written in 1955, is a demure, affectionate apostrophe to a black girl who drowned during an outdoor baptism. The poem bears Jarrell's characteristic rejection of false comfort. Like John Crowe Ransom's duo "Janet Waking" and "Bells for John Whiteside's Daughter," the tender girl lies sedately entombed in the South's hard red clay. With a bittersweet jest, the poet mimics bouncing jump-rope rhymes by chanting "They looked for you east, they looked for you west, / And they lost you here in the cuckoo's nest." Tweaking the crisp, curly hair and ebony complexion, the poet remarks that her dark-skinned ghost startles even the sharp-eyed owl. Decking her spirit's progress through the wild are delicate glimmers of lightning bugs and "darning-needles that sew bad girls' mouths shut," the touches of terror that remind the reader of death's permanent silencing.

The leisured, protracted perusal of Lady Bates' death raises goose bumps for the juxtaposition of a girlish gentility and the persistence of Night, an ambiguous cavalier who rescues the girl from a future of hard knocks. Set against the chain gangs and kitchen jobs of hard-handed Southern racism, the premature loss of an innocent soul suits the unblinking inscription in "the Book of Life." Recorded among other "poor black trash" tragedies, the short life bears Jarrell's characteristic sweet melancholy offset by a teasing cruelty that taunts, "Reach, move your hand a little, try to move — / You can't move, can you?"

The gently evocative "Lady Bates" prefigures somber, disappointed female figures in Jarrell's later works, particularly "The Woman at the Washington Zoo" and "Next Day." Published in 1960 as the title poem in the collection *The Woman at the Washington Zoo*, "The Woman at the Washington Zoo," a work of Jarrell's mature years, was a favorite for recitations during the emotion-charged early years of American feminism. The poem has a subdued reverie at the beginning and sketches the inner landscape of a passive uniform-clad figure walking among cages and fearfully observing the exhibits. In the surreal atmosphere of Washington, saris on embassy women are not uncommon. At the zoo, the diaphanous patterned silks rival the gorgeous rippling hide of the leopard. At the same time, the startling colors clash with the speaker's "dull null" navy, a rigid, dutiful, stultifying fabric that will follow her joyless days and deck her corpse.

The speaker mourns that she is a voiceless entity caged in flesh, an unwilling sacrifice to mortality. Terrified at a soul-withering desk job, she pleads with the self-imposed bars to "open, open!" Unlike the zoo animals, she acknowledges the measure of her life and chafes at the pageant of the capital city, where "the world" passes by her desk without alleviating despair and loneliness. Starved for passion, she visualizes a man-shape in the vulture, a gallant, red-helmeted figure who has "shadowed" her like approaching death, which the poet glimpses in fly-blown meat torn by buzzards. Ending this scary eye-to-eye experience, the plaint in the last three lines is one of Jarrell's most compassionate cries, rising to an imperative: "You know what I was. / You see what I am: / change me, change me!"

A lament for the unfulfilled 1960s woman, "Next Day," from *Sad Heart at the Supermarket: Essays and Fables* (1962) is one of Jarrell's inventive psychological portraits. As the female persona studies the merchandise of the grocery soap aisle, the bubbly optimistic names—Cheer, Joy, All—mock her attempts at self-expression when she creates exotic menus from wild rice and Cornish hens. Without success, she attempts to "overlook" the mundane by distancing herself from a flock of average shoppers. As though words can mask her misgivings, she asserts, "I am exceptional."

The first of ten stanzas begins a series of stanza-to-stanza run-on lines, which link the querulous voice to a station wagon, the typically suburban conveyance that carries her away from the unseeing bagboy. A flash of nostalgia returns her to youth, when men noticed her. Now, she is an untempted, middle-aged, upper middle-class housewife with a dog and maid for companionship. Starved for attention, she languishes.

The straightforward, conversational narrative unleashes a discontent similar to the office drone in "The Woman at the Washington Zoo." Disappointed by former choices, the speaker longs for a change other than death, a finite transformation that she witnesses in the rearview mirror. At a friend's funeral the previous day, the made-up corpse seemed to admire the speaker's

152

youth. Jarrell presses the character to an acknowledgment—"I stand beside my grave." The fearful frankness of the concluding lines depicts a quandary of the modern age—a confusion and terror at the ordinariness of a life made precious by its brevity.

DISCUSSION AND RESEARCH TOPICS

(1) Compare empathy toward violent death in Jarrell's "The Death of the Ball Turret Gunner" and "Mail Call" to that of Donald Davidson's "Ode to the Confederate Dead" and Karl Shapiro's poem "The Leg" and the hapless battlefield casualties in Dalton Trumbo's *Johnny Got His Gun*, Mariano Azuela's *The Underdogs*, and Erich Maria Remarque's *All Quiet on the Western Front*.

(2) Analyze Jarrell's lucid re-creations of the female outlook in "Next Day" and "The Woman at the Washington Zoo." Contrast his depiction of malaise with that of poets Anne Sexton and Sylvia Plath.

(3) In "Next Day," the female speaker says, "I am exceptional." Is she? Why or why not?

SELECTED BIBLIOGRAPHY

CHAPPELL, FRED. "Remembering Randall Jarrell." *Raleigh News and Observer,* 13 May 1990, 1B.

JARRELL, RANDALL. *The Complete Poems.* New York: Farrar, Straus & Giroux, 1969.

"Noted Poet Randall Jarrell Killed by Car at Chapel Hill." *Greensboro Daily News,* 15 October 1965, 1, 19.

PRITCHARD, WILLIAM H. *Randall Jarrell: A Literary Life.* New York: Farrar, Straus and Giroux, 1990.

QUINN, SISTER BERNETTA. *Randall Jarrell*. Boston: Twayne, 1981.

"Randall Jarrell." *Contemporary Authors*. Gale Research. galenet.gale.com

RUBIN, LOUIS D., JR., comp. and ed. *The Literary South*. Baton Rouge: Louisiana State University Press, 1979.

SHAPIRO, KARL. *Randall Jarrell*. Washington, DC: Library of Congress, 1967.

SIMPSON, EILEEN. *Poets in Their Youth, A Memoir*. New York: Vintage Books, 1982.

GWENDOLYN BROOKS (1917–)

A landmark poet, novelist, and autobiographer, Gwendolyn Elizabeth Brooks is treasured for an abiding humanity strongly grounded on the experiences of wife and mother. A symbol of commitment to her race, she became the first black American to win a Guggenheim Fellowship, American Academy of the Arts and Letters Grant in literature, and the Pulitzer Prize. She is immersed in the rhythms, themes, and language of the black American. She committed her art to the commonalities and hardships of living in a racist society.

Brooks is a native of Topeka, Kansas, born on June 7, 1917, the eldest of three children. Rooted in Chicago's South Side, she kept detailed notebooks from age six, because she was determined to become a spokesperson for black people.

Brooks' education at Hyde Park Branch, Wendell Phillips High, and Englewood High was uninspiring, primarily because it presented Brooks no black role models among teachers and staff and few nonwhite peers. Withdrawn, she read from the foremost white authors of the day—T. S. Eliot, e. e. cummings, William Carlos Williams, Ezra Pound, John Crowe Ransom, and Wallace Stevens—and began learning the intricacies of sonnet, alliteration, and wit. At age 13, certain she would one day be a member of America's best, she buried a sheaf of verse in the backyard for later discovery. Three years later, her mother escorted her to readings of James Weldon Johnson and Langston Hughes. Johnson had little to say, but Hughes eagerly nudged Brooks toward a career in poetry.

Brooks graduated from Wilson Junior College, then married poet Henry Lowington Blakely, Jr., writer for Wilson Press and father of their children, Henry and Nora. While on the faculty of Chicago Teacher's College, she graduated to professional poet with *A Street in Bronzeville* (1945), a landmark series of portraits highlighting the verve of city-dwellers. That same year, she won the Midwestern Writers' Conference Poetry award for the third year as well as recognition as one of *Mademoiselle's* ten outstanding women of 1945, which afforded her introductions to Richard Wright and Ralph Ellison.

After her publisher rejected a novel proposal, Brooks shifted to woman-centered verse. She highlighted the ambiguities of women's lives with a mock epic, "The Anniad," in *Annie Allen* (1949), winner of the 1950 Pulitzer Prize for poetry. She experimented with a semiautobiographical novel, *Maud Martha* (1953), a repressed self-study that sidesteps family frustrations, and issued a children's compendium, *Bronzeville Boys and Girls* (1956), a continuation of Chicago-based observations.

The burgeoning civil rights movement influenced Brooks' independent period. No longer courting white readers, she produced *The Bean Eaters* (1960), a collection of idiosyncratic verse that editors often pilfer for representative black verse to flesh out multicultural texts. Buoyed by critical response to *Selected Poems* (1963), she wowed critics with a dark, groundbreaking ballad series, *In the Mecca* (1968), based on her secretarial work for an evangelist. The text is a sophisticated satire of city opulence from the vantage point of a domestic worker, Mrs. Sallie, who searches a city center for Pepita, her lost child. The narrative concludes with praise for black heroes Malcolm X and Medgar Evers.

Brooks' verse sharpened in *Riot* (1969), *Family Pictures* (1970), *Aloneness* (1971), *Broadside Treasury* (1971), and *Jump Bad* (1971). This flood of new writings anticipated the height of her skills displayed in an urgent, fiercely militant collection, *The World of Gwendolyn Brooks* (1971), the last manuscript she entrusted to a white publisher. She contracted with black presses and published an impressionistic autobiography, *Report from Part One: The Autobiography of Gwendolyn Brooks* (1972), which showcases memories and photos of her younger brother Raymond.

Richer, fuller statements of black loyalties infuse Brooks' *The Tiger Who Wore White Gloves* (1974), *Beckonings* (1975), *Primer for Blacks* (1980), *To Disembark* (1981), *The Near-Johannesburg Boy and Other Poems* (1986), *Gottschalk and the Grande Tarantelle* (1988), and *Winnie* (1988). With the anthology *Blacks* (1987), Brooks began publishing through her own press. Her many achievements include election to the National Institute of Arts and Letters, and, in 1973, appointment to the poetry consultancy of the Library of Congress. A distinguished professor of English at Chicago State University, Brooks was the impetus for the Gwendolyn Brooks Center for Black Literature and Creative Writing, a continuation of her support for the next generation of artists.

CHIEF WORKS

Early on, Brooks displayed a finely tuned, yet accessible poetic vision. A favorite, "The Mother" (1945), looks into the mind of a woman troubled by repressed grief for aborted non-babies. Composed in somewhat artificial rhymed couplets, the text breaks into a liberating candor with the emergence of "I" in the second stanza. As though suffering wavelike contractions, the speaker moves to confession in line 21. With a late-developing reverence for life, the speaker acknowledges through repetition a regret that her lost children "were never made."

A lyric sequence, *The Womanhood* (1949), draws on structured questions about motherhood. The second stave, "The Children of the Poor," uses the fourteen-line Petrarchan stanza to frame questions of legacy. Implicit in a cry against judgments of "my sweetest lepers" is the mother's self-blame for giving birth to children condemned as "quasi, contraband." Out of kilter is the coming of age of her "little halves" in autumn, when their fruits freeze before ripening. Segueing to a conclusion with "True," she notes that blacks intent on being less black miss the "silver" under their darkness and never pause to mine a "treasure of stars."

On the outer edge of the coming civil revolt, "A Bronzeville Mother Loiters in Mississippi" (1960) expresses through melodramatic urgency a miscarriage of justice in a nation where "Nothing and nothing could stop Mississippi." The poem narrates a vignette in which a white woman dwells apart from the "milk-white maids" and dashing prince-rescuers of anthologized verse. As she prepares breakfast for her family, she mourns the demonizing of a young black teen, yet watches as a malodorous hatred, "big / Bigger than all magnolias" engulfs her family. In reply to the poem's high drama, "The Last Quatrain of the Ballad of Emmet Till" (1960) closes obliquely on the victim's mother. The starkness of reds and blacks summons a single image: "Chaos in windy grays / through a red prairie." Heavy with the poet's conviction that imperfections cloud America's past glories, the poem anticipates upheaval.

Prefiguring a generation captivated by rap some three decades hence, "We Real Cool" (1960) frames a time line out of street jive, alliterated monosyllables, and the dicer's roll of seven. Situated "at the Golden Shovel," the eight-stage litany honors with sharp-edged irony the self-adulating pool sharks. Cool for dropping out of school, cruising the streets, and romancing self-destruction, the deluded males, like self-cloned victims, move from sin to gin to an erotic tease ("Jazz June") before succumbing to an unnamed killer. A flip warning, the poem throws back in the faces of knowing teens the premature death that becomes an eighth player in their trite street drama.

DISCUSSION AND RESEARCH TOPICS

(1) In many of her poems, Brooks focuses on mothers and motherhood. Write an essay in which you discuss Brooks' treatment of motherhood. Is being a mother a positive experience to Brooks? Support your argument by citing her poems.

(2) Summarize the social and educational milieu of the speakers in Brooks' "Negro Hero," "Ulysses," "Kitchenette Building," and "The Coora Flower."

(3) Characterize the portraiture of Brooks' "A Bronzeville Mother Loiters in Mississippi" and "The Sundays of Satin-Legs Smith."

SELECTED BIBLIOGRAPHY

CHAPMAN, ABRAHAM, ed. *Black Voices: An Anthology of Afro-American Literature*. New York: New American Library, 1968.

DAVIDSON, CATHY N., and LINDA WAGNER-MARTIN. *The Oxford Companion to Women's Writing in the United States*. New York: Oxford University Press, 1995.

"Gwendolyn Brooks." *Contemporary Authors*. Gale Research. galenet.gale.com

HINE, DARLENE CLARK, ELSA BARKLEY BROWN, and ROSALYN TERBORG-PENN, eds. *Black Women in America: An Historical Encyclopedia*. Bloomington: Indiana University Press, 1993.

PLOSKI, HARRY A., and JAMES WILLIAMS, eds. *The Negro Almanac.* Detroit: Gale Research, 1989.

SMITH, JESSIE CARNEY, ed. *Notable Black American Women.* Detroit: Gale Research, 1992.

WRIGHT, STEPHEN CALDWELL, ed. *On Gwendolyn Brooks: Reliant Contemplation.* Ann Arbor: University of Michigan Press, 1996.

ROBERT LOWELL (1917—1977)

Distinguished in family and literary career, Robert Traill Spence Lowell, Jr., flourished as a teacher, poet, translator, and playwright. His flight from an aristocratic background, numerous emotional breakdowns, and three failed marriages contrasts the bond he shared with the stars of modern American poetry— Randall Jarrell, John Berryman, William Carlos Williams, and Anne Sexton, all supportive friends who called him "Cal." He was alienated from white-gloved elitists and their over-refined notions of family, home, and church, and he reshaped himself through poetry that delved into New England's sins and reevaluated American ideals. His contentment took root in the classroom amid student writers who looked up to him as mentor. To the literary world, he was the American prophet of a new poetic freedom, a structurally uninhibited lyricism that was true to self, speech, and history.

Lowell was born in Boston, Massachusetts, on March 1, 1917, and was kin to poet Amy Lowell. After elementary studies at the Brimmer Street School, he studied at St. Mark's School to prepare for entrance into Harvard. In his second year of college, he eluded his father's control by transferring to Kenyon College and boarding with Allen Tate and Caroline Gordon. He studied literary criticism under poet John Crowe Ransom and graduated *summa cum laude* in 1940.

Lowell brought assorted baggage from his New England background to his personal and professional life. For his rigid piety, critics called him the "Catholic poet." His marriage to fiction writer Jean Stafford foundered because of his infidelities, depression, and alcoholism. In 1941, the couple lived in Baton Rouge while he taught at Louisiana State University, then resettled in Boston. At the height of World War II, Lowell spent five months in jail for refusing to register for the draft. He gained parole in March 1944 and undertook janitorial duties at the nurses' quarters of St. Vincent's hospital. He recounts the experience through "In the Cage" in *Lord Weary's Castle* (1946), an antiauthoritarian volume that won him the 1947 Pulitzer Prize for poetry.

In 1951, Lowell suffered full-blown manic depression, which burdened him until his death. After marrying critic Elizabeth

Hardwick, he settled on Marlborough Street near his childhood home, entered psychoanalysis, and enjoyed a period of stability. While teaching and lecturing at Iowa State University, Kenyon School of Letters, Boston University, and Harvard, he produced his best known free verse in *Life Studies* (1959). The collection, which won a National Book Award, tapped the energy and audacity of Beat poetry and recorded Lowell's break with Catholicism, soul-bearing confessions, and revelations of dishonor and scandal among some of Boston's most revered families.

Lowell's buoyant years saw the issue of *For the Union Dead* (1964), which showcases one of the most anthologized titles, and the Obie-winning play *The Old Glory* (1965), a trilogy based on Nathaniel Hawthorne's "My Kinsman, Major Molineux" and Herman Melville's novella *Benito Cereno*. During this vigorous, assertive era of the Vietnam War, Lowell produced *Near the Ocean* (1967), two dramas; *Prometheus Bound* (1967); *Endecott and the Red Cross* (1968); and *Notebook 1967–1968* (1968), a diary in unrhymed sonnet form that lauds colleagues Allen Tate, John Crowe Ransom, Randall Jarrell, and T. S. Eliot. Following Lowell's marriage to his third wife, British author Lady Caroline Blackwood, and the birth of a son, he found hope in lithium treatment. He began detailing the emotional crisis and renewal in a deeply allusive sonnet series entitled *The Dolphin* (1973), winner of a second Pulitzer Prize.

To his detriment, Lowell explored personal events in indiscreet verse, which he performed at public readings. A final collection, *Day by Day* (1977), a pensive series weakened by obscurity and repetition, won a National Book Critics Circle award. *Imitations*, containing modernizations of Homer, Sappho, Rilke, Villon, Mallarme, and Baudelaire, won the 1962 Bollingen Prize; *Poetry* (1963) received a Helen Haire Levinson Prize. Shortly after abandoning England and his wife to return to Elizabeth Hardwick, on September 12, 1977, Lowell died unexpectedly of congestive heart failure in a New York City taxi. He was eulogized at Boston's Episcopal Church of the Advent and buried among his ancestors. *Collected Poems* was issued in 1997.

CHIEF WORKS

Much of Lowell's early poetry contains meaty themes and sonorous voicing. A seven-part lament in iambic pentameter, "The Quaker Graveyard in Nantucket" (1946) was dedicated to his cousin, lost at sea during World War II and commemorated as the drowned figure dredged up from the Atlantic in stave I. The poet launches forth in grand style with compound words—for example, whaleroad, dead-lights, heel-headed, and dreadnaughts—and frequent allusions to the Old Testament and to Captain Ahab, drowned skipper of the Pequod in Herman Melville's *Moby Dick*. As though the universe demands payment for an untimely drowning, the winds beat on stones and gulls grasp the sea by the throat. The address grows more impassioned in stave III, which depicts the "whited monster," Moby Dick, as Jehovah, who, in Genesis 3:14, identified himself to Moses, "I am that I am." The cry of godfearing Quaker sailors concludes with their assurance that God shelters the faithful.

Bound with erratic rhymes (roll/Hole, into the fat/Jehoshaphat) and slant rhymes (world/sword), stave III builds on the image of piety with a cry from Psalm 130, reiterated in the Latin mass, "Out of the depths I have cried unto thee, O Lord." At a high emotional point on the edge of apocalypse, the poet demands atonement with "Who will dance / The mast-lashed master of Leviathans / Up from this field of Quakers in their unstoned graves?" In grim alliterated pictures of the whale's destruction, the poet questions how the destroyer of the great beast will hide his sin, which risks a God-hurled punishment. A complex image of "Jonas Messias," a composite of Jonah and Christ, requires an act of martyrdom as dire as steel gashing flesh, an allusion to Christ, whose side a Roman soldier pierced at the end of the crucifixion.

The puzzle of Lowell's poem, stave VI, veers from the agitation of previous lines to dense images focused on the veneration of Our Lady of Walsingham, an English shrine near Norfolk called "England's Nazareth." The Slipper Chapel, where pilgrims have traditionally entered in bare feet to pray, honors a medieval saint, Lady Richeldis de Faverches, who saw and heard the Virgin Mary in 1061. Returned to Nantucket, where an irate oak emotes above an empty grave, the poem questions again New England's past sins of greed and destruction of nature, depicted as the harvesting of the sea and the fouling of its floor with corpses. The final line, an allusion to the rainbow that God displayed to Noah in promise of no more deluges, is an intended puzzle. Weighted with Old Testament gravity and apocalyptic significance, it prefigures unforeseen redemption, a miraculous Christian rescue through divine grace.

Lowell's mastery of varying tones and settings produces some surprising contrasts. A pivotal example of confessional, "Skunk Hour" (1956) is a tormented soliloquy that overlays deep despair with comedy. One of Lowell's autobiographical triumphs, the poem honors poet Elizabeth Bishop. It is an existential experience derived from Lowell's nightly car rides and conveys the naked desperation he felt on an August night. The monosyllabic "skunk" becomes a description of Lowell's mood. In rhymed sestets, the poem moves slowly into New England's coastal milieu before capturing the dark decline of the soul that precedes a spirit-boosting glimpse of sanity.

The poet models its atmosphere, pacing, and focus on Bishop's "The Armadillo," which she dedicated to him in 1965. The motoring speaker ponders the "hermit / heiress" buying up shoreline, a "fairy / decorator" laying in orange net, and "our summer millionaire," all caricatures of the short-term vacationers who invade the New England coast. In an inward state of mind, as he drives his sedan over a skull-shaped hill, an allusion to Christ approaching Golgotha, the poet-speaker returns to a spiritual dark night. Approaching lover's lane, he acknowledges the black mood by comparing parked cars with downed ships. With a deft twist, he ends the fifth stanza with self-accusation—a plaintive, "My mind's not right."

Lowell's ear for the crass commercialism and mindless media barrage notes a figure dressed in L. L. Bean finery and a car radio bleating "Love, O careless Love." A curious out-of-body image pictures his hand strangling his "ill-spirit." The candor is admirable. A depleted ego recognizes that "I myself am hell," a restatement of Satan's misery in John Milton's *Paradise Lost*. Building to stanzas V and VI, the poet hits bottom. Self-abusive, he feels himself in hell and erases himself with a two-word declaration, "nobody's here—."

Without pause, the short lines converge on a single animal figure going about the normal activity of hunting a meal. The appearance of the mother skunk at the head of a line of little ones blends humor with the absurdity of defiant animals boldly scavenging in the heart of town. As the softly-padded feet march along Main Street, their striped backs mirror the painted dividing line. Beneath a comfortless spire, the imagery draws back to Golgotha in the naming of the Trinitarian Church, a pompous, "chalk-dry" figure.

In a more contemplative mood, "Memories of West Street and Lepke," a bold first-person tour of jail, relates the poet's incarceration among extremists ranging from the radical vegetarian Abramowitz and an antiwar Jehovah's Witness to the balding Lepke Buchalter, syndicate chief of "Murder Incorporated." The free-verse narrative, which appeared in *Partisan Review* in Winter 1958 alongside "Skunk Hour," rambles amiably over a curiously domestic setting. From the post World War II economic upsurge known as the Eisenhower Years, Lowell flashes back to his "fire-breathing" youth when serving time for "telling off the state and president" seemed noble. Marked by the nonchalance of the lobotomized killer and the smugness of young Republicans, the era bobs along, seemingly unaware of coming "sooty . . . entanglements" resulting from "lost connections," veiled references to future national troubles.

Those concerns, in the form of civil rights protests and peace demonstrations, took shape in the 1960s. Written in 1964, "For the Union Dead," a 17-stanza eulogy, he originally titled "Colonel Shaw and the Massachusetts' 54th" to honor the white leader of the first all-black troop in the Union army. Composed in declamatory style, the topic and form bring Lowell back to his thematic and metrical beginnings.

The straightforward narrative is a chain of associated images. Opening on a child's view of the Boston aquarium, it progresses to the barbarous tearing down and rebuilding on Boston Common in sight of the statue of Colonel Robert Gould Shaw, famed exponent of black involvement in the war to end slavery. Beginning in line 32, the poet lauds Shaw, whose sculpted pose stands "as lean as a compass-needle," as though directing the nation toward racial equality. Praised in natural images for ten lines, the historic figure, a small man, is as vigilant as an angry wren guarding her nestlings, and as gently taut as a running greyhound. Line 40 concludes with a poignant reminder that Shaw, once dedicated to his task of producing black infantrymen to fight the Confederacy, could not "bend his back," an image of military posture blended with the fact that Shaw died in a battle he could not elude. To his honor, he remains where jeering rebel soldiers interred him—piled along with fallen black warriors in a common grave at Fort Wagner, South Carolina, the site of their futile assault.

With self-conscious mannering, the poem segues from Civil War era abolitionism to the 1940s with a lament that Boston has no statue to "the last war," which could refer to World War II, the Korean War, or even an end-of-time cataclysm. A photo on Boylston Street depicting a Mosler safe that survived the atomic bombing of Hiroshima disparages contemporary culture for its commercialism. The nation has entered an irreversible decline. As the poem reaches its thematic conclusion, the lines narrow to two beats, then a blunt spondee, "he waits." For the poet, the long-awaited end to racial division is an ephemeral ideal on which Colonel Shaw rides. With the bursting of the bubble, the poet shifts back to the aquarium for a letdown—the liberated fish change into finned automobiles slipping easily through modern-day Boston, where money greases the ride.

In 1977, Lowell produced one of his most personal assessments in "For John Berryman." Remembering his colleague as "lit up," possibly by enthusiasm or drunkenness or both, Lowell fondly recalls his generation's self-serving myth-making by labeling themselves "the cursed." As the poets of the 1950s graduated from students to teachers, they welcomed alcohol at the same time that they embraced the intoxication of poetry. Lowell refers to death in "You got there first," as though dying were a hurdle in a race. In a candid evaluation of mortal fears, the poet acknowledges that the thought of John in the afterlife eases Lowell's fears of what lies beyond.

DISCUSSION AND RESEARCH TOPICS

(1) Compare the ruined men in Lowell's "The Quaker Graveyard in Nantucket" and Randall Jarrell's "The Death of the Ball

Turret Gunner." Determine how both poets augment a fear of death with images of disintegrating bodies.

(2) Discuss the various human relationships in "Memories of West Street and Lepke." What is Lowell's opinion of people considered as "fringe elements" of society?

(3) Isolate elements of Elizabeth Bishop's "The Armadillo" that carry over to Lowell's "Skunk Hour."

(4) Summarize sources of moral decline in Lowell's "The Mills of the Kavanaghs" and "Falling Asleep over the Aeneid." Contrast the poet's judgments against his forebears with William Faulkner's assessments of the Compson family in the novel *The Sound and the Fury*.

(5) Analyze depictions of alcoholism in Lowell's "For John Berryman" and E. A. Robinson's "Mr. Flood's Party." Determine how drinking can liberate at the same time that it enslaves.

SELECTED BIBLIOGRAPHY

"The Chameleon Poet." *Time,* 6 June 1969, 112.

FEIN, RICHARD J. *Robert Lowell*. Boston: Twayne, 1970.

HAMILTON, IAN. *Robert Lowell: A Biography*. New York: Vintage Books, 1983.

PARKINSON, THOMAS, ed. *Robert Lowell: A Collection of Critical Essays*. Englewood Cliffs, NJ: Prentice-Hall, 1968.

"Robert Lowell." *Contemporary Authors*. Gale Research. galenet.gale.com

SIMPSON, EILEEN. *Poets in Their Youth, A Memoir*. New York: Vintage Books, 1982.

RICHARD WILBUR (1921–)

A skilled poet, editor, and teacher, Richard Wilbur is that rarity of the era, the cheerful poet. During World War II, his poetic voice emerged from experiences in southern France and Italy, where he first began writing with one purpose: to impose order on a world gone to pieces. He is notable for rejecting the me-centered confessionals of his contemporaries, and he has divided his lyric perfectionism between original collections and award-winning translations of Voltaire's *Candide* and the plays of Jean Racine and Molière. Along with an extraordinary number of citations for excellence, he has earned his share of lumps for avoiding tragedy and concealing ambivalence. Most of all, critics seem intent on castigating him for skirting the modern and postmodern obsessions with politicized verse and stylistic experimentation.

Richard Purdy Wilbur is a native New Yorker, born on March 1, 1921. He was a resident of Montclair, New Jersey, and graduated from Montclair High School and from Amherst, where he encountered poet-teacher Robert Frost. Before entering the army infantry, Wilbur married Mary Charlotte Hayes Ward, mother of their children: Ellen Dickinson, Christopher Hayes, Nathan Lord, and Aaron Hammond. After the war, Wilbur studied at Harvard and taught for three years as a junior fellow. After completing an M.A., with no intention of continuing as a poet, he published two major titles, *The Beautiful Changes* (1947) and *Ceremony and Other Poems* (1950).

From 1952 to 1953, Wilbur settled in Sandoval, an artists' enclave northwest of Albuquerque, New Mexico. After teaching English at Wellesley, he moved on to Wesleyan University, where he served on the faculty for twenty years. Early in his writing career, he earned the Harriet Monroe prize, Edna St. Vincent Millay Memorial award, Oscar Blumenthal prize, and two Guggenheim fellowships. He completed a masterwork, *Things of This World: Poems* (1957), which won both the Pulitzer Prize and National Book Award, and followed with *Advice to a Prophet* (1961) and *Walking to Sleep* (1969). In his mature years, he collaborated with playwright Lillian Hellman and composer Leonard Bernstein on a musical setting of Voltaire's utopian fantasy *Candide* (1957) and translated three of Molière's comedies: *The Misanthrope* (1955), *Tartuffe*

(1963), and *The School for Wives* (1971). The second of these earned him the Bollingen Prize for translation.

During the 1980s and 1990s, Wilbur remained active as teacher and poet. He served Smith College as writer in residence and the Library of Congress as its second Poet Laureate of the United States. His more recent publications include *New and Collected Poems* (1988) and *A Game of Catch* (1994), children's verse in *More Opposites* (1991) and *Runaway Opposites* (1995), and two additional translations, *The School for Husbands by Molière* (1992) and *The Imaginary Cuckold* (1993).

CHIEF WORKS

With a touch of mock-heroic, Wilbur's "The Death of a Toad" (1950) ennobles a small being savaged by a lawn mower in a scenario as delicately interwoven as an impressionist painting. The meticulous shaping of line lengths—from four to six beats and back down to four, four, and three—suits the precise rhyming pattern of aabcbc. The purpose of so much discipline of language emerges from the lighthearted beats that elevate a dying amphibian to the all-seeing eye of nature. Hidden in green bower, he grows still as the life force drains away. Misinterpreted as a sage, the body gives up its life, but leaves the eye alert.

Wilbur carries the poem beyond the toad's death to the impression it leaves on the viewer. The poet tweaks the imagination with the multiple possibilities of "dies / Toward some deep monotone," a suggestion of synesthesia (describing a sense impression with words normally used to describe a different sense impression) in the pun die/dye, and the merger of monochromatic sound and the single color that camouflages the maimed body. The compact action thrusts the expiring toad toward loftier destinations in the third stanza. Removed to an amphibian afterlife, the toad spirit leaves behind the still corpse, which seems to observe across cut grass in the middle distance the ignoble death of the day.

Similarly luxuriant in image, rhyme, and sibilance, "A World Without Objects Is a Sensible Emptiness" (1950) is a poetic interpretation on a line by English metaphysical poet Thomas Traherne. In grandly measured beats, the poet contrasts the aridity of the spiritual desert to the soul-nourishing light of the real world. With double address to the mounted magi, grandly upraised and borne away at a stately gait, the poet calls to his wandering spirit, represented by the camel train. The call serves as a retort to critics who reject Wilbur's disdain of dense, emotionally twisted verse. Rather than search for illusory gold, he impels his imagination to richer rewards in the real world as opposed to the outward reach for "fine sleights of the sand," a pun on "sleight of hand" or trickery. Unlike the mirages that "shimmer on the brink," the "light incarnate" of Bethlehem's star over Christ's manger suits the spirit's need.

At a mellower stage of artistry, Wilbur composed his famous dramatic monologue, "The Mind-Reader" (1976). In the tradition of Robert Browning's "Andrea del Sarto," the speaker muses on loss. From a drifting vision of a sun-hat cartwheeling over a wall, the speaker moves to a more mundane pipe-wrench jolted off a truck and a book fallen from the reader's hand and slipped over the side of an ocean-going steamer. In each action, the objects are lost during a forward motion, which contrasts the static pose of the mind-reader. At line 20, the clairvoyant inserts four lines to differentiate between objects that slip from consciousness and others imprisoned in deliberate forgetting, a hint that his own psyche chooses oblivion over memory.

The poem moves inward in line 24 to a lengthy recall of how, in childhood, the mind-reader earned a reputation for locating lost objects. To explain the art, the speaker enlarges on the mental landscape, a difficult sweep of ground over which memory searches for misplaced items. Employing three models—eyes searching a crowd, a key enwebbed in tangled threads, and a faded snapshot in an album—the speaker asserts that nothing good or bad is truly forgotten, neither "Meanness, obscenity, humiliation / Terror" nor "pulse / Of Happiness."

The poem grows more personal in line 68 with a description of the mind-reader's daily fare. Seated in a café and identified by scraggly gray hair and persistent smoking, he drinks away the day and night while assisting a stream of questers searching for answers to their problems. The mind-reader's method calls for the seeker to write the question on paper. While the speaker smokes and plays the part of Delphic oracle, he uses practical wisdom of human nature to locate an answer. Implicit in the explanation is the speaker's unstated misery. Confessing to fakery and to his own hurt is the truth of the mind-reader's act, "I have no answers." In the falling action, his retreat into free drinks suggests that skill in reading others' sufferings is a carefully staged hoax. Beyond the facts that he recovers, he presses his own consciousness to observe nothing but oblivion.

DISCUSSION AND RESEARCH TOPICS

(1) Compare Wilbur's playful verse in *Opposites, More Opposites*, and *Runaway Opposites* to Mary Hunter Austin's child-centered *Children Sing in the Far West*.

(2) Contrast the post–World War II sensibilities of Wilbur's "The Beautiful Changes" with the incisive scientific eye of William Carlos Williams' "Queen Anne's Lace."

(3) What does the image of light in "A World Without Objects Is a Sensible Emptiness" symbolize?

(4) Compare the kinetic images of Sandra Hochman's "The Goldfish Wife" with Wilbur's "Love Calls Us to the Things of This World." Determine why he calls for "clear dances done in the sight of heaven."

SELECTED BIBLIOGRAPHY

EDGECOMBE, RODNEY STENNING. *A Reader's Guide to the Poetry of Ricahrd Wilbur.* Tuscalosa: University of Alabama Press, 1995.

HOUGEN, JOHN B. *Ecstasy Within Discipline: The Poetry of Richard Wilbur.* Atlanta, Ga.: Scholar's Press, 1996.

PERLOFF, MARJORIE. "Poetry 1956: A Step Away from Them." wings.buffalo.edu/epc/authors/perloff/1956.html

"Richard Wilbur." *Contemporary Authors.* Gale Research. galenet.gale.com

"'Walking to Sleep' and Richard Wilbur's Quest for a Rational Imagination." Twentieth Century Literature. library.northernlight.com/cgi-bin/pdserv?cbrecid=LW1997-923-4-27787&cb=0#doc

JAMES DICKEY (1923–1997)

In answer to the question "Does regional verse still flourish?" James Lafayette Dickey, a giant among mid-to-late twentieth-century Southern poets, provided a yes—a definitive sense of place and person. Dickey, who is grouped with Randall Jarrell, William Styron, Ralph Ellison, and Ernest Gaines, has earned praise for probing internal monologues and for studies of life forces, which thrust into scenes of joy, pain, birth, confrontation, survival, and death. His style, a blend of visionary and humanistic, accommodated a wide-ranging curiosity that refused to be satisfied by surface knowledge.

Dickey was an Atlantan, born February 2, 1923. He excelled in football at North Fulton High and was struggling through his freshman year at Clemson when he enlisted in the United States Army Air Corps. While he was based near Luzon during World War II, he flew a hundred missions over Okinawa and Japan with a decorated bomber squadron, the 418th Night Fighters. On returning from the war, he graduated *summa cum laude* with a B.A. from Vanderbilt. After he completed an M.A. from Vanderbilt, he taught one semester on the English faculty of Rice Institute, then was recalled to the military to train pilots. He earned an ace's renown and an Air Medal in the Korean War for bravery in combat.

Because of his service in two wars, Dickey took a long time to produce verse. In postwar adulthood, he taught once more at Rice and the University of Florida while publishing in *Partisan Review*, *Harper's*, and *Atlantic Monthly*. While on the staff of McCann-Erickson in New York, he wrote copy for Coca-Cola and crafted advertisements for Lay's Potato Chips and Delta Airlines.

After Dickey spent five and a half years juggling office responsibilities while submitting poetry to little magazines, he published two collections, *Into the Stone and Other Poems* (1960) and *Drowning with Others* (1962). A Guggenheim Fellowship temporarily placed him in Europe in 1961 to compose and study language while he wrote *Helmets* (1964), a collection of war poems. In 1963, he returned to the classroom as writer-in-residence at Reed College, San Fernando Valley State University, and George Washington University while completing *Interpreter's House* (1963) and *Two Poems of the Air* (1964).

Dickey surprised those who typified him as a slightly scruffy good-timer. Under the influence of Theodore Roethke, Dylan Thomas, James Agee, and a Southern literary group known as the Fugitive Agrarians, he mastered technique and structure. Among his verse characterizations are astronauts of the first Apollo moon landing, a woman suffering heart disease, and a man battling cancer.

Dickey arrived when he received a National Book Award for *Buckdancer's Choice* (1965). At this time he lived on Lake Katherine in Columbia, South Carolina, with his wife, Maxine Syerson Dickey, and younger son Kevin. He reached a new audience with an ominous best-selling adventure novel, *Deliverance* (1970), set on an undesignated river north of Atlanta. Two years later, the story made an even more menacing film.

Dickey achieved less critical impact in the last decades of his career, when he published *The Eye-Beaters, Blood, Victory, Madness, Buckhead and Mercy* (1970), *The Zodiac* (1976), and *Puella* (1982), as well as two volumes of poetic prose: *Jericho: The South Beheld* (1974), illustrated by painter Hubert Shuptrine; and *God's Images* (1977). His novels include *Alnilam* (1987) and *To the White Sea* (1993), and five critical volumes: *The Suspect in Poetry* (1964), *Babel to Byzantium: Poets and Poetry Now* (1968), *Self-Interviews* (1970), *Sorties* (1974), and *Night Hurdling: Poems, Essays, Conversations, Commencements, and Afterwords* (1983).

Dickey died on January 19, 1997, from alcoholism and lung fibrosis.

CHIEF WORKS

In 1964, Dickey published "Cherrylog Road," an exuberant, comic boy-meets-girl that abandons the ritual conventions of courtship. Nostalgic, yet standing clear of the scene, the poet exhibits his characteristic masculine energy by dramatizing a daredevil's flirtation with danger. For structure, he chose a tumbling eighteen-stanza framework relieved of a strong metric order by frequent enjambment and rhythmic inconsistencies. In pulsing iambic trimeter, the speaker, an uninitiated motorcyclist indulging his fantasy in an auto junkyard, anticipates a tryst with Doris Holbrook. Acknowledging that Doris's father is capable of flogging his wayward daughter and stalking her seducer, the youth accepts the threat, enjoys a breathless coupling, then charges "Up Highway 106," his future determined by the audacity of forbidden sex.

A near-parody of Alfred Noyes's "The Highwayman," Dickey's narrative breaks into the frenetic adolescent mindscape. Opening on the sexual implications of the Cherrylog road, a reference to a town in northwest Georgia as well as a fused image of female virginity and engorged phallus, the poet becomes a voyeur ranging over heaped automotive junk in pursuit of sex-driven youth. The clutter of the 1934 Ford, Chevrolet, and Essex inspires ego-active imaginings of moonshine running and racing, both products of the South. In the sedate Pierce-Arrow, the central intelligence can play the stuffed shirt. In the back seat, partially walled off by a broken glass panel intended to separate chauffeur and passenger, he engages the interphone to dramatize the role of sanctimonious benefactor to an orphanage.

The dominant event, a boy's carnal escapade with a willing partner, pulls the adventurer out of daydreams into an instinctive release of pent-up tension. Powered solely by risk and joyous lust, he anticipates the sweet union previously arranged for a hot afternoon made hotter by teen hormones. As an introduction to the constants of the chase, the poet toys with "parts" and "chassis." A subtle movement closes the car door from within for privacy; three repetitions punch out an intense, hasty thrusting as the boy "held her and held her and held her." Brisk alliteration and witty imagery depict the blacksnake stalking the mouse "with deadly overexcitement," a sexual crescendo that erupts in depersonalized "breathless batting" as the stuffing bursts from the ruined seat cover. The passionate consummation ends abruptly without tender farewell. Dickey, who identifies wholeheartedly with his callow protagonist, maintains the male perspective in the crouch of the motorcyclist "wringing the handlebar for speed" as he pledges himself to a lifetime of such hurried bliss.

A shift in Dickey's standard three-beat line departs from an expedited rhythm to a slower, more contemplative cadence in the 176 lines of "Falling," the chilling focal work of *Falling, May Day Sermon, and Other Poems* (1981). Long, sweeping visual images break into phrases punctuated by spaces rather than commas. Based on an actual event—the misstep of a stewardess who fell through the emergency door of a plane—the poem parcels out the deadly plunge in curiously protective stop-action shots. The strobed melodrama pictures a neatly-groomed form dressed according to airline regulations as she is altered from employee to casualty.

A free flow of details honors the protagonist who dies through no fault or omission of duty. Simultaneously, like a police officer or insurance investigator, the witness examines the accident from numerous possibilities: "hung high up in the overwhelming middle of things," "a marvelous leap," and "riding slowly." Sense impressions intersperse with explicit action words—for example, collapsing on "stupendous pillows" and whirling "madly on herself." As enhancements of the terror of a free fall from on high, images of towns, houses, lakes, and a Greyhound bus below counter impressions that stray from simple observation of momentum and shifting physical states to images of lovemaking, an owl preying on a chicken yard, and an innocent rabbit, which softens and elongates the slide toward certain death.

As physical forces compel the body toward earth, the poet, like a lover, caresses the outstretched arms, air-buoyed breast, and bare legs with a sensuous eye for female beauty. He withholds hope of survival in lines 68 and 69, which comment that she might live if she had plunged into water. By line 75, the victim's mind set, which is "now through with all," follows a surreal progression from life focus to acceptance of mortality to emergence as a mythic deity honored by corn-growing farmers below. Line 85 notes the unlikely occasion of a "correct young woman" meeting death over Kansas in so catastrophic a fashion as though singling out the incident as a sign of divine intervention.

Celebrating the airborne grace of the fall in audacious imagery, the poet departs from cold fact with an inventive extraction of spirit from the doomed body. As though reconstituting her in midair, he retrieves her from inelegant sprawl to the skilled aerodynamics of "bank" and "roll," a pilot's terminology. Near death, she transcends horror in the image of "the holy ghost / Of a virgin." In brief comic relief, the poet envisions her shedding underclothes one by one, losing an abnormal, "monobuttocked" shape with the removal of her girdle, which lands on a clothesline. The "superhuman act" of hurtling through the sky carries sexual overtones in "let her come openly trying at the last second to land / On her back." Impacting with earth, the fragile form imbeds itself in loam in a stark collision that interrupts "her maiden flight." Relinquishing a "brief goddess / State," she offers up a last breath. The final "Not and tries less once tries tries AH, GOD—" elevates her passing to a titanic struggle, the epitome of the human effort to grasp life.

DISCUSSION AND RESEARCH TOPICS

(1) Compare the portraiture of Randall Jarrell's poem "The Woman at the Washington Zoo," Sylvia Plath's "The Disquieting Muses," or Katherine Anne Porter's short story "The Jilting of Granny Weatherall" with James Dickey's female sufferer in "Angina."

(2) Characterize the tone and outlook of "The Performance" in light of Dickey's experiences in World War II and the Korean War.

(3) Locate evidence of the influence of Ezra Pound on Dickey's rapid-fire imagery in "Night Bird" and "Falling."

(4) How does Dickey control the act of falling in "Falling"? Does the rhythm of the poem affect the movement of the action? If so, how?

(5) Contrast Dickey's selection of "The Strength of Fields" for Jimmy Carter's inaugural with choices made by Robert Frost and Maya Angelou for similar state occasions.

SELECTED BIBLIOGRAPHY

BLOOM, HAROLD, ed. *James Dickey*. New York: Chelsea House, 1987.

BOTTOMS, DAVID. "Remembering James Dickey." *Atlanta Journal-Constitution*, 26 January 1997, B1.

CALHOUN, RICHARD J., and ROBERT W. HILL. *James Dickey*. Boston: Twayne, 1983.

DICKEY, BRONWEN. "He Caught the Dream." *Newsweek*, March, 24, 1997, 19.

DICKEY, JAMES. *Buckdancer's Choice*. Middletown, CT: Welseyan University Press, 1965.

———. *The Selected Poems*. Hanover, NH: University Press of New England, 1998.

DIEDRICHS, DICK, and KNUTE BERGER. "James Dickey." *Charlotte Observer*, 3 February 1980, 1D+.

"Everyone's Notion of a Poet." *Time*, April 20, 1970, 92.

"James Dickey." *Contemporary Authors*. Gale Research. galenet.gale.com

Morrow, Lance. "A Prophetic Delver." *Time*, February 3, 1997, 75.

POWELL, DANNYE ROMINE. "'Deliverance' Author James Dickey, Dead at 73, Was Master of Both Fiction, Poetry." *Charlotte Observer*, 21 January 1997, 1A+.

———. *Parting the Curtains: Interviews with Southern Writers*. Winston-Salem, NC: John F. Blair, 1994.

PRICE, REYNOLDS. "James Dickey, Size XL." *New York Times Book Review*, 23 March 1997, 31.

STARR, WILLIAM W. "At 70, Dickey Revels in Continued Creativity." *Charlotte Observer*, 14 February 1993, 1F.

DENISE LEVERTOV (1923-1997)

Poet and critic Denise Levertov, an antiwar, antinuclear activist who was moved to public testimonial, unified life and beliefs with art. Her work was a response to a calling. In her words, she chose to live in an all-out state of alert, "open to the transcendent, the numinous." Assertive in politics and language, she eludes categorization as feminist or seer. Perhaps she is best described as an emerging American eclectic; she accommodated contemporary idioms as the language best suited to her well-plotted, luminous verse.

Of Welsh and Russian-Hasidic descent, Levertov was the daughter of Beatrice Spooner-Jones and the Reverend Paul Philip Levertov, a Jew turned Anglican. A native of Ilford, Essex, England, born on October 24, 1923, she was educated at home, where European Jews gathered during pre-Holocaust tensions. Her interests—art, French, and ballet—tended toward the genteel until the 1930s, when her family voiced their protest of Mussolini's fascism and supported Spanish independence, Eastern Europe's refugees, and the League of Nations. After completing her education privately and publishing *The Double Image* (1946), she married American author Mitchell Goodman, bore a son, and settled in the United States, where she became a naturalized citizen in 1955.

A descendant in verse of H. D. and William Carlos Williams, Levertov came under the influence of Charles Olson and Robert Duncan, poets of the Black Mountain school, yet steered her own course. She taught at Tufts and Stanford and published spare naturalist-populist verse in *Here and Now* (1957), *Overland to the Islands* (1958), and *With Eyes at the Back of Our Heads* (1959). In 1961, she became poetry editor of *The Nation* and issued probing, disturbing verse in *The Jacob's Ladder* (1961) and *O Taste and See: New Poems* (1964). She toured Southeast Asia to protest American involvement in Vietnam, the subject of a collection of pacifist writings, *Out of the War Shadow* (1967), and a soulful triad, *The Sorrow Dance* (1967), *Relearning the Alphabet* (1970), and *To Stay Alive* (1971). In addition to verse, she collaborated with Edward Dincock, Jr., on a translation, *In Praise of Krishna: Songs from the Bengali* (1967).

Like many of her contemporaries, Levertov took up feminist themes, which she addressed in *Footprints* (1972), *The Freeing of the Dust* (1975), *Life in the Forest* (1978), and *Candles in Babylon* (1982). While teaching at Tufts, Brandeis, and Stanford, she remained focused on her art in *Oblique Prayers: New Poems with Fourteen Translations* (1984), *Breathing the Water* (1987), *A Door in the Hive* (1989), *Evening Train* (1992), and *Tesserae* (1995), and two essay collections, *The Poet in the World* (1973) and *Light Up the Cave* (1981). By the time of her death from lymphoma in Seattle, Washington, on December 20, 1997, she had accumulated a wide readership.

CHIEF WORKS

Levertov introduces her forebears in "Illustrious Ancestors" (1958). The Hasidic grandfather, the rabbi from "Northern White Russia," learns the "language of birds" from nature-centered concentration during his devotions. Similarly pragmatic, a Welsh grandfather, "Angel Jones of Mold," incorporates his mysticism in the real world by stitching his thoughts into his garments. At the poem's conclusion, the poet begins with "Well" her inclusion of birds, hard data, and the tailor's needle in her life's work. In silence, she contemplates the thin-air quality of internalized stimuli.

Composed four years after Levertov's divorce, "A Woman Alone" (1978) delights in "blessed Solitude," the reward to an aging woman lost in a paradox of "sober euphoria." Stepping over breezy enjambments from a memory of passion to an involved late-night conversation that prefaces sleeping alone among books, she has no need to banish self-pity, which "dries up" of its own volition. More fearful of attrition than manlessness, the poet-speaker pictures an active old age, "a wanderer, / seamed and brown." Slightly ridiculous as "Mrs. Doasyouwouldbedoneby" from *The Water-Babies*, she acknowledges that the world rejects that winsome Victorian fantasy. At home in the realities of urban life, she chooses instead to be "tough and wise" in a newfound contentment.

Published the year after her mother's death, "Death in Mexico" (1978) traverses the final stages of life. The poem moves through a self-revelatory grief to contrasting forms as a garden returns from the imposed ideal to the wild. As though depicting in metaphor the retreat of health over a five-week decline, the text vivifies the "squared circle" of her mother's garden destroyed in a month after twenty years of tending. Prefiguring a processional to the grave, line 31 pictures the gardener, borne past her garden on a stretcher, as too blind to focus on the transformation of her garden. Building on the image of blurred vision, the poet-speaker turns to the obdurate masks of stone "gods and victims," whose fixed gaze allows no response to life, even that which crawls like a vine or scorpion over the face. Alienated by death and Mexican exotica, the speaker pictures the garden as her mother's hostage, summarily retrieved into its natural surroundings.

DISCUSSION AND RESEARCH TOPICS

(1) What are Levertov's impressions of her ancestors in "Illustrious Ancestors"? Cite lines of the poem that support your answer.

(2) Determine Levertov's complex woman-centered point of view in "A Woman Alone." Does the speaker in the poem relish being alone? If so, why? If not, why not?

(3) What does Mexico symbolize in Levertov's "Death in Mexico"? How much of an impact does Mexico play in the poem?

(4) Analyze the interplay of humor and self-image in Levertov's "Song for Ishtar."

(5) Summarize the pervasive unease in Levertov's "The Ache of Marriage," "Divorcing," and "About Marriage."

SELECTED BIBLIOGRAPHY

DAVIDSON, CATHY N., and LINDA WAGNER-MARTIN. *The Oxford Companion to Women's Writing in the United States.* New York: Oxford University Press, 1995.

JANSSEN, RONALD R. "Denise Levertov: Among the Keys." *Twentieth Century Literature* (Fall 1992): 263–290.

LINTHWAITE, ILLONA, ed. *Ain't I a Woman!* New York: Wings Books, 1993.

SHAPIRO, DAVID. "Dreaming of Design: Reading Denise Levertov." *Twentieth Century Literature* (Fall 1992): 299–305.

A. R. AMMONS (1926–)

A science-minded businessman late bloomed into rustic bard, Archie Randolph Ammons unintentionally achieved a visionary optimism through lyric analogies. He was influenced by Walt Whitman, Ezra Pound, Robert Frost, and William Carlos Williams. He has earned critical respect for verse essays, meditations, and anthems replete with rural pragmatism, contemporary misgivings, and a vibrant but guarded holiness. Deriving focus from Henry David Thoreau's hermitage at Walden Pond and structure from Wallace Stevens' exacting phrasing, Ammons has forged a unique succinctness. His logic derives from patterns in nature.

A native of the poor North Carolina sandhills outside Whiteville, Ammons was born on February 18, 1926. His link with nature stems from life on a farm, where the regeneration of nature was an everyday occurrence. A United States Navy veteran of the Pacific theater, he began writing poems during long night watches at sea. After graduating from Wake Forest University with a degree in chemistry, he married Phyllis Plumbo, mother of their son, John Randolph. He did advanced work in English at the University of California at Berkeley, which matched Ammons' concreteness with a poet's curiosity. His twelve-year pre-literary background includes a principalship of a Hatteras, North Carolina, elementary school and serving as officer of Friederich & Dimmock Inc., a New Jersey manufacturer of laboratory glass.

Beginning in the 1950s, Ammons injected vigor into American poetry. He earned little attention for his first self-published collection, *Ommateum, with Doxology* (1955), which uses the multiple eyes of an insect as metaphor for the fragmented poetic vision. After a nine-year pause, he issued *Expressions of Sea Level* (1964), the preface to a staff position at Cornell and a growing shelf of poetry collections. He allowed himself an unusual experiment—typing a daybook on a piece of adding machine tape, which resulted in a lengthy, digressive narrative, *Tape for the Turn of the Year* (1965). Sure-footed at last with formal verse, he blended poignant puzzles with humor in *Corsons Inlet: A Book of Poems* (1965), *Northfield Poems* (1966), and *Selected Poems* (1968), a success that earned him a Guggenheim Fellowship. Mid-career titles continued the rhythm of innovation in *Uplands* (1970), *Briefings* (1971), and *Sphere: The Form of a Motion* (1974). A pinnacle of his mature verse, *Collected Poems 1951–1971* (1972), won a National Book Award.

Firmly wedded to studying physical nature, Ammons interspersed classroom work with increasingly welcomed collections: *Diversifications* (1975), *The Snow Poems* (1977), *Selected Longer Poems* (1980), *A Coast of Trees* (1981), *World Hopes* (1982), *Sumerian Vistas* (1987), *The Really Short Poems* (1991), *Garbage* (1993), and *Glare* (1998), a venture into funkier rhythms, eccentric subjects, and colloquial speech. For his visionary grace, he has earned numerous awards, including the Lannan Poetry award, National Book Critics Circle award, Bollingen Prize, MacArthur Foundation award, and fellowships from the American Academy of Arts and Letters and the MacArthur Foundation.

CHIEF WORKS

A casual verse anthem to the dynamics of nature, "The City Limit" (1971) demonstrates Ammons' ability to match an emotion with reality. In a straightforward rhetoric achieved through five parallel adverb clauses and an answer begun at the end of line 14, the poet observes the rightness of nature. Robustly assertive, he imposes a rigid graphic discipline on observations of a power he names "the radiance." The resultant equilibrium between natural cycles of decay and reemergence offsets a fear wrought by "the glow-blue / bodies and gold-skeined wings of flies swarming the dumped / guts of a natural slaughter." Beyond the haphazard urban "coil of shit" that defines "the city limits," his facile creation of glory out of garbage leads naturally to the "May bushes" and a restrained praise for order.

Critics declare Ammons' concept of God a form of visionary romanticism. Combining loss with emerging faith, "Easter Morning" (1981) reflects candidly on divinity. Sparsely punctuated, but guided by confessional, the narrative follows a spiritual pilgrim through grief over passing generations. In the fourth stanza, a simple statement captures the crux: "the child in me that could not become / was not ready for others to go." In the child's blunt cry of "help, come and fix this," he speaks for the human family in the pervasive fear that "we / can't get by."

In line 53, the speaker perches on the end of childhood and envisions "the flash high-burn / momentary structure of ash," which prefigures a more lasting burn in the final image. In line 71, he banishes doubt by observing the stages of flight executed by "two great birds." Investing them with the incompleteness of earthly lives, the observer remarks that they "flew on falling into distance till / they broke across the local bush and / trees." In the disappearance of the birds, he praises "bountiful / majesty and integrity," his summation of patterns in nature.

DISCUSSION AND RESEARCH TOPICS

(1) Determine the direction, shape, and clarity of Ammons' best nature poems. Comment on his intent to order in verse an impersonal, constantly shifting universe.

(2) Contrast Ammons' portrayal of an emotion with reality in "The City Limit."

(3) What does the title "The City Limit" mean? What does the city symbolize?

(4) How does Ammons conceive of God in "Easter Morning"? Does God play an active role in human life according to the poem?

(5) Compare the wonder and sufficiency of the soaring bird in Ammons' "Easter Morning" with Gerard Manley Hopkins' "The Windhover."

(6) Summarize how Ammons resolves questions of religious faith in "Hymn," "The Foot-Washing," "Christmas Eve," and "The Dwelling."

SELECTED BIBLIOGRAPHY

AMMONS, A. R. *Glare*. New York: W. W. Norton, 1997.

"A. R. Ammons." www.diacenter.org/prg/poetry/94_95/amhecht.html

"A. R. Ammons." *Contemporary Authors.* Gale Research. galenet .gale.com

LEPKOWSKI, FRANK J. "'How Are We to Find Holiness?': The Religious Vision of A. R. Ammons." *Twentieth Century Literature* (Winter 1994): 477–499.

RUBIN, LOUIS D., JR., comp. and ed. *The Literary South.* Baton Rouge: Louisiana State University Press, 1979.

——, et al., eds. *The History of Southern Literature.* Baton Rouge: Louisiana State University Press, 1985.

ALLEN GINSBERG (1926–1997)

A disciple of American liberties found in the writings of Walt Whitman, Herman Melville, Henry David Thoreau, and Ralph Waldo Emerson, Irwin Allen Ginsberg was a latter-day prophet of freedom. Unconventional in life and art, he was a gay anarchist and Jew-turned-Buddhist who flaunted eccentricity as a badge of distinction. He was a dissenter and political spokesman for leftists, union organizers, and proponents of unfettered sex and psyche-delic drugs, and he pursued the ideal and visionary along with the creative in pop culture.

Apart from the wealth of analysis attached to his work, Ginsberg's literary doctrine was simple and personal: Poetry equals sanity. His blunt sexuality and unconventional ravings chal-lenged notions of propriety and decorum left over from seven-teenth-century puritanism, compounded by eighteenth-century conservatism and nineteenth-century prudery. Spurned by purists as a drugged-out degenerate, but admired by contemporaries as a libertarian crusader, he earned respect from a sprinkling of the lit-erary in-crowd, including poet William Carlos Williams.

Ginsberg was born of a liberal Jewish working-class back-ground on June 3, 1926, in Newark, New Jersey, and reared in Paterson. His Russian immigrant parents, Naomi Levy and high school English teacher Louis Ginsberg, conditioned him to buck conservative trends by supporting spontaneous expression, radical Communism, and nudity. He graduated from Paterson High School in 1943.

Labeled a gay drug experimenter while completing a B.A. at Columbia University, Ginsberg resided with fellow free spirits in Harlem. To accentuate his mounting rebellion, he studied Franz Kafka and William Blake and hung out at the West End Café, one of the first locations connected with the birth of the Beat move-ment. During his erratic college years, he was suspended for two semesters for scrawling obscene words on his dorm room window and allowing Jack Kerouac to stay as unofficial roommate.

After working as a welder, dishwasher, and deckhand, Ginsberg served the *New York World Telegram* as a copy boy and *Newsweek* as a reviewer. During his tenure in San Francisco, he discovered congenial artists in North Beach, which thrived at the end of the McCarthy era in outrageous, anticonservative artistic bliss. Acknowledged with a letter of introduction from William Carlos Williams, he launched the Beat movement in 1955 at his "Happy Apocalypse," a public reading of "Howl," an apocalyptic diatribe against modern corruption. City Lights Bookshop published Ginsberg's *Howl and Other Poems* (1956), which effectively channeled his rage into self-conscious experimental verse. The volume's controversial content preceded his arrest on an obscenity charge against publisher Lawrence Ferlinghetti, who, in 1957, weathered a highly publicized trial and acquittal.

Ginsberg did not limit himself to the California scene. He taught at the University of British Columbia, appeared in twenty movies, formed a lifetime relationship with mate Peter Orlovsky, and recited verse in the British Isles, Russia, Czechoslovakia, Poland, India, Peru, and Chile. During his residency in Greenwich Village, New York, he shared a 7th Street apartment with Kerouac and William Burroughs while completing *Kaddish and Other Poems* (1961), a verse biography of his mother. Ginsberg's correspondence with Burroughs appeared as *The Yage Letters* (1963). He drew police surveillance while picketing the Vietnam War in New York and the 1968 Democratic National Convention in Chicago, and authorities ejected him from Cuba in 1965 for protesting anti-gay treatment at state schools. *The Fall of America: Poems of These States* (1973), a lament for the poet's deceased mother, won a National Book Award.

While living on the ultraliberal university campus at Berkeley, California, Ginsberg published *First Blues: Rags, Ballads, & Harmonium Songs, 1971–1974* (1975). *As Ever* (1977) reprises his letters to fellow Beat poet Neal Cassady. His *Journals Early Fifties Early Sixties* (1977) covers travels in Greece and reveals an anti-establishment bent, which he celebrated with poetry readings at the Second Bisbee Poetry Festival in Bisbee, Arizona, in 1980. In a wacky but sincerely rebellious spirit, he cofounded the Jack Kerouac School of Disembodied Poetics in Boulder, Colorado, where he codirected curriculum and taught poetry each summer.

Following Ginsberg's death on April 15, 1997, his funeral at Temple Emanu-El in San Francisco turned into a media circus. Old friends and admirers exulted that the poet would have loved it.

CHIEF WORKS

Howl, Ginsberg's Dantean masterwork, dominated the poet's canon to his last years and formed a catechism for young bohemians in search of a mentor and mythmaker. In old age, he wished aloud that he had the vigor to start again and denounce more recent government repression with *Howl II.* A dynamic sermon composed in Old Testament rhythms, rich active verbs, explicit nouns, and ordinary speech, the original *Howl* condemns authoritarians for forcing the fringe, later called beatniks or hippies, into subhumanity. He anchored his furor on a shared experience with Carl Solomon, whom he met while both were receiving insulin shock treatment for mental illness at Columbia Presbyterian Psychiatric Institution. The shock factor of astonishing juxtapositions—for example, the hungry figure plunging under a meat truck in search of an egg; boxcar bums traveling toward "grandfather night"; the use of shocking terms like *cunt, balls,* and *gyzym*; and personal memories of a sexual relationship with N. D. [Neal Cassady]—precipitated an investigation by San Francisco police, who censored the work for obscenity.

To control wave on wave of painful memories, a catalog of evils, and disdainful prophecy, Ginsberg tames elongated lines with sight mechanisms, primarily parallel entries preceded by repetitions of the pronoun "who." The list of complaints cites unrelated places—Atlantic City, Newark, Baltimore, Los Alamos—and intersperses jubilant acts of straight and gay sex with state coercion, alienation, despair, suicide, and expatriation. His exaggerations of injustice weave a black-on-white tapestry of suppression by which "the absolute heart of the poem of life [is] butchered out of their own bodies." Like a challenge, the innovative verve of *Howl* presses into the reader's face a new poetic style either exciting or exasperating, depending on the point of view.

In less frenzied style, Ginsberg employs the same free verse for "A Supermarket in California," a satire on American plenty. The poem opens with an address to his literary idol and spiritual mentor, Walt Whitman. Despairing for the haven that Whitman prophesied, Ginsberg's apostrophe closes on the "black waters of Lethe," a romantic cliché for oblivion. Juxtaposing human shoppers among inanimate vegetables and fruit, the poet moves to a verse biography of Whitman, a solitary man obsessed by lust for young bag boys. Ginsberg idealizes his relationship with the nineteenth-century poet in images of artichoke tasting. Once out in the street with his dream companion, the poet makes a pun on "shade to shade," a vision of a ghost shadowed by trees along the sidewalk. Like Ginsberg, Whitman, a wartime medic, lived in difficult times as Union fought Confederate. The poem closes on the formidable "courage—teacher," whom the ferryman Charon abandons on a smoking bank of the underworld.

Ginsberg pursues his signature tumbling style in "Sunflower Sutra," a pseudo-religious poem written in 1956 following a vision of William Blake reciting "Ah! Sunflower." The text, which reads with the honesty of a diary entry, opens on somber lament. Alongside friend Kerouac, the grieving poet obsesses over polluted streams devoid of fish and rusted machinery until Jack points out one hopeful entity, a sunflower. In technically powerful lines enlivened with similes, the poet summarizes America's downhill slide. In alliterated monosyllables, he decries "the smut and smog and smoke" of trains. Dramatically, powerfully, the poem rises to an intense melancholy in line 9: "O my soul, I loved you then."

Ginsberg seems overwhelmed with the violation of technology, which he characterizes as "artificial worse-than-dirt." Continuing in a flood of alliterated pairings, he humanizes the wreckage around him in slang anatomical terms. With mannered exaggeration, he differentiates sunflower from locomotive, humorously warning, "forget me not!" The glorified sunflower becomes the cavalier's sword. Stuck in his belt, it arms the idealist, who lectures "anyone who'll listen." In the final line of the vision, which he sets apart by a dash, the poet embraces the internal sunflower beauty of self while rejecting the outer shame that fouls society.

"America," a self-conscious national evaluation composed in the same period, speaks with the ringing self-righteousness of the inquisitor. The pace is deliberately slow, the tone brow-beating, almost intimidating. Less like oratory than a nose-to-nose confrontation, the poem departs from the long-lined lyricism of "Sunflower Sutra" with harshly end-stopped, verbal accusations against the poet's native land. In snarly discontent, he badgers America like a parent scolding a child, blaming the nation for ignoring want and war and for forcing Ginsberg to "want to be a saint." His insistence on run-on sentences creates a peevish atmosphere, which suits a boyish confession, "I smoke marijuana every chance I get."

The second stave jerks at the lapels of Ginsberg's homeland with a curt, "I'm addressing you." In rebellion against the vision of America published in *Time* magazine, the poet makes his discovery, "It occurs to me that I am America." By pairing self and country, the speaker considers national enemies his personal foes. To remind the nation of its blunted purpose, he trivializes contemporary concerns over marijuana, sexuality, and censorship in the opening line of the third stave, which accuses America of fostering a "silly mood."

The poem champions the underdog by name, ordering America to stop tormenting a labor agitator and two radicals unjustly accused of murder. Mixed in are Spanish Loyalists and the racially charged cases of the Scottsboro boys, two celebrated cases that Americans abandoned. With a brief return to sentence overload, the poet spews out childhood memories of Communist cell meetings and abandons straightforward rhetoric for the comic Old West Indian dialect from such television series as "The Lone Ranger." In a final dedication to task, the speaker declares himself unfit mentally, morally, and physically for anything but the people's poetry. Phrasing his intent in cliché, he pledges with mock-seriousness to put his "queer shoulder to the wheel."

DISCUSSION AND RESEARCH TOPICS

(1) Discuss the role of authoritarian power in *Howl*. How does Ginsberg buck authority in the work?

(2) In *Howl*, Ginsberg cites various cities spread throughout the United States. What role do these cities play in the work? Is Ginsberg's vision an urbanized vision, or does it encompass rural settings as well?

(3) Write an essay in which you discuss whether or not the images in *Howl* are obscene. If the work were written today, would the government's reaction to it be different? Why or why not?

(4) Contrast Ginsberg's pessimism in *Howl* with Hart Crane's ecstatic vision of America's greatness in *The Bridge*.

(5) Contrast Ginsberg's portrait "To Aunt Rose" with the lyric biography of Rita Dove's *Thomas and Beulah*.

(6) Contrast the speaker of "America" with the speaker of *Howl*. Is one speaker more pessimistic than the other? If so, which speaker, and why?

(7) Chronicle the parallel growth of beat expression with imagism, impressionism, and modern verse.

SELECTED BIBLIOGRAPHY

"Allen Ginsberg." www.charm.net/~brooklyn/People/AllenGinsberg.html

"Allen Ginsberg." *Contemporary Authors*. Gale Research. galenet.gale.com

BRAME, GLORIA GLICKSTEIN. "One Beacon of Sanity: An Interview with Allen Ginsberg." www.pce.net/elf/archives/v6n2019a.htm

EBERHART, RICHARD. "West Coast Rhythms." *New York Times*, 12 September 1956.

HAMLIN, JESSE. "San Francisco Says Goodbye to a Bard." *San Francisco Chronicle*, 21 April 1997. www.ginzy.com

MERSMANN, JAMES F. *Out of the Vietnam Vortex: A Study of Poets and Poetry Against the War*. University Press of Kansas, 1974.

MILES, BARRY. *Ginsberg: A Biography*. New York: Simon & Schuster, 1989.

MOORE, JIM. "Public Heart: An Interview with Allen Ginsberg." www.bookwire.com/hmr/REVIEW/moore.html

W. S. MERWIN (1927–)

A mystic symbolist, mythmaker, and master of dense verse, poet William Stanley Merwin concerns himself with America's isolation and rootlessness. Through careful compartmentalization, he reflects on the future by absorbing himself with preliterate people, primal sources, pacifism, pollution, and the themes of fragmentation, loss, and social and moral regression. His writing is never trivial. Elegant and freighted with warning, his verse combines passionate focus, logic, and lyricism in a consistent flow that engages as generously as it stymies and unnerves the unwary.

A New Yorker born September 30, 1927, Merwin grew up in Union City, New Jersey, where he wrote hymns at age five. When his family relocated to Scranton, Pennsylvania, he came to love landscapes not yet strip-mined, fouled, and plundered, a focus of his despairing laments. At age 18, Merwin met a poetic giant, Ezra Pound, whose eccentricity struck him as original and unshakable. The meeting preceded Merwin's own development into a unique seer. Like the Hebrew prophet Jeremiah, he began speaking a message terrible and forbidding to his contemporaries.

On scholarship at Princeton, Merwin found what he had been seeking while reading poetry in the library and combing the outlying area for horses to exercise. He completed a B.A. in English at age 20. Poet John Berryman and critic R. P. Blackmur encouraged his early writings. During seven years of residency in Europe, he translated Spanish and French classics for the BBC's London office. In 1956, Merwin settled in Cambridge, Massachusetts, as playwright in residence at Poet's Theater, issuing *Darkling Child* (1956), *Favor Island* (1958), and *The Gilded West* (1961). He served *Nation* as poetry editor and, in 1961, edited *West Wind: Supplement of American Poetry* for the London Poetry Book Society. In the mid-1960s, he was on staff at Roger Planchon's Theatre de la Cité in Lyons, France.

Merwin's *A Mask for Janus* (1952), a collection of traditional songs, ballads, and carols, earned the approval of W. H. Auden and the Yale University Younger Poets series. *The Dancing Bears* (1954), a volume rich with fable, probes alienation, as does *Green with Beasts* (1956), a bestiary, or animal book, expressing lessons learned from animals. More family-oriented is *The Drunk in the*

Furnace (1960), a collection of verse portraits. After an unproductive period, Merwin recaptured his poetic voice for *The Moving Target* (1963), an experiment in flowing rhetoric that employs a halting line marked by long pauses, but uninhibited by punctuation. A cult favorite, *The Lice* (1969), predicts the destruction of those who lose their connections with divinity and nature. Composing these harsh poems was so devastating to Merwin that he feared he would never write again. He reclaimed his vision with *Animae* (1969) and a Pulitzer Prize winner, *The Carrier of Ladders* (1970), a tribute to history's role in self-redemption. He refocused on the present in *Writings to an Unfinished Accompaniment* (1973), followed by a somber work, *The Compass Flower* (1977).

After shifting residence to Hawaii in the late 1970s, Merwin took heart in new encounters with seascapes and native culture, as displayed in the adapted haiku of *Finding the Islands* (1982). Returning to boyhood, he issued *Opening the Hand* (1983), which preceded another somber work, *The Rain in the Trees* (1987), and *Travels* (1993). In addition to anthologies, he published prose stories, essays, and vignettes in *The Miner's Pale Children* (1970), *Houses and Travelers* (1994), and *Unframed Originals: Recollections* (1994). Winner of the PEN translation prize, he also published *Selected Translations: 1948–1968* (1979), as well as translations of the Cid, Sanskrit love verse, medieval epics, and numerous other literary works.

CHIEF WORKS

Merwin's "The Drunk in the Furnace" (1960) is a meditation on a sleeper in an abandoned smelting furnace in the Pennsylvania hills. The poet balances his narrative within four pentameter quatrains, each begun and ended with half-lines of two or three beats. In the first stanza, the setting of the hat-like "hulking black fossil" alongside a "poisonous creek" points to the locals' ignorance, implying both lack of education and the original Latin meaning of "don't know." By the second stanza, a wisp of smoke awakens the unidentified observers to an intruder capable of "a pale / Resurrection," a playful hint at the viewers' shortsighted Christianity.

Drawing on his youth in a Presbyterian rectory, Merwin prolongs the play on fundamentalism in the last two stanzas, noting that the source of the drunk's "spirits" is mysterious. Drunk on alcohol, he falls "like an iron pig" on car-seat springs, a contrast of dead weight against buoyancy. Again, the poet bolsters meaning with the implied image of pig iron, a product of Pennsylvania's smelters. The conclusion links hell with the furnace, an earthly damnation of those who pollute nature. Returning to the image of springs, Merwin concludes with the viewers' "witless offspring," the Pied Piper's rats who scurry to the source of singing. A witty play on words, "agape" describes their rapt faces as well as the Greek concept of love freely offered.

In an unusual form of celebration, Merwin imagines the annual date of his demise in "For the Anniversary of My Death" (1967). To typify the opposite of life, he envisions silence traveling into space "like the beam of a lightless star." In the second stanza, the experience of non-being allows him to flee the surprising qualities of earthly life, which drapes him like "a strange garment." Among memorable experiences, he singles out "the love of one woman," an unfinished statement that leaves questions in the reader's mind about its obviously private significance. When the speaker is refined into spirit and no longer answers to life, he can truly know divinity—the source of "three days of rain," a wren's song, and clearing weather.

Grimly regretful of human waste, "For a Coming Extinction" (1967) expresses Merwin's pessimism about the earth's future. Line lengths vary from double beats in lines 1 and 4 to longer statements of four or five stresses. Addressed to the gray whale, an endangered species, the four-stanza poem honors the animal as an emblem of all endangered nature, including the "seas nodding on their stalks." The absence of punctuation creates uncertainty, as with the ominous conclusion of stanza 3: "the future / Dead / And ours." As though atoning for loss, the poet-speaker promises the whale that it will have company among long-extinct beings, "The sea cows the Great Auks the gorillas," who predicted the eventual extinction of other living beings. He concludes with a repetition of "Tell him" and stresses that humanity has hastened nature's death out of arrogance.

Similarly heavy with evanescence, "Losing a Language" (1988), one of Merwin's most famous poems, responds to a fragility in human communication in the first line, which focuses on the single breath that transmits sentences. The loss of sensitive forms of expression precipitates misunderstanding. Language tethers slip away, leaving gaps between people. Dismissing the message of the old, the youngest members value fewer experiences. The fifth couplet mourns changes in children, whom the outside world urges to devalue their elders "so that they can be admired somewhere / farther and farther away." At the poem's climax, line 16, the poet-speaker states the terrible outcome: "we have little to say to each other."

The remaining six couplets express the failed interactions of a language-dead society. The new find the old "wrong and dark." Reflecting the warnings of H. G. Wells's "1984," the apprehensive poet-speaker warns that the collapse of language prefaces an atmosphere of lies. In an evolving Babel, "nobody has seen it happening / nobody remembers." Lacking the means to prophesy mounting chaos, people can no longer discuss the elements of life that are slipping away.

DISCUSSION AND RESEARCH TOPICS

(1) What does the furnace in "The Drunk in the Furnace" symbolize?

(2) Characterize the townspeople in "The Drunk in the Furnace". Is Merwin critical of them? If so, how does he show this criticism in the poem?

(3) What role does the drunk play in "The Drunk in the Furnace". How does Merwin characterize the drunk?

(4) What is the speaker's opinion of death in "For the Anniversary of My Death"? Does the speaker fear or accept death? What in the poem supports your answer?

194

(5) Is Merwin a pessimistic poet? Cite his poetry to support your answer. Also, contrast Merwin, T. S. Eliot, and Adrienne Rich as sentinels on the frontiers of doom. Determine which poet is most spiritually uplifting and why.

(6) Summarize Merwin's opinions on language and human communication in "Losing a Language." Does he suggest a way to improve communication?

SELECTED BIBLIOGRAPHY

DAVISON, PETER. "Swimming Up Into Poetry." *Atlantic,* August 28, 1997: www.theatlantic.com/atlantic/atlweb/poetry/antholog/merwin/pdmerwin.htm

FRAZIER, JANE. "Writing Outside the Self: The Disembodied Narrators of W. S. Merwin." *Style* (Summer 1996): 341–351.

HOWARD, RICHARD. "The Vixen." www-polisci.mit.edu/Boston Review/BR21.c/Reviews.html

"M. S. Merwin." *Contemporary Authors.* Gale Research. galenet.gale.com

"On Reading W. S. Merwin." instar.com/mall/janus/merwin.htm

ST. JOHN, DAVID. "The Last Troubadour." *Kenyon Review* (Summer/Fall 1997): 197.

JAMES WRIGHT (1927-1980)

Admired for depicting the little dramas lived by the lonely and alienated, poet James Arlington Wright probed the distances between people. A lyric romanticist in the tradition of Robert Frost and E. A. Robinson, Wright profited from classes with teachers John Crowe Ransom and Theodore Roethke. His literary output was phenomenal: seven poetry collections and seven volumes of translated verse, plus a prose anthology and seven posthumous volumes. The conversational ease of his voicing, fidelity to detail, and immediacy of subjects are evident in such titles as "A Note Left in Jimmy Leonard's Shack," "Confession to J. Edgar Hoover," and "At the Executed Murderer's Grave."

Wright was born into a family of Irish talkers and storytellers on December 13, 1927, in Martins Ferry, Ohio. His Midwestern working-class roots held firm through three decades of poetic portraits drawn from heartland realities. During the Depression, his father suffered layoffs from the Hazel-Atlas glass factory. Wright thrived on public speaking in grade school and began writing verse in high school. After being drafted into the United States Army during World War II, he wrote his mother to forward copies of Gerard Manley Hopkins' verse and Elizabeth Barrett Browning's *Sonnets from the Portuguese*. After he was mustered out while serving in occupied Japan, he took advantage of the G. I. Bill and entered the only school that showed interest, Kenyon College.

After Wright shifted his concentration from vocational education to English and Russian literature, by 1952 he had published in twenty journals and earned the Robert Frost Poetry Prize, election to Phi Beta Kappa, and a B.A. degree. He attended the University of Vienna on a Fulbright Fellowship. At the University of Washington, he studied under poet Theodore Roethke and completed a dissertation on Dickensian comedy, then earned a Ph.D. in 1959. Simultaneously, he held a post as English instructor at the University of Minnesota while completing *The Green Wall* (1957), winner of a Yale Series of Younger Poets award. Three years later, he won the Ohiona Book Award for *Saint Judas* (1960).

Wright published *The Lion's Tail and Eyes: Poems Written Out of Laziness and Silence* (1962) with William Duffy and Robert Bly. Wright's break with traditionalism was influenced by his intimate study of German and Spanish masters, as demonstrated in *The Branch Will Not Break* (1963) and *Shall We Gather at the River* (1968). Throughout this period, he published regularly in some fifteen journals.

Wright held subsequent teaching positions at Macalester College, Hunter College, and State University of New York. His *Collected Poems* (1971) won a Pulitzer Prize. He was active for the remainder of the 1970s, when his elegies were issued in *Two Citizens* (1973), *I See the Wind* (1974), *Old Booksellers and Other Poems* (1976), *Moments of the Italian Summer* (1976), and *To a Blossoming Pear Tree* (1978). Much of the self-pity and despair of his early works disappeared after Wright conquered alcoholism and married his traveling companion Edith Anne Runk, whom he incorporated in a series of "Annie" poems. At his death from throat cancer on March 27, 1980, friends and colleagues eulogized him at Riverside Church in New York City. Posthumous works include *This Journey* (1982), *The Temple in Nimes* (1982), and *Above the River: The Complete Poems* (1992).

CHIEF WORKS

In 1963, Wright composed a twelve-line lyric to his hometown entitled "Autumn Begins in Martins Ferry, Ohio." A brief hymn to the working class, the poem accounts for the phenomenon of high school sports heroics. Almost like a verse essay, the first stanza introduces place and economic motivation in laborers who invest their dreams in gridiron hero worship. The second stanza contrasts the testosterone-driven hunger for winners and the excluded females. Levering on "Therefore," Wright concludes his brief treatise with the next generation, who "grow suicidally beautiful" by acting out an artificial valor in theatrical combat at "Shreve High football stadium."

Composed in the same year, "Having Lost My Sons, I Confront the Wreckage of the Moon: Christmas, 1960" (1963) is a stark, yet winsome elegy. As is typical of Wright, he identifies the time in the title and the setting—"on the South Dakota border"—in line two. The poem's tension mounts to a peak in lines 15 and 16 with "I am sick / Of it, and I go on." As though touring the gravesites of "Chippewas and Norwegians," the poet-speaker admires the moonlight, which dazzles the eye with points of light. In spiritual repose, like a mystical father of the nation's sons, he ponders "the beautiful white ruins / Of America."

In the same style, "A Centenary Ode: Inscribed to Little Crow, Leader of the Sioux Rebellion in Minnesota, 1862" (1971), an oddly assertive history, is based on the death of the famed militant whose remains were first dumped at a Hutchinson slaughterhouse, then put on display by the Minnesota Historical Society. The poem moves beyond racism to social violence wrought by the Civil War. At the emotional pinnacle, the poet-speaker remarks to Little Crow, "If only I knew where to mourn you, / I would surely mourn. / But I don't know." Double spacing forces a rhetorical pause, as though the reader must hear out a hesitant voice laden with regret, not only for a dishonored leader but for the foundation of America on the graves of its Indians.

The unexpected detail of the wartime career of "Old Paddy Beck, my great-uncle" reminds the reader of a nation's shame, depicted as the loss of "the dress trousers." With a mild jog of thought from past to present in "Oh," the poet-speaker speaks distractedly of hobos, then segues to the personal with "I don't even know where / My own grave is." Almost embarrassingly frank about self-imposed exile, he departs from the usual breast-beating over past racism against natives and Africans to remind the reader that casual brutality, both past and present, compromises not just the republic, but also the individual citizen.

Wright displays another side of compassion in "Small Frogs Killed on the Highway" (1971). He adjusts the linear emphasis by varying from the single introductory adverb "Still" in line 1 to a lengthening span that reaches its height in line 10. An emotive hymn to the lowest levels of life, the poem disarms the reader with a contrast between the drivers' careless acts and the jubilant "tadpoles . . . dancing / On the quarter thumbnail / Of the moon."

The poet's celebration of self-regeneration anticipates a broader vision in "The Journey" (1982), a frozen moment set above Anghiari in the Tuscan hills of Italy. An upbeat discovery, the study of a spider poised on a web amid dust and corruption is an ambiguous image that could as easily apply to a local woman, "poised there, / While ruins crumbled on every side of her." Unlike his contemporaries, Wright carries implications to a straightforward statement—for example, "[don't] lose any sleep over the dead."

DISCUSSION AND RESEARCH TOPICS

(1) How does Wright characterize the middle class in "Autumn Begins in Martins Ferry, Ohio"? Does he positively or negatively portray this class?

(2) In "Autumn Begins in Martins Ferry, Ohio," what does the term "grow suicidally beautiful" mean? Is Wright tongue-in-cheek here?

(3) Contrast the underlying philosophy of Wright's "Small Frogs Killed on the Highway" or "Lightning Bugs Asleep in the Afternoon" to that of Robert Lowell's "Skunk Hour."

(4) How does "Old Paddy Beck, my great-uncle" evoke shame? In the poem, what is shameful?

(5) Compare James Wright's polemics in "Confession to J. Edgar Hoover" to contemporary political commentary in the works of Edna St. Vincent Millay, Joy Harjo, and Allen Ginsberg.

(6) Summarize the delight in imperfection that Wright develops in "With the Shell of a Hermit Crab," "All the Beautiful Are Blameless," and "The Ice House."

SELECTED BIBLIOGRAPHY

BAKER, DAVID. "James Wright." *Kenyon Review* (Spring 1996): 157–161.

"Hermann Hesse's Poems, Translated by James Wright." pubweb.nwu.edu/~srmina/pal.html

"The Pure Clear Word: James Wright's Literary Manuscripts." www.metronet.lib.mn.us/lol/umn-wril.htm

ANNE SEXTON (1928–1974)

A college dropout turned housewife, fashion model, and jazz singer, Anne Gray Harvey Sexton is an unusual source of self-revelatory verse that prefaced an era of modernist confessional. An ambivalent feminist, she spoke for the turmoil in women who despised the housewife's boring fate, yet she suffered guilt over ventures into angry complaint and personal freedom. A relentlessly honest observer capable of springing from disillusion to flashes of perception, she celebrated physical details of womanhood, naming menstruation, masturbation, incest, adultery, illegitimacy, and abortion, and pondered drug dependence, madness, and suicide. Long parted from religion, she retained the fault-consciousness and self-loathing of Roman Catholicism. Her freedom of expression engaged female literary figures at the same time that it distressed poet James Dickey.

Sexton was born on November 9, 1928, in Newton, Massachusetts, to a prominent family. She grew up strong-willed, outstandingly attractive, and confident, a surface poise that masked misgiving. She attended Wellesley public schools and Rogers Hall, an exclusive boarding school.

After a year at Garland Junior College, an elite Boston finishing school, Sexton eloped to North Carolina at age 19 with Alfred Mueller "Kayo" Sexton II, whom she had dated for a month. He dropped out of premedical courses at Colgate to work in his father-in-law's business; Anne clerked in a bookshop. During their tumultuous marriage, the couple lived in Massachusetts, Baltimore, and San Francisco. They produced daughters Linda Gray and Joyce Ladd.

While Kayo fought in the Korean War, Linda's birth precipitated Sexton's depression, exacerbated by ambivalence toward motherhood and voices compelling her to die. Unsuited to domesticity and infant care, she required intermittent hospitalization at Westwood Lodge. At her doctor's direction, she relieved anguish through confessional writing. Her earliest efforts focus on conflict between housekeeping and creative expression.

Writing verse helped stabilize Sexton's mind after a 1956 suicide attempt and earned her a scholarship to the Radcliffe Institute for Independent Study. After forming a professional friendship with Maxine Kumin at a poetry workshop at Boston Center for Adult Education, Sexton developed into a major talent, characterizing psychiatric analysis and grief for her dead parents in verse. Her literary growth was swift and intense. In 1961, she became the first poetry scholar at the Radcliffe Institute for Independent Study.

Central to Sexton's themes are the exasperating self-study, frank admissions of personal fault, and death urges that lace the writings of her idols, Robert Lowell, Theodore Roethke, and Sylvia Plath. Sexton's initial collections—*To Bedlam and Part Way Back* (1960) and *All My Pretty Ones* (1962), nominated for a National Book Award and winner of the Helen Haire Levinson Prize—preceded a fellowship from the American Academy of Arts and Letters, nomination for a National Book Award, and multiple invitations for readings. In the wake of a European tour and publication of the children's books *Eggs of Things* (1963) and *More Eggs of Things* (1964), coauthored with Maxine Kumin, and *Selected Poems* (1964), Sexton achieved a Pulitzer Prize for *Live or Die* (1966), containing personal and aesthetic ponderings over unresolved grief.

During a three-year reprieve from suicidal fantasies, Sexton pursued mature, darkly humorous verse in *Poems by Thomas Kinsella, Douglas Livingstone and Anne Sexton* (1968) and *Love Songs* (1969) and saw the production of a play, *Mercy Street* (1963). While teaching at Boston University and Colgate, she exposed social fraud by restating Grimm's fairy tales in *Transformations* (1971) and issued a third children's title, *Joey and the Birthday Present* (1971), also coauthored by Kumin. Newly turned to interest in religion, she wrote *The Book of Folly* (1972), filled with themes of anti-woman violence, incest, abortion, drug addiction, neurosis, and insanity.

Following an appointment to the Pulitzer Prize jury in 1973, Sexton completed *The Death Notebooks* (1974), a vivid statement of a death urge. Addicted to alcohol and tranquilizers, she despised her torpid, bloated body. She divorced Kayo with some hesitance, even though he was physically and emotionally abusive to her and their daughters. She entered McLean Hospital for treatment but left the hospital disheveled, ashen, and thin, and survived less than eleven months.

At the time of her suicide by carbon monoxide gas on October 4, 1974, in the garage of her home in Weston, Massachusetts,

Sexton, wrapped in her mother's fur coat and clutching a glass of vodka, ended a troubled, chaotic life. She died just as she was emerging as a champion of self-fulfillment. At a memorial service, Adrienne Rich decried the self-indulgence of suicidal personalities; Denise Levertov noted in an obituary that Sexton had confused creativity with self-annihilation.

Sexton's personal, many-sided poems and intimate writings appeared in posthumous editions—*The Awful Rowing Toward God* (1975), a juvenile title, *The Wizard's Tears* (1975), the play *45 Mercy Street* (1976), *Anne Sexton: A Self Portrait in Letters* (1977), and *Words for Dr. Y: Uncollected Poems with Three Stories* (1978). A compendium, *Complete Poems*, was issued in 1981, and another, *No Evil Star: Selected Essays, Interviews and Prose*, in 1985.

CHIEF WORKS

In 1960, at the beginning of her rise to prominence, Sexton wrote "Her Kind," a controlled three-stanza confessional that concluded *To Bedlam and Part Way Back*. The poem illustrates the author's immersion in a New England tradition, the roundup of hapless females to be tormented and executed during the Salem witch persecutions. In one of the poet's characteristic split personalities, through a double first-person presentation, she merges consciousness with a subversive, energized woman shunned by the pious as she is hunted for witchcraft. The loosely structured four-beat lines follow a rhyme scheme of ababcdc, linked by mostly monosyllabic end words. Each stanza concludes with the markedly forthright three-beat iambic refrain, "I have been her kind," which names her jazz ensemble, Anne Sexton and Her Kind. Images of darkness and freakishness dominate the first stanza, which stresses a compulsion to roam outside the confines of civility. The dual-natured character is both witch and violator of the domestic womanhood that inhabits the "plain houses" below.

Lonely and driven, the speaker ranges beyond civilization to surprisingly inviting caverns, where she fills the warm emptiness with a rat pack of possessions. Arranged on orderly shelves are oddments derived from past episodes of eccentricity and madness.

Like good children, her companions, worms and elves, eat her suppers. Innately "disaligned," they submit to reshaping, a personal reference to Sexton's organic poetry and failed attempts of psychological analysis and treatment with Thorazine. At the end of the stanza, she defends the speaker as "misunderstood," a defense of her own erratic behaviors.

The poem returns to well-lighted places as an unidentified carter drives the speaker toward execution. Wracked by flames and the wheel, an allusion to a medieval torture device on which victims were simultaneously rotated, pierced, and stretched, the speaker appears to greet villagers, who reside in the bright houses she once soared above in her flight from conventionality. Although her arms are nude and vulnerable, in her last moments, she is boldly unashamed of previous deeds and attitudes. Eagerly, proudly, the witch-poet embraces the identity of other brave, possessed women. Like them, she yields to torment for violating polite womanhood.

An equally fantastic view of womanhood appears in "Housewife." A ten-line free verse poem composed in 1962, its tight imagery depicts a house as a physical entity with heart, mouth, liver, and intestines. The woman, a self-sacrificing drone imprisoned in flesh-toned walls, kneels as she performs daily drudgery, scrubbing the house that has devoured her. The poet characterizes male authority figures as rapists, the intrusive cripplers who shatter woman's wholeness. Like Jonah, the Old Testament sailor swallowed and disgorged by a whale, the male householder penetrates a woman-centered home like an incestuous son returning to his mother's womb. The speaker stresses the oneness of all women, in particular, mother and daughter. The poet's matrophilia is a positive impulse that allows Sexton to love her mother and herself, the producer of two daughters.

Written in the same time period, "The Truth the Dead Know" commemorates Sexton's grief for her parents, who died in 1959 within three months of each other—her mother from breast cancer, her father from cerebral hemorrhage. The speaker recalls her father's funeral in June, when she left the formal funeral to walk alone from the church as though turning her back on God and ritual. Later, at the shore, the poet recalls sunlight that glitters like a candle and the surf, which swings to land like an iron gate. The wind, as impersonal as falling stones, drives inland from "white-hearted water," a suggestion of bloodlessness and diminished passion. Simultaneously with nature's functions, the speaker touches a loved one and affirms life.

The final quatrain bears out an alternating rhyme scheme, which links perfect and imperfect rhymes of church/hearse, grave/brave, cultivate/gate, sky/die, stones/alone, and touch/much. In the concluding lines, Sexton allies shoes/refuse with stone/knucklebone, a hard-edged conclusion that jars like a fist to the eye. The impertinence of her tone in "And what of the dead?" loses its initial sassiness as she subsides to death images. She envisions the dead lying shoeless in tombs as rigid as "stone boats." However, the brief flicker of sobriety is a boxer's sucker punch, a feint that precedes a right hook in her defiance of mortality.

Perhaps her most read work on mortality, "Sylvia's Death," scrolls out like a long, emotion-charged farewell. It was written on February 17, 1963, six days after the suicide of poet Sylvia Plath, and published in 1966. Sexton had assisted the Unitarian minister in selecting lines to read at a memorial service. In retrospect of Plath's need for closure, Sexton determined that her friend had chosen an appropriate homecoming. The comment weighs heavy in light of her own choice of self-destruction.

Speaking intimately of the addictive yearning for death, Sexton calls to her friend, asking how she could crawl into an oven to die, abandoning Sexton for a liberating death that they had both foresworn as though giving up cigarettes or chocolate. Personal memories of a cab ride in Boston obscure events that the two shared as they debated the issue of suicide. Personifications of death, "our boy," the "sleepy drummer," hammer at the poet's consciousness with a lust for death. The news that Sylvia has at last committed the long-contemplated act leaves a taste of salt, no doubt generated by tears. Critics debate whether the source of Sexton's weeping is grief or self-pity or a blend of the two.

The poet reaches out to the "stone place" in which Sylvia is buried and acknowledges that they once shared death like membership in a club. Sexton identifies the yearning for release from undisclosed pain as a mole that permeates Plath's verse, a perky underground being whose blind vitality contrasts the stillness of the buried corpse. The poem closes with three addresses to Sylvia—startling images that glimpse her as mother, duchess, and "blonde thing."

DISCUSSION AND RESEARCH TOPICS

(1) What does Sexton's ambivalence toward self-study share with Emily Dickinson's "Tell all the Truth but tell it slant"?

(2) Contrast the loss of self in violence and martyrdom in "Her Kind" with similar scenarios in Richard Wright's narrative poem "Between the World and Me" or Margaret Atwood's dystopian novel *The Handmaid's Tale*.

(3) What does the repeated phrase "I have been her kind" in "Her Kind" mean? Does the phrase have universal significance for Sexton?

(4) In "Her Kind," how does Sexton characterize loneliness? Is being lonely a positive or wholly negative quality?

(5) Discuss Sexton's image of womanhood in "Housewife."

(6) Discuss the speaker's relationship to her parents in "The Truth the Dead Know." Does the speaker seem overly saddened by her parents' deaths?

(7) Compare the tone and imagery of "The Truth the Dead Know" with Sexton's "A Curse Against Elegies" or "The Touch." Determine which poem is the more powerful and universal and which is more personal.

SELECTED BIBLIOGRAPHY

"Anne Sexton." www.kutztown.edu/~reagan/sexton.html

DAVIDSON, CATHY N., and LINDA WAGNER-MARTIN. *The Oxford Companion to Women's Writing in the United States*. New York: Oxford University Press, 1995.

HALL, CAROLINE KING BARNARD. *Anne Sexton*. Boston: Twayne Publishers, 1989.

MIDDLEBROOK, DIANE WOOD. *Anne Sexton: A Biography*. Boston: Houghton Mifflin, 1991.

SEXTON, LINDA GRAY. *Searching for Mercy Street: My Journey Back to My Mother*. Boston: Little, Brown, 1998.

SEXTON, LINDA GRAY, and LOIS AMES, eds. *Anne Sexton: A Self-Portrait in Letters*. Boston: Houghton Mifflin, 1977.

ADRIENNE RICH (1929–)

A multitalented writer, polemist, and literary theorist, Adrienne Cecile Rich is an exponent of a poetry of witness and dissent, a poetry that voices the discontent of those generally silenced and ignored. Prophetic of the bitterness that emerged from 1960s feminism, antiwar protests of the 1970s, and the 1990s gay rights movement, her mature poems breached caution to strike at resentment against sexism and human victimization. In token of shifts in her generation's consciousness, her own awakening extols the personal epiphanies that free the underclass. Radical in content, consciously power-wielding in style, her works embrace language as a liberating, democratizing force.

Rich was born in Baltimore, Maryland, on May 16, 1929. Against the intellectual battleground of a Jewish father and Protestant mother, in childhood, she produced two respectable dramas: *Ariadne: A Play in Three Acts and Poems* (1939) and *Not I, But Death* (1941). After her father introduced her to poetry, she focused on Robert Frost, Wallace Stevens, and William Butler Yeats. A Phi Beta Kappan, she graduated *cum laude* from Radcliffe the year she won the Yale Younger Poets Prize for *A Change of World* (1951). The book contained W. H. Auden's introduction, a literary coup for a beginning poet.

In 1953, Rich broke with her father because she married Harvard economist Alfred Haskell Conrad. Ostensibly domesticated, she served as faculty wife and mother to sons David, Paul, and Jacob, all born in a span of four years. As family demands shaped and defined her, she limited literary activity to *The Diamond Cutters and Other Poems* (1955), a muted, asexual effort that imitates the themes and forms of Yeats and Auden. She broke away from imitation with *Snapshots of a Daughter-in-Law: Poems 1954–1962* (1963), a dramatic pre-feminist drubbing of motherhood, sexual dominance, and suppressed anger. These hard-handed themes echo her discontent, which had smoldered for a decade as she mastered the techniques of sexual politics. In a darker mood, she followed with *Necessities of Life* (1966), the introduction to a series of poems on alienation and despair.

When her husband took a post at City College of New York in 1966, Rich instructed poor nonwhite students for SEEK, a remedial

English program geared to open admissions. She echoed the idiom and dynamism of protests against patriarchy and the Vietnam War by publishing *Selected Poems* (1967), *Leaflet: Poems 1965–1968* (1969), and *The Will to Change: Poems 1969–1970* (1971), published a year after her marriage ended and her husband committed suicide. Freed from tight metrics, she produced *Diving into the Wreck: Poems 1971–1972* (1973), which revisits the mythic parameters of the male-female relationship.

Speaking as an omniscient presence, in subsequent works, Rich championed marginalized groups in scenes that challenge the white male overlord. She began teaching English at City College and composed *When We Dead Awaken: Writing as Re-Vision* (1972), a frank autobiographical essay and challenge to literary politics, and *Of Woman Born: Motherhood as Experience and Institution* (1976), a prose exposé of the inequalities that undermine modern marriage. A bolder statement fueled *Compulsory Heterosexuality and Lesbian Existence* (1980), a terse monograph that disclosed her lesbianism.

Rich's powerful, evocative work suited late-twentieth-century poetry texts and anthologies and energized feminist coursework in women's studies departments in American colleges and universities. She reprised titles from *Twenty-One Love Poems* (1976) in an expanded volume, *The Dream of a Common Language: Poems 1974–1977* (1978). Feminism and an independence mark two prose collections, *On Lies, Secrets and Silence: Selected Prose 1966–1978* (1979) and *Blood, Bread and Poetry: Selected Prose 1979–1987* (1986); and verse in *A Wild Patience Has Taken Me This Far: Poems 1978–1981* (1981); *Sources* (1984), an exploration of Jewish roots; and *The Fact of a Doorframe: Poems Selected and New 1950–1984* (1984), a backward glance at the territory she had explored.

After three years at Douglass College, Rich left teaching to settle in western Massachusetts with her mate, poet Michelle Cliff. She produced reflective verse on lesbian feminism, anti-Semitism, and gender violence in *Your Native Land, Your Life* (1986), *Time's Power: Poems 1985–1988* (1989), *An Atlas of the Difficult World: Poems 1988–1991* (1991), and *What Is Found There: Notebooks on Poetry and Politics* (1993). Filled with a jubilant self-discovery, the urgent later works compel young students still innocent of the greed and coercion around them.

CHIEF WORKS

In her first leap from male-dominated metrics and themes, Rich produced "Snapshots of a Daughter-in-law" (1963), a visually charged odyssey. Ironically akin to the dense verse of T. S. Eliot, the text moves through ten measured glimpses, each challenging the truth of preconceptions about the female individualist. The focus, a Shreveport belle, enters stanza 1 with studied grace. Well-schooled in womanliness, she performs a musicale, one of Chopin's piano confections. By the end of the poem, the persona has achieved a transformation "long about her coming." No longer the precious, static model of femininity, she accepts the challenge to "be more merciless to herself than history."

The poem's inner structure is a self-willed passage over a treacherous mindscape. From a psyche "moldering like wedding-cake," the daughter-in-law departs from self-abuse and from becoming masculinized, like "the beak that grips her." Jettisoning the trappings of fashion and custom, she battles "ma semblable, ma soeur!"—"my double, my sister!" The doppelganger motif places the speaker in merged roles—challenger and challenged—as she sheds constraint and uselessness, typified as "the whatnot every day of life."

Crucial to Rich's re-creation of woman is the rejecion of stereotypes—the sweetly laughing girl of Horace's odes, the externally programmed lute player of Thomas Campion's ditty. At the climax, the point beyond which life can never return to its old structures, Rich questions whether sorrow itself is a revitalizing force. Stanza 7 answers the question. For the first time, the poet cites a bold woman writer, Mary Wollstonecraft, a pioneer who suffered multiple criticisms for declaring that each must find "some stay," the unshakeable anchor that steadies the rebel against convention. Unwilling to be a mere oddity, the one woman gifted with rare talents, the poet epitomizes change. Like the helicopter freighted with goods, she exults in a cargo

> delivered
> palpable
> ours.

Her selection of a vertical delivery suggests that, for the motivated feminist, a satisfying arrival is a straight shot to earth, guided by gravity.

Rich has forged a reputation for powerful examinations of human politics. The most urgent of her explorations, "Diving into the Wreck" (1973), is less compressed than the previous poem, but no less urgent. She edges cautiously into the past through a controlling metaphor, the calculated moves of the deep-sea diver. The poet cloaks the first-person speaker in so much equipment that the identity is obscure. Armed with the myths of the past, the camera of the present, and a knife for unknown menace, the speaker departs a "sun-flooded schooner" by way of the mundane ladder. Again, like the helicopter drop that concludes "Snapshots of a Daughter-in-Law," the motion is downward, a free fall to reality.

The stanzas, like cells in a movie, separate actions into the individual elements of a dive-climbing down, anticipating the ocean underfoot, drawing on containerized oxygen to power the body for peril. In line 36, the speaker warns of twin dangers: anoxia (a lack of oxygen), then the euphoria that threatens to overwhelm purpose. As is true of most of Rich's canon, purpose controls the persona. With straightforward optimism, the speaker acknowledges, "I came to see the damage that was done / and the treasures that prevail." In strict parallelism in lines 62–63, the purpose surmounts the myth, establishing a mature, open mind-set. The pointed exposure of a female figurehead establishes that the wreckage is woman herself.

The discovery of lines 71–77 is the merger of sexual selves, male with female. The androgynous view strips analysis of a need to identify the speaker. The he/she persona immediately segues into another self, the victim, "whose drowned face sleeps with open eyes." Rich's explicit picture establishes that the harm done to the downed vessel has further corroded instruments that might have guided the way. In the final stanza, Rich reminds the reader of a crucial fact: that "We are, I am, you are" the seekers who carry past, present, and weapon against the unknown. For Rich, the future remains unrecorded.

DISCUSSION AND RESEARCH TOPICS

(1) Compare Adrienne Rich, Audre Lorde, Joy Harjo, Wendy Rose, James A. Wright, and June Jordan as witnesses of wrongs done to women. Determine which poets best characterize Rich's belief that "Poems are like dreams: in them you put what you don't know you know."

(2) Discuss Rich's views of female individualism in "Snapshots of a Daughter-in-law."

(3) How does the speaker in "Snapshots of a Daughter-in-law" achieve a personal transformation? What is this transformation?

(4) What does the wreck symbolize in "Diving into the Wreck"?

(5) Discuss the downward motion in "Diving into the Wreck" in terms of the speaker's personal growth. How does this downward motion compare to that found in "Snapshots of a Daughter-in-law"?

(6) Explain Rich's belief that women themselves must reshape the pattern of female existence to excise old expectations of "the Victorian Lady of Leisure, the Angel in the House, and also of the Victorian cook, scullery maid, laundress, governess, and nurse," which she characterized in *Of Woman Born*.

SELECTED BIBLIOGRAPHY

"Adrienne Rich." www.poetry.books.com/nrich.htm

"Adrienne Rich." *Contemporary Authors*. Gale Research. galenet. gale.com

"Adrienne Rich Refuses to Accept National Medal." www.hotlink. com/8797.html

DAVIDSON, CATHY N., and LINDA WAGNER-MARTIN. *The Oxford Companion to Women's Writing in the United States*. New York: Oxford University Press, 1995.

ROTHSCHILD, MATTHEW. "Adrienne Rich." *Progressive* (January 1994): 31–36.

SYLVIA PLATH (1932–1963)

Sylvia Plath, a precocious enigma of the 1960s, battled perfectionism and precipitous mood swings while pursuing a career as a teacher and poet. She was born in Jamaica Plain, a suburb of Boston, Massachusetts, on October 27, 1932. In early childhood, she lived in Winthrop on Massachusetts Bay. Left fatherless at age 8, she lived with her mother's parents and attended school in Winthrop and college at Wellesley. She later acknowledged uncertainty about her father through bee imagery in "Stings," "The Swarm," "The Bee Meeting," and other poems.

After publishing the story "And Summer Will Not Come Again" in *Seventeen* magazine and the poem "Bitter Strawberries" in *Christian Science Monitor* in 1950, Plath earned a scholarship to Smith College and majored in English literature and composition. She published additional poems in *Harper's*. A subsequent story, "Sunday at the Mintons," won a *Mademoiselle* scholarship, a position on the magazine's college board, and a summer internship in New York.

In August 1953, Plath attempted suicide. She underwent electroconvulsive therapy at McLean Hospital in Belmont, Massachusetts. She returned to Smith in February 1954 and earned a B.A. in English, graduating *summa cum laude* with membership in Phi Beta Kappa. She subsequently studied English literature as a Fulbright scholar at Newnham College, Cambridge, and then married British poet Ted Hughes in June 1956.

Plath taught at Smith, then worked as a hospital secretary in Boston while concentrating on writing. Her diary captures the negativism that paralyzed and bedeviled her. She felt lonely and isolated at school. The best she could offer her bruised self was a grade of "middling good." The year after Ted Hughes published a critical success, *The Hawk in the Rain*, she failed twice, neither earning a Saxton Fellowship nor publishing verse.

After seeking guidance from Robert Lowell and Anne Sexton, Plath won a Guggenheim Fellowship in 1959. She continued working in the clerical department of Massachusetts General Hospital while undergoing therapy. The family returned to London in December 1959, months before the birth of daughter Frieda Rebecca and a subsequent move to a Devon manor house. Plath published *The Colossus and Other Poems* (1962) and completed a radio play, *Three Women: A Monologue for Three Voices* (1962), and *The Bell Jar* (1963). The latter, a powerful psychological novel and autobiographical study of schizophrenia, she issued under the pen name Victoria Lucas.

Plath entered a productive period in 1962, when a renewed vigor and daring took her into ever-deepening levels of psychic expression. Her health and emotional stability declined with the birth of a son, Nicholas Farrar. She was antagonized by her husband's adulteries, and she burned a stack of manuscripts (her own and Hughes') and filed for divorce. Seeking renewal in the visionary works of William Butler Yeats, she moved the children to Chalk Farm in London. During a wretched winter, after supplying each crib with a mug of milk and stuffing the crevices with towels, on February 11, 1963, she committed suicide by overdosing on barbiturates and inhaling gas from the kitchen stove.

Plath was much missed. Her friend, poet Anne Sexton, composed a Unitarian eulogy and wrote a verse tribute. Literary fans and cultists welcomed posthumous publication of *Ariel* (1965), a verse study of the patriarchy of her husband and father. Additional titles—*Crossing the Water: Transitional Poems* (1971), *Winter Trees* (1972), and *Letters Home: Correspondence, 1950–1963* (1975), edited by her mother—strengthened Plath's place among feminists. Hughes issued his ex-wife's prose (minus one he chose to destroy) in *Johnny Panic and the Bible of Dreams and Other Prose Writings* (1977), *The Collected Poems* (1981), and *The Journals of Sylvia Plath* (1982). On the strength of these works, Plath earned the 1982 Pulitzer Prize for poetry. Her work continues to influence the writings of a new generation of feminists.

CHIEF WORKS

In 1959, Plath wrote "The Colossus," a painstaking evaluation of her deceased father. After three decades of labor, the speaker's plastic reconstructions fail to re-create the man she knew only from childhood memories. The astonishing controlling image of a fallen giant places the speaker in the seriocomic role of a Lilliputian, who climbs ladders and traverses the oversized brow and pate of a fallen Gulliver. Locked in the hell of ambivalence, she explores fantasies meant to free her from loss, betrayal, and remorse.

Charged allusions to Aeschylus's *Oresteia* and the Roman Forum dignify the dead father as they tinge a lifelong search with subtle shades of tragedy. The poet-speaker allies herself with the Greek Agamemnon's doomed twins, Orestes and Electra, who destroyed themselves by attempting to avenge the father's murder. A pivotal image—"married to shadow"—tethers the harried speaker to an Electra Complex, the Freudian name for a young girl's abnormal adoration of her father. As though abandoned on a faraway island, she ceases to anticipate rescue from an idealized father.

In 1961, Plath composed "Morning Song," a re-creation of childbirth. Like coded messages, her personal memories lie hidden among metaphors of parenthood. Conceived in love, the infant arrives to an ungentle world. The poet enhances fragility with the midwife's slap, the dual meaning of "sole" in "footsole," and the vulnerable hairless head and naked limbs. The image of the child as a "New statue. / In a drafty museum" prefigures later views of bodies as sculpture. In the third stanza, the mother retreats from importance like a cloud dispersed by wind. During the first night, she accustoms herself to infant breathing, pink complexion, and the demanding cry. With self-deprecating humor, she sees herself as "cow-heavy," a bovine shape in floral nightdress hurrying to nurse a newborn. One of her most optimistic works, the poem characterizes normalcy and hope.

Composed at the height of her creativity, "Daddy" (1962) resorts to childish, mannered naughtiness and the ebullience of jump-rope rhyme to express a more complex defiance and rage at a father who confined his daughter like a foot laced into a shoe. Returning to the image of the fallen statue, the poet reveals personal recollections of Nauset Beach and her father's Polish ancestry. Departing from anguish, the mouthy brat envisions herself stuttering in German, then succumbing to Nazi torments at "Dachau, Auschwitz, Belsen." In the seventh stanza, the choice of "chuffing" for the sound of trains deporting Jews returns to the baby language that began the poem. The word, a pun on "chough," draws on the connection between hovering blackbirds and carrion.

Wordplay continues as she degrades her father with the words "the brute / Brute heart of a brute like you."

The convergence in stanzas 11 through 16 illustrates why critics disagree in their assessment of Plath's skill. Clever and inventive in the drumming beats and assonance of *oh* and *oo* sounds in "go," "glue," "screw," "you," and "through," the picture of a cloven-footed demon biting a child's heart precedes self-destruction. No longer the sturdy, willful persona of the opening stanzas, the poet-speaker suffers from suicide attempts, the patchwork of psycho-analysis, and a "fat black heart," a guilt-soaked conscience which she plants in her father's breast. A mental picture of the tormenter adept at rack and screw compels her to say "I do, I do," an oral implication of perverse sex and emotional marriage to the father. In the guise of a vengeful bride of Dracula, she kills off the real and the imagined father, a monstrous, self-damning double murder intended to set her free.

In this same period, Plath produced "Ariel," a spare, densely packed vision. Like piano scales, the deranged persona speaks brief lines. Ecstatic and energized, she produces word pictures compressed to maximize motion. Named for a sprite who did the will of Prospero in Shakespeare's *The Tempest*, the poem draws on a memory of riding a horse named Ariel before sunup. A controlling assonance—"I," "White / Godiva," "rider," "flies," "drive," "eye"— suits the gallop, which liberates as it brings the speaker nearer extinction.

The image of the furrow, an allusion to female genitalia, builds with an overlay of the blood-red berry juice. The flow of semen into her body renders her powerless, as though she dangled in air. Sexual connotations continue with "Thighs, hair; / Flakes from my heels," a reference to the missionary position, which places the female on bottom during intercourse, where she attains leverage with her feet. The poem diverges into a new direction in stanza 7, which recalls childbirth. The first-person mother evolves into a death-dealing arrow, the self-destroyer. Envisioning suicide, she epitomizes freedom as unbridled flight toward a burning sun, a symbol of power and regeneration.

Also written in her last three months, "Lady Lazarus" strikes out with a lacerating tone. An allusion to the dead man whom Christ revived, the poem enlarges on glimpses of a rotting corpse stripped of its burial napkin. Terrible in fleshless skull and decay, the deceased revitalizes in stanza 7, like a cat that retains nine of its fabled lives. The poet-speaker, livid with rage and self-pity, envisions a third reclamation from death, with crass, peanut-eating gawkers pushing to get a look at the unwrapping of her body. The revelation recharges the corpse, as though empowered by a sideshow appeal to the crowd.

In chronological order, the poet-speaker recalls the first suicide attempt, then the second, when she "rocked shut / As a seashell." With a neurotic joy in the art of suicide, she claims, "I do it exceptionally well," an artful statement made by Sylvia-the-poet about Sylvia-the-madwoman. Still angry at viewers, she insists on charging them for "eyeing of my scars," "the hearing of my heart." As though chanting to terrify tormentors, she intones through repetition, implied rhyme, and paired rhymes a surreal return to the victims of Nazi persecution. To both God and Satan, she warns that her rejuvenation is lethal to men.

A posthumous work, "Blackberrying" (1965), retreats from anguish to a pastoral setting, where the speaker gathers and eats ripe berries, a controlling metaphor for art poised atop constraints, depicted as thorns. Pitting sweet-juiced spheres against the price for gathering, the speaker accumulates an ominous fruit, which she characterizes as black eyes. The darkness mirrors black birds protesting in the sky. They ride air currents as gracefully as fly ash blown from a fire, a blended image of cremation and release. In line 13, the speaker doubts that the alley-shaped hedges will allow her a glimpse of the sea, an implication of spiritual release in the afterlife.

The remainder of "Blackberrying" addresses the obstacles to Plath's personal freedom and art. The lushness of berries leads her to a bush so ripe that it is decked in flies, hellish insects whose translucent wings stand out like the sheer panels of an oriental screen. By the end of stanza 2, the speaker moves beyond berrying to stand in the damp gust of sea air, "slapping its phantom laundry in my face." The housewife image links to the taste of salt, an allusion to the poet's hatred of domestication. After achieving the final push to the sea, the speaker looks out on space, a metaphor for the purity of death. The sound of the sea reminds her of hammerings against her stubbornness.

From the same time period, a crossover piece, "Fever 103," parallels the metrics of "Lady Lazarus" with its abrupt question, exclamation, and confession, but reflects the resignation of her last works. Picturing illness as a trip to hell, the poet imagines herself undergoing purification. Wrapped in sin, she hears "tinder cries," a pun on tender/tinder to heighten the flimsiness of human tissue, soon to be burned away amid the smell of an extinguished candle flame. The smoke that circles her frame reminds her of Isadora Duncan, the dancer accidentally strangled when her scarf tangled in the spokes of the Bugatti convertible in which she was riding.

Building on the death of Isadora, the poet protests the snuffing out of delicate infants, like hothouse orchids, a double image of hanging planter and the hovering aura of lavender smoke. As the hallucinatory imagery returns to history, death steals aboard technology, annihilating the rare leopard with radiation and the innocents at Hiroshima, who, in 1945, were incinerated in an atomic explosion that ended World War II. In stanza 10, the poet returns to self, the victim who flickers between life and death. The raging, self-destructive fever, depicted in the repetition of "The sin. The sin," turns the victim's head into a macabre Japanese lantern, which gives off an astounding glow resembling the flushed petals of a camellia. In a kaleidoscopic shift to the final image, she pictures lust falling away as the spirit, purged to its original state, rises to heaven.

DISCUSSION AND RESEARCH TOPICS

(1) Analyze the success of confessional modes in Plath's *The Bell Jar* and poems from *Ariel*. Account for severe criticisms of self-indulgent neurosis.

(2) Compare Plath's startling images of confinement and coercion in "Purdah" with those in poems by Anne Sexton, Audre Lorde, and H. D.

(3) Summarize lines from Plath's prose and verse that capture her ambivalence toward male authority figures, in particular, her husband and father.

SELECTED BIBLIOGRAPHY

BLOOM, HAROLD, ed. *Sylvia Plath*. New York: Chelsea House, 1989.

DAVIDSON, CATHY N., and LINDA WAGNER-MARTIN. *The Oxford Companion to Women's Writing in the United States*. New York: Oxford University Press, 1995.

HUGHES, TED. *Birthday Letters*. New York: Farrar, Straus & Giroux, 1998.

OATES, JOYCE CAROL. "The Death Throes of Romanticism: The Poems of Sylvia Plath." *Southern Review* (Summer 1973): 501–522.

PLATH, SYLVIA. *Letters Home: Correspondence, 1950–1963*. New York: Bantam Books, 1975.

ROSE, PHYLLIS, ed. *The Norton Book of Women's Lives*. New York: W. W. Norton & Co., 1993.

"Sylvia Plath." *Contemporary Authors*. Gale Research. galenet.gale.com

"Sylvia Plath Links." cityhonors.buffalo.k12.ny.us/city/reference/English/plath.html

AMIRI BARAKA (1934–)

A model of the self-made African-American national, poet and propagandist Imamu Amiri Baraka is a leading exponent of black nationalism and latent black talent. Baraka, who was originally named Everett LeRoi Jones, earned a reputation for militancy among radical contemporaries Stokely Carmichael, Huey P. Newton, and the Black Panthers. He has thrived as activist, poet, and playwright of explosive oratories produced on the stages of New York, Paris, Berlin, and Dakar, Senegal.

Baraka was born on October 7, 1934, in Newark, New Jersey, to upscale parents. He attended Rutgers University and Howard University on scholarship, but was ousted due to his poor performance. After graduate work at Columbia University and the New School for Social Research and a dismissal from the United States Air Force for suspicious activities, he influenced the black community's economy and politics and earned a reputation as a polemical dramatist and Beat poet.

Baraka's early success derives from a play, *A Good Girl Is Hard to Find* (1958), and *Preface to a Twenty-Volume Suicide Note* (1961), an introduction to a life's work revealing the black man's pain. While living with wife Hettie Cohn in Manhattan, he established *Yugen*, a neo-bohemian review, and Totem Press. He journeyed to Cuba in 1960, which radicalized his thinking about oppression in the third world. Newly energized, he wrote *Blues People: Negro Music in White America* (1963), and edited *The Moderns: An Anthology of New Writings in America* (1963). The bluntness of his radical thinking, as displayed in *The Dead Lecturer: Poems* (1964), influenced the establishment of the American Theater for Poets.

Baraka's early flash of brilliance did not go unnoticed. In his late twenties, he earned a John Hay Whitney Fellowship and an Obie for the violent drama *Dutchman* (1963), a taut, menacing vehicle for black consciousness-raising. It succeeded off-Broadway the same year he produced *The Toilet, The Baptism,* and *The Slave.* The latter is an explosive drama depicting racist confrontations of the times. A kingpin of the Black Arts Movement by 1964, Baraka was visiting scholar at the University of Buffalo. After his adoption of a Muslim name, he settled in Harlem to write *J-E-L-L-O* (1965), a denunciation of a public figure, and autobiographical fiction, *The System of Dante's Hell* (1965), which earned him a Guggenheim Fellowship. His work sharpened in *Home: Social Essays* (1966) and fueled the drive for the Black Arts Repertory Theater School, one of New York City's cultural landmarks. He completed *Arm Yourself or Harm Yourself* (1967) and collaborated with Larry Neal on *Black Fire: An Anthology of Afro-American Writing* (1968).

Outside these literary coups, Baraka's Marxist-Leninist activism has placed him in positions of power. In March 1972, he led the National Black Political Convention in Gary, Indiana, which drew 3,500 delegates from the United States and the Caribbean and prefaced a permanent consortium, the Congressional Black Caucus. While residing in Newark, he focused on black activism and Afro-Islamic culture with the establishment of Spirit House, a gathering spot and drama center. After his arrest on a concealed weapons charge, he pursued black nationalism through an Afrocentric cult, the Temple of Kawaida.

As Baraka developed black community, his artistry altered from dense obscurities to the positive, youth-centered style of Langston Hughes. His anthology, *Black Magic: Sabotage, Target Study, Black Art: Collected Poetry 1961–1971* (1969), demonstrates his emergence as an American writer respected by outspoken peers. Perpetually in print, he produced short fiction in *Tales* (1967) and issued additional nonfiction, *In Our Terribleness: Some Elements and Meanings in Black Style* (1969) in collaboration with Billy Abernathy; *Raise Race Rays Raze: Essays Since 1965* (1971); and *Afrikan Congress: A Documentary of the First Modern Pan-African Congress* (1972).

In his mature years, Baraka published *The Motion of History, Six Other Plays* (1978), containing the pageant *Slave Ship*, which was staged off Broadway. He anthologized verse in *Selected Poetry of Amiri Baraka/LeRoi Jones* (1979) and previously unpublished autobiography in *Selected Plays and Prose of Amiri Baraka/LeRoi Jones* (1979). At age 50, he issued *The Autobiography of LeRoi Jones* (1984), followed by more prose commentary in *Reflections on Jazz Blues* (1987). His honors include a National Endowment for the Arts award and a Guggenheim fellowship.

CHIEF WORKS

"An Agony. As Now" (1964), derived from his early radicalism, dissociates selves in a tormented first-person speaker. Driven mad with toxic emotion, the unacknowledged self lives in the sensory experiences of a hated outer self. His distaste takes shape in the songs his double sings and the women he loves. Like the man in the iron mask, the internal self looks out through metal at an interaction with the world that he neither understands nor condones.

Beginning in line 12, pain takes on a greater distraction as the schizoid state becomes less tolerable. Repetitions of "or pain" recycle the poet-speaker's misery as he attempts to name the source and type of hurt. The suffering outdistances his notion of God as it reaches for a "yes" in line 27, the beginning of resolution. With controlled self-direction, the speaker forces himself to see and acknowledge beauty. In the final five lines, the trapped inner speaker batters the outer shell that refuses to feel normal love. The outer man, incapable of compromise, gazes at the sun and scorches the pulp-tender inner being.

A long verse ode, "A Poem for Willie Best" (1964), retrieves the humanity of modern-day Jim Crow, a black actor who functioned in film as "Sleep'n'eat." The poem opens on Best's head, a symbol of his disembodied talent, which performs while ignoring a suffering heart. Carefully aligned alliteration (all/hell, beggar bleeds) and assonance (time/alive) precede a rich image of doom in slippery-sided hell "whose bottoms are famous."

In Baraka's trademark poetic geometry, stave II pictures the dimensionless point of the head viewed from "Christ's / heaven" and emphasizes God's disinterest in the black man's anguish. Pilloried, the black Christ figure can expect no aid, for "No one / will turn to that station again." In succeeding staves, the poet-speaker ponders the use of sexual release as repayment for racial degradation but interrupts his angst in stave VII to plead, "Give me / Something more / Than what is here." The reasoning is crushingly simplistic: Relief must come from the outside world, for "my body hurts."

In line 128, the poet-speaker begins a resolution calling for balance. Punning on a homonym ("Can you hear? Here / I am again"), the insistent voice turns from easing the body to seek comfort in spirit. The speaker is tired of losing. He justifies the demand as only fair. Retreating into casual violence as a form of self-reclamation, the "renegade / behind the mask" lists the black qualities and behaviors stereotyped by the white world. Still misidentified, the suffering Willie Best, his name a mockery of what the white world expects of a talented black, awaits "at the crossroads," a symbol of martyrdom on the cross.

Five years after "An Agony. As Now" and "A Poem for Willie Best," Baraka composed "Black People: This Is Our Destiny" (1969). He launches his verbal challenge in an oratorical, out-of-syntax style drawn from the tradition of storyteller and ecstatic preacher. Visionary in its obscurities, the text spins out the reality of black fate. The pulsing rhythm forges ahead in noun clusters— "the gases, the plants, the ghost minerals/the spirits the souls the light in the stillness." The poet shocks in line 15 with a jarring declaration that there is "nothing in God." On its descent, the poem gathers speed once more before halting at the pause in line 17 and plunges into a bold statement of the future. Drawing on a belief that blacks were the first humans to evolve from primates, Baraka sees his idealism as a holy commission to "evolve again to civilize the world."

DISCUSSION AND RESEARCH TOPICS

(1) Compare Baraka's internalization of racism in "An Agony. As Now" with Richard Wright's identification with a lynching victim in "Between the World and Me."

(2) Contrast Baraka's throbbing phrases and inventive punctuation with that of the Beat poets, in particular, Allen Ginsberg.

SELECTED BIBLIOGRAPHY

"Amiri Baraka." csm.astate.edu/~engphil/gallery/baraka.html

"Amiri Baraka." www.biography.com/find/bioengine.cgi?cmd=1 &rec=15249

ANDERSON, MICHAEL, et al. *Crowell's Handbook of Contemporary Drama.* New York: Thomas Y. Crowell Co., 1971.

PLOSKI, HARRY A., and JAMES WILLIAMS, eds. *The Negro Almanac.* Detroit: Gale Research, 1989.

WENDY ROSE (1948–   )

A blend of poet, historian, painter, illustrator, and anthropologist, Wendy Rose rejects marginalization. Issued under her birth name Bronwen Elizabeth Edwards and the pseudonym Chiron Khanshendel, as well as Rose, her realistic writings, watercolors, and pen-and-ink sketches defy those who relegate native American artisans to a passing fad. As spokesperson for ecology, women, and the dispossessed, she maintains a balanced outlook devoid of bitterness. She is intent on making positive connections, and she uses verse to mark spiritual boundaries.

A native of Oakland, California, of Hopi, Miwok, and Scottish-German ancestry, Rose was born on May 7, 1948, and grew up in a predominantly white environment. After attending Cabrillo College and Contra Costa College, she earned a B.A. and M.A. in cultural anthropology from the University of California at Berkeley, where she entered a doctoral program while teaching ethnic and native American studies. To account for her support of the Light of Dawn Temple, a San Francisco occult research center, she published a premier volume, *Hopi Roadrunner Dancing* (1973). She followed with verse in *Long Division: A Tribal History* (1976), *Academic Squaw: Reports to the World from the Ivory Tower* (1977), *Poetry of the American Indian* (1978), *Builder Kachina: A Home-Going Cycle* (1979), and a Pulitzer Prize nominee, *Lost Copper* (1980), an anguished statement of the native American blended identity. Departing from the negativity of earlier works, she composed *What Happened When the Hopi Hit New York* (1982) and *The Halfbreed Chronicles and Other Poems* (1985), self-illustrated volumes that recapture the beauties of chant and establish her admiration for fellow native authors Leslie Marmon Silko, Paula Gunn Allen, and Joy Harjo.

While coordinating American Indian studies at Fresno City College, Rose edited *American Indian Quarterly*, a vehicle for her struggle to be known as more than a native American relic. Candor has earned her other positions with the Smithsonian Native Writers' Series, Women's Literature Project of Oxford University Press, Modern Language Association Commission on Languages and Literature of the Americas, and Coordinating Council of Literary Magazines. Her more recent volumes include *Going to War with All My Relations: New and Selected Poems* (1993), *Bone Dance: New and Selected Poems, 1965–1993* (1994), and *Now Poof She Is Gone* (1994).

CHIEF WORKS

In retort to insensitive faculty at Berkeley, "Academic Squaw" (1980) taunts her detractors with a pejorative self-labeling title. The poet employs the image of battered bone as the springboard to a native American sense of self. As though glorying in fragility and imperfection, the poet-speaker depicts her ancestry as a smudged design with "bowl-rim warped / from the beginning." Fleshing out a human frame with "jumping blood," saliva, and melted eyes, she marvels that so haphazard an ancestry allows a "random soul" to survive. The patchwork imagery moves to a surprise rhyme (trained/drained) and a defiant address, "Grandmother, / we've been framed." The sturdy ending suggests that Rose, like her native fore-mothers, has no intention of building a life around victimization.

"If I Am Too Brown or Too White for You" (1985), one of Rose's dialogues spoken to an unidentified "you," clarifies her place as in-dividual and poet in a world obsessed with categorizing. Toying with visual images, she moves from two colors in the title to the bold introduction of "a garnet woman" who is neither "crystal arithmetic" nor a "cluster." To account for her dreams and black-bird pulse, she builds on the notion of a semiprecious stone that re-flects the color of blood, a layered image that suggests pure and mixed blood ancestry as well as the bloodshed that followed the ar-rival of Europeans to the Western Hemisphere.

To express the Anglo world's obsession with race, Rose envi-sions a seeker selecting polished river stone by color. She employs the term "matrix / shattered in winter," which draws on the ety-mology of matrix from "mater," Latin for mother. Native produc-tivity suffered in a wintry era, the 1870s, when white society conquered native American tribes. Imperfect, clouded, and mixed in the late twentieth century, the stone's interior shelters a "tiny sun / in the blood," the pure aboriginal element that gives rise to song. By claiming a tie with the native story keeper, Rose nour-ishes that portion of Indian heritage that can't be drubbed out or winnowed away. Her verse establishes the value of native poems as embodiments of native chant, a sacred utterance that defines and elevates.

DISCUSSION AND RESEARCH TOPICS

(1) Account for the dream vision at the heart of Rose's "To the Hopi in Richmond" and "Oh My People I Remember."

(2) Summarize images of femininity in Rose's "Newborn Woman, May 7, 1948."

(3) Characterize Rose's creation of dialogue between a poetic voice and the epigraph of "I expected . . .," "Three Thousand Dollar Death Song," "What the Mohawk Made the Hopi Say," and "Halfbreed Chronicles."

(4) Contrast autobiographical concerns in Rose's "Neon Scars," "Vanishing Point: Urban Indian," and "Naming Power" with personal reflections in the confessional poems of Elizabeth Bishop, Anne Sexton, Robert Lowell, and James A. Wright.

SELECTED BIBLIOGRAPHY

BERNER, ROBERT L. "World Literature in Review." *World Literature Today* (Autumn 1995): 845.

DAVIDSON, CATHY N., and LINDA WAGNER-MARTIN. *The Oxford Companion to Women's Writing in the United States.* New York: Oxford University Press, 1995.

"Discovering Multicultural America." Gale Research. galenet.gale.com

FAST, ROBIN RILEY. "Borderland Voices in Contemporary Native American Poetry." *Contemporary Literature* (Fall 1995): 508–537.

"Wendy Rose." *Contemporary Authors.* Gale Research. galenet.gale.com

"Wendy Rose." www.nativeuathors.com/search/bio/biorose.html

JOY HARJO (1951–)

Feminist screenwriter and poet Joy Harjo relishes the role of "historicist," a form of storytelling that recaptures lost elements of history. Typically listed alongside native writers Paula Gunn Allen, Mary Crow Dog, Wendy Rose, and Linda Hogan, she strives for imagery that exists outside the bounds of white stereotypes. As a force of the Native American renaissance, she speaks the pain and rage of the Indian who lacks full integration into society. Harjo's antidote to despair is a vigorous reclamation of living. Her poems resonate with Indian journeys and migrations; her characters combat the cultural displacement that fragments lives and promotes killing silences.

Of Muscogee Creek, Cherokee, French, and Irish ancestry, she was born Joy Harjo Foster on May 9, 1951, in Tulsa, Oklahoma. She is a lifelong music lover who plays jazz saxophone and enjoys community stomp dances. After switching majors from art to poetry, she earned a B.A. in creative writing at the University of New Mexico and completed an M.F.A. at the University of Iowa, followed by cinema study at the College of Santa Fe in 1982. In addition to teaching at the universities of Arizona, Colorado, New Mexico, and Montana, she has served as Native American consultant for Native American Public Broadcasting and the National Indian Youth Council and director of the National Association of Third World Writers.

Influenced by the works of Flannery O'Connor, Simon Ortiz, Pablo Neruda, and Leslie Marmon Silko, Harjo began publishing in feminist journals, including *Conditions*, and in the anthologies *The Third Woman* (1980) and *That's What She Said* (1984). Her early work in *The Last Song* (1975), *What Moon Drove Me to This?* (1980), and *She Had Some Horses* (1983) ponders the place of women in a blended Anglo-native world. She rose above the "native poet" label with *In Mad Love and War* (1990), an examination of the vengeance unleashed by failed romance. Her feminism enhanced two cinema scripts, *Origin of Apache Crown Dance* (1985) and *The Beginning*. In 1994, she produced "The Flood," a mythic prose poem that links her coming of age to the "watermonster, the snake who lived at the bottom of the lake."

At the end of the twentieth century, while retaining her focus on gender and ethnic disparity, Harjo turned to universal themes. *The Woman Who Fell from the Sky* (1996), a volume of prose poetry, pairs creation and destruction. She juxtaposed benevolent native female voices in an anthology, *Reinventing Ourselves in the Enemy's Language: Contemporary Native Women's Writing of North America* (1997). In addition, she edits *High Plains Literary Review, Contact II,* and *Tyuonyi.* Her honoraria include fellowships from the National Endowment for the Arts and Arizona Commission on the Arts, a first place from the Santa Fe Festival for the Arts, American Indian Distinguished Achievement award, and a Josephine Miles award.

CHIEF WORKS

One of Harjo's early triumphs, "The Woman Hanging from the Thirteenth Floor Window" (1983) describes conflict in the tense drama of an unnamed woman who hangs between survival and doom. Subtle touches characterize her personal torment as "her mother's daughter and her father's son." Crucial to the woman is motherhood and the impetus to lie still and cuddle a sleeping infant rather than "to get up, to get up, to get up" at the command of a harassing male, generalized as "gigantic men."

Harjo's coverage of impending suicide stresses "lonelinesses." In line 46, in view of pitiless women and others who clutch their babes like bouquets while offering aid, the speaker establishes that suffering and choice are an individual matter. From chewing at harsh truths, the hanging woman's teeth are chipped. The precarious either/or of her posture remains unresolved in the last four lines, suggesting that death in life mirrors the fatal leap.

A contemporary grudge piece, "New Orleans," explores the poet's trove of history-as-memory during a trek down the Mississippi to New Orleans. The speaker-traveler—obviously Harjo herself—carries preconceptions of an undercurrent of blood, of "voices buried in the Mississippi / mud." The native perspective emerges with wry humor: The poet-speaker envisions a trinket seller destroyed by magic red rocks that repay the unwary for wrongs that date to the European settlement of the New World. A deft shape-shift depicts the speaker, searching for a familiar Indian face, as a swimmer submerged in gore, "a delta in the skin."

As a well-honed tale withholds its climax, the non-linear poem, somewhat late in line 37, finds its target: Hernando De Soto, the death-dealing Spanish conquistador inflamed by the myth of El Dorado. In a city connected with black slavery, where merchants sell tawdry "mammy dolls / holding white babies," the topic ignores white-on-black crimes to needle De Soto, guilty of Latino-on-Indian violence. Shifting from the "lace and silk" luxuriance of New Orleans to the home-centered Creek, the poem claims that the Creek "drowned [De Soto] in / the Mississippi River." (History's version of the event tells of a Catholic burial in the river after he died of fever.) Like Louisiana graves that "rise up out of soft earth in the rain," the ghost of De Soto imbibes his fate and gyrates in a Bourbon Street death dance with "a woman as gold / as the river bottom."

Narrative outside history dominates Harjo's long works. Dedicated to poet Audre Lorde, "Anchorage" (1983) turns to prehistory through one of Harjo's characteristically long introductions. This time, glacial "ice ghosts . . . swim backwards in time" to the alluvial era when volcanoes forced their way to the surface. She transposes straightforward text into native dance rhythms and pictures the parallel dance lines of air over subterranean ocean:

> where spirits we can't see
> are dancing
> joking getting full
> on roasted caribou, and the praying
> goes on.

As indicated by the punning title, natives anchor their lives in primal urges—the rhythmic dance, humor, feasting, and worship that celebrate oneness with nature.

The themes of continuity, momentum, and resilience fuel the remaining twenty-eight lines. The traveler, accompanied by Nora, strolls down city streets. Disdainful of a society that turns an aged Athabascan grandmother into a spiritually battered bag lady "smelling like 200 years / of blood and piss," the pair alter their confident step with a soft reverence for life. Two streets over, they pass the jail and marvel at Henry, survivor of a burst of gunfire outside a Los Angeles liquor store. Native humor bubbles through bitterness to toast "the fantastic and terrible story of all of our survival," a solidarity that transcends urban chaos.

In 1990, Harjo captured violence and vengeance in "Eagle Poem," a traditional Beauty Way chant. Visually evocative and spiritually stimulating, in ceremonial rhythm, the prayer acknowledges forms of communication other than sound. Parallel phrasing propels the lines along with the physical and spiritual invocation: "To sky, to earth, to sun, to moon / To one whole voice that is you." Merging with the circling eagle, the speaker achieves a sacral purity and dedicates self to "kindness in all things." The act of breathing establishes kinship with universal rhythms. Animism transcends mortality, which the speaker touches lightly as though the end of life were only one stage of perpetual blessing. In traditional closure, the speaker asks that all be accomplished "In beauty. / In beauty."

DISCUSSION AND RESEARCH TOPICS

(1) Compare Harjo's racial recall through poetic myth in "Vision," "Deer Dancer," and "New Orleans" with novelist Toni Morrison's "rememory" in *Beloved* and Louise Erdrich's recovered myth in *Tracks*.

(2) Account for the use of horses as a metaphor for warring internal demons in Harjo's *She Had Some Horses*.

(3) Contrast Harjo's faith in re-created history, as demonstrated in the poems "The Real Revolution Is Love," "Autobiography," "For Anna Mae Pictou Aquash, Whose Spirit Is Present Here and in the Dappled Star," or "For Alva Benson, and For Those Who Have Learned to Speak," with the historic confession in Robert Lowell's "For the Union Dead" and "The Quaker Graveyard in Nantucket."

(4) Apply to Harjo's ethic the command of Ozark poet C. D. Wright: "Abide, abide and carry on. Give physical, material life to the words of your spirit. Record what you see. Rise, walk and make a day."

SELECTED BIBLIOGRAPHY

ALEXIE, SHERMAN. "She Had Some Horses: The Education of a Poet." *Teachers & Writers* (March–April 1995): 1–3.

BRUCHAC, JOSEPH. "Interview with Joy Harjo." *North Dakota Quarterly* 53 (1985): 220–234.

DAVIDSON, CATHY N., and LINDA WAGNER-MARTIN. *The Oxford Companion to Women's Writing in the United States.* New York: Oxford University Press, 1995.

"DISCovering Multicultural America." Gale Research. galenet. gale.com

GOODMAN, JENNY. "Politics and the Personal Lyric in the Poetry of Joy Harjo and C. D. Wright." *MELUS* (Summer 1994): 27–35.

KALLET, MARILYN. "In Love and War and Music." *Kenyon Review* 16 (1989–1990): 5–13.

LEEN, MARY. "An Art of Saying: Joy Harjo's Poetry and the Survival of Storytelling." *American Indian Quarterly* (Winter 1995): 1–16.

"Voices from the Gaps: Women Writers of Color." www-engl.cla. umn.edu/lkd/vfg/Author/JoyHarjo

RITA DOVE (1952–   )

The first black and youngest author to serve as poetry consultant to the Library of Congress, Rita Frances Dove considers herself the heir of Phillis Wheatley, slave poet of the colonial era. A complex intellectual, Dove has edited *Callaloo*, *Gettysburg Review*, and *TriQuarterly* and served at Harvard on the Afro-American Studies Visiting Committee while producing some of the twentieth century's most controlled, viscerally satisfying imagery. She has earned praise for concrete immediacy. Her low-key, high intensity poems are distillations brewed by night until predawn from private imaginings and wordplay at her one-room cabin outside Charlottesville, Virginia. Her finished verse spirials out of everyday images and shards of sound, thought, and long-nurtured memory.

Dove was born in Akron, Ohio, on August 28, 1952. She discovered her gift for word manipulation in early childhood. Dove intended to make the most of her talents. After earning a National Merit Scholarship and ranking among the nation's top 100 high school seniors in 1970, she accepted a Presidential Scholarship and a tour of the White House. Although she was a Phi Beta Kappa inductee and stellar graduate of Miami University, she disappointed her parents by taking creative writing workshops while pretending to study law. After a change of heart in her junior year, she also dismayed teachers by embracing poetry as a career goal. She completed her education on a Fulbright/Hays Scholarship at the University of Tübingen. While she was a teaching fellow at the Writer's Workshop of the University of Iowa, she earned an M.F.A. in creative writing and issued a first volume, *Ten Poems* (1977).

In 1979, Dove married novelist Fred Viebahn, father of their daughter, Aviva Chantal, and translator of German editions of Dove's verse. Blending political undercurrent into personal memoir, she began submitting to national poetry journals and published *The Only Dark Spot in the Sky* (1980) and a poetic slave memoir entitled *The Yellow House on the Corner* (1980). While teaching at the University of Arizona, she composed *Museum* (1983), a hymn to history and culture that moved toward a more mature expression beyond the limitations of personal experience. The height of this collection is "Parsley," a depiction of Rafael Trujillo's slaughter of 20,000 Caribbean blacks on the basis of their pronunciation of *perejil,* the Spanish word for parsley.

Dove reached literary maturity with a dramatic coup, *Thomas and Beulah* (1986), a forty-four-poem tribute to her Southern-born maternal grandparents. The work reads like a novel. Dove based the intimate glimpses on the stories of her grandmother Georgianna, who brightened widowhood by reliving romance and marriage in shared memories. The book won the 1987 Pulitzer Prize for poetry, the first awarded to a black female since Gwendolyn Brooks' prize in 1950.

Dove followed with *The Other Side of the House* (1988) and *Grace Notes* (1989); juxtaposed with short fiction in *Fifth Sunday* (1985); a novel, *Through the Ivory Gate* (1992); the one-act play *The Siberian Village* (1991); and a verse drama, *The Darker Face of the Earth* (1994). Among her honoraria are appointments as juror for the 1991 Pulitzer Prize and National Book Award for poetry, the 1985 chair of poetry grants for the National Endowment for the Arts, and many honorary doctorates.

CHIEF WORKS

With "Geometry," Dove employs a lyric three-line stanza to express delight in writing verse. She derives the title from a brother's recommendation that she visualize shapes while working out geometric proofs. Selecting robust verbs for a series on remodeling, she re-creates the poet's work as knocking out walls, removing windows, and forcing the ceiling up. To characterize the whole process, she retreats from activity with a satisfied sigh. The walls, made clear, free the odor of carnations, a funeral flower that takes its name from the Latin for flesh because the blossom gives off an odor like a decaying corpse. Thus, her energetic removal of restraints is also a reprieve from dismal reminders of mortality.

To meld into a conclusion, Dove breaks the last line of stanza II and hurries on to stanza III with joy in being "out in the open." The invitation to look beyond confinement grows out of magical realism. For example, like cartoon shapes, the uptilted windows, tinged with sunlight, change into butterflies, a complex image of optimism and flight. Unconstrained in the act of composing poetry, Dove moves toward truths that await proving.

"Adolescents—I," the beginning of a gemlike triad numbered I—III, presents teenage girls in secret conference. Dove describes the sight with symbol—the daring conspirators kneel behind "grandmother's porch," a reference to the rigid, elevated outlines of the previous society. Teased by grass at ground level, they speak a child's immature truism—"a boy's lips are soft." As though looking toward the roles of wife and mother that await them, they characterize the feeling of a kiss with a prophetic, gently sibilant simile, "as soft as baby's skin." The meager light of a firefly precedes the lighting of street lamps, both small wattages that begin the illumination of a "feathery" adolescent awareness.

At the head of Dove's accomplishments, *Thomas and Beulah* (1986) is a major contribution to her family's lore. Dove has acknowledged in interviews that her ambitious work moved from a series of snapshots for a family album to more imaginative characterization. Among the changes necessary for her poetry was an alteration of Grandmother Georgianna's name to Beulah, which suits the meter. Dove concludes the series with a chronology of events that stand out in an otherwise unremarkable family history.

The action accounts for the lasting marriage of two endearing nobodies: Tennessee-born Thomas wed to Beulah, a Georgia native whose family settled in Akron, Ohio, after they joined the Great Migration of Southern blacks to industrial centers of the Midwest. Their historical union spans from December 1924 to Thomas's death at the end of July 1963. The significant and not-so-significant events that coincide with their private achievements and crises together underweave Dove's appraisal of a commonplace couple who influenced her first decade of life.

Dove presents both points of view—male and female—and instructs the reader to peruse them in sequence. Opening on Thomas, the poet follows the pre-feminist thinking of the era by allowing the husband to dominate. She dots his share of the text with details that characterize a fictionalized version of her half-Cherokee grandfather. In the poem, he is an Appalachian mountaineer short on prosperity, but long on good looks and musical talent. Gifts to his intended are simple, yet as intimate as a scarf, "the yellow silk / still warm from his throat / around her shoulders." Gently probing the foundations of a family, Dove depicts his fluttering heart as "slowly opening" to domesticity. As though convincing himself of worthiness, he promises, "I'll give her a good life."

Dove allows history to drift in and out of understated scenes. In an up mood, Beulah selects the color of their "sky blue Chandler" for a family visit back to Tennessee; in 1943, a personal and national decline overwhelms Thomas as he departs a movie theater under a veil of despair. Like a doting parent, in "Aurora Borealis," the poet breaks through the character's subconscious. With stodgy, clipped finality, the authoritarian voice commands, "Thomas, go home." By halting on "home," Dove implies that the husband's answer to qualms and self-doubt is found in the solidity and comfort of his marriage to Beulah.

Beulah's mental landscape meanders far from that traversed by Thomas. As though unaware of the greater cosmos, in "Sunday Greens," Beulah seasons her cooking with hambone during the spare Depression years when precious little meat clung to spare frames. In flitting daydreams, she eludes fragrance of beebalm pomade by linking it to a distant cityscape. Looking out to the world, she fixes on "Turkish minarets against / a sky wrenched blue."

Dove's strongest feminist commentary derives from the housewife's private burden in "Dusting," the poet's most analyzed, anthologized poem. Keeping physically and mentally busy, Beulah challenges a nagging despair with fantasy. While hands combat the "grainstorms" with a gray dustrag, her mind flies free of housewifery to ponder the name of a boy who kissed her at the fair. Was it Michael? As though polishing her life, she rubs the furniture to a bright shine. Too late, an answer comes to her—Maurice, an exotic not-Thomas kind of name. In subsequent entries, Dove pursues her grandmother's emotional displacement. The grit of "Dusting" returns in the form of "Nightmare," a twenty-four-line torment that ends with a memory of her mother's cry—"you'll ruin us"—for opening an umbrella indoors, a violation of folkways.

The verse cycle closes with "The Oriental Ballerina," a shifting, iridescent picture story centering on the dancing figurine that spins and dips atop a jewelry box more suited to budding women than old ladies. Beulah, aged and widowed, lies in a ghost-ridden room and perceives the dancer as a Chinese woman on the opposite side of the globe, where "they do everything upside down." Her association of classical ballet with Asia rather than France, where it began, suggests that her knowledge of culture is limited.

With the skill of a pointillist painter, Dove daubs the remains of her grandmother's memories on a verbal canvas with too-candid flashes—"papered in vulgar flowers," "background the color of grease," and a disheartening reminder that the veneer of Beulah's existence can never rise above "cracked imitation walnut." The details anchor the room in a humdrum, working-class environment. Obviously, Beulah has few treasures to feed her fantasy.

The aged speaker is left husbandless and bedfast beside crumpled, camphor-soaked tissues and an invalid's straw poking out of the glass like an accusing finger. Beyond Beulah's idealism of a petite dancer atwirl on her toes, the poet remarks, "the rest is shadow." Yet, bright rays against dull walls explode the invalid's limited view into reflected patterns. Like theatrical light tricks, a dazzling transformation spatters the dismal room with "shabby tutus." The sun-fed illusion becomes the poet's blessing on a failing grandparent whose memory retains all that is left of a marriage. Still capable of fleeing place and body, Beulah thrives on the active fantasy that sustained her from early marriage through widowhood to the receding boundaries of her life.

DISCUSSION AND RESEARCH TOPICS

(1) Contrast the gentle tone of Dove's "Adolescence—I" with Gwendolyn Brooks's ironic "We Real Cool." Comment on the cost of adolescent coming-to-knowledge.

(2) Apply the term "lyric narrative" to Thomas and Beulah. Determine which segments are most lyric and which are earthbound in straightforward narration.

(3) Compare Dove's historical, female-centered scenarios with those of poets Anne Sexton, Cathy Song, and Lorna Dee Cervantes or of fiction writers Isabel Allende, Gabriel García Marquez, Maxine Hong Kingston, and Laura Esquivel.

SELECTED BIBLIOGRAPHY

DAVIDSON, CATHY N., and LINDA WAGNER-MARTIN. *The Oxford Companion to Women's Writing in the United States*. New York: Oxford University Press, 1995.

DOVE, RITA. *Selected Poems*. New York: Pantheon Books, 1993.

HINE, DARLENE CLARK, ELSA BARKLEY BROWN, and ROSALYN TERBORG-PENN, eds. *Black Women in America: An Historical Encyclopedia*. Bloomington: Indiana University Press, 1993.

PETERSON, KAREN S. "White House's Epic Evening with Poets Laureate." *USA Today,* 21 April 1998, 8D.

"Rita Dove." www-engl.cla/umn.edu/lkd/vfg/Authors/RitaDove

"Rita Dove." *Contemporary Authors*. Gale Research. galenet.gale.com

"Rita Dove." *Current Biography.* New York: H. W. Wilson Co., 1994.

"Rita Dove Page." members.aol.com/bonVibre/rdove.html

SMITH, JESSIE CARNEY, ed. *Notable Black American Women*. Detroit: Gale Research, 1992.

VENDLER, HELEN H. *The Given and the Made: Strategies of Poetic Redefinition*. Cambridge: Harvard University Press, 1995.

WALLACE, PATRICIA. "Divided Loyalties; Literal and Literary in the Poetry of Lorna Dee Cervantes, Cathy Song, and Rita Dove." *MELUS* (Fall 1993): 3–20.

WALSH, WILLIAM. "Isn't Reality Magic? An Interview with Rita Dove." *Kenyon Review* (Summer 1994): 142–155.

WHITE, JACK E. "Rita Dove." *Time,* October 15, 1993, 88–89.

CATHY SONG (1955–)

A Hawaiian of Chinese and Korean ancestry, Cathy Song centers her verse on island themes and activities and understated pastoral settings. Her language is standard English inset with words and phrases from Pacific and Asian sources. She has gained credence for lifting the mundane from homely backgrounds to produce a lyric strangeness offset by teasing and, at times, startling analogies.

Song was born in Honolulu on August 20, 1955, to airline pilot Andrew and seamstress Ella Song. Their marriage, a "picture bride" arrangement, and the resulting closeness with her grandparents, influenced Song's concepts of male-female relationships and the tri-generational home. Coming of age in Wahiawa, Oahu, she began writing in high school and pursued a career in writing. She obtained a B.A. in English from Wellesley College and an M.A. in creative writing from Boston University. At age 21, she published a short story in *Hawaii Review* and continues submitting works to *Greenfield Review*, *Tendril*, *Dark Brand*, *Asian-Pacific Literature*, and *Bamboo Ridge: The Hawaii Writers' Quarterly*.

A first collection, *Picture Bride* (1983), which won the Yale Younger Poets Award and a National Book Critics Circle award nomination, personalizes the slow assimilation of women into society. Song draws inspiration from modern Southwestern painter George O'Keeffe's flower portraits. Song names each section for a flower and exalts O'Keeffe's work in "From the White Place" and "Blue and White Lines after O'Keeffe."

After marrying medical student Douglas McHarg Davenport, Song composed a second anthology, *Frameless Windows, Squares of Light* (1988), which develops her meditative vision while furthering themes of family history. With island poet Juliet S. Kono, she coedited and contributed poetry and prose to *Sister Stew* (1991). Three years later, she published a third volume, *School Figures* (1994). Her writing has earned the Hawaii Award for Literature and a Shelley Memorial Award.

CHIEF WORKS

Song's blend of deceptive quiet and spontaneous self-study powers "The White Porch" (1983). A subtly erotic piece bound up in the commonalities of a woman's day, the poem unfolds in a three-stage presentation. The tender chiming between "I" and "you" begins in the first stanza, which is set on a family porch at 12:05 p.m. Languorous diction pictures time stretched out like a lawn and compares wet hair to "a sleeping cat," an introit to the inswept sexual passions that emerge with feline grace. Line 21 begins the upward spiral of sensuality as the female speaker acknowledges "this slow arousal."

The intrusion of a third person, the speaker's mother, literally grabs attention by grasping the daughter's braided rope of hair, a symbol of patterned proprieties. The hair, no longer lush from a fresh shampoo, continues to unite images as the mother's ring snags strands, a suggestion that parental control is a minor intrusion on the daughter's mature passion. Like the knotted hair, the mother curls into "tight blankets" as the daughter loosens her hair and signals a welcome to her lover.

From the same period, "Beauty and Sadness" studies femininity in the "women of Edo." Dedicated to Utamaro, the opening lines picture the artist, a "quick, nimble man," as an unseen presence, similar to the waiting lover in "The White Porch." The images stress fragility in "skinlike paper" and "fleeting loveliness," the source of the poem's melancholy. The second stanza masses luxuriant images of sight, smell, and touch that transform women into "beautiful iridescent insects, / creatures from a floating world." The mood begins a downward sweep in the third stanza as the models display an outer beauty balanced by melancholy. The trembling lip takes on the surface tension of a blood droplet, a comparison that tops vulnerable veins with a transparent skin of female elegance.

In the concluding stanza, the poet's delicate picture sequence captures both the act of sketching loveliness and the brief moment of pose that strikes the artist's eye. Although Song dedicates the work to the artist, her verse speaks for the women. Untouched by

Utamaro, they change into "dusty ash-winged moths"; their indifference and emotional withdrawal separates them from artistic technique.

DISCUSSION AND RESEARCH TOPICS

(1) Summarize shifting and intertwined relationships in Song's "Picture Bride." Enlarge on the images of blended cultures with comparisons to marriages described in the writings of Maxine Hong Kingston, Jeanne Wakatsuki Houston, Michael Dorris, and Amy Tan.

(2) Characterize Song's female personae in "The Youngest Daughter," "Lost Sister," "Blue Lantern," "Waialua," "China Town," "The White Porch," and "The Seamstress."

(3) Discuss how Song's poems express Audre Lorde's concept of poetic voyaging to inner sources.

SELECTED BIBLIOGRAPHY

BLOYD, REBEKAH. "Cultural Convergences in Cathy Song's Poetry." *Peace Review* (September 1998): 393–400.

DAVIDSON, CATHY N., and LINDA WAGNER-MARTIN. *The Oxford Companion to Women's Writing in the United States.* New York: Oxford University Press, 1995.

"DISCovering Multicultural America." Gale Research. galenet.gale.com

GAFFKE, CAROL T., and ANNA J. SHEETS, eds. *Poetry Criticism.* Volume 21. Detroit: Gale Research, 1998.

WALLACE, PATRICIA. "Divided Loyalties; Literal and Literary in the Poetry of Lorna Dee Cervantes, Cathy Song, and Rita Dove." *MELUS* (Fall 1993): 3–20.

GENERAL BIBLIOGRAPHY

BAYM, NINA, gen. ed. *The Norton Anthology of American Literature,* 5th edition. New York: W. W. Norton & Co., 1998.

BLAIN, VIRGINIA, PATRICIA CLEMENTS, and ISOBEL GRUNDY. *The Feminist Companion to Literature in English.* New Haven, CT: Yale University Press, 1990.

BLANKENSHIP, RUSSELL. *American Literature: As an Expression of the National Mind.* New York: Henry Holt & Co., 1931.

BLOOM, CLIVE, and BRIAN DOCHERTY, eds. *American Poetry: The Modernist Ideal.* New York: St. Martin's Press, 1995.

BRADBURY, MALCOLM, gen. ed. *The Atlas of Literature.* London: De Agostini, 1996.

BROOKS, CLEANTH, and ROBERT PENN WARREN. *Understanding Poetry,* 4th edition. New York: Holt, Rinehart & Winston, 1976.

BROOKS, CLEANTH, R. W. B. LEWIS, and ROBERT PENN WARREN, eds. *American Literature: The Makers and the Making.* New York: St. Martin's Press, 1973.

BUCK, CLAIRE, ed. *The Bloomsbury Guide to Women's Literature.* New York: Prentice Hall, 1992.

Cambridge Biographical Dictionary. New York: Cambridge University Press, 1990.

CHAPMAN, MARY LEWIS, ed. *Literary Landmarks: A Guide to Homes and Memorials of American Writers.* Williamsburg, VA: Literary Sketches Magazine, 1974.

EHRLICH, EUGENE, and GORTON CARRUTH. *The Oxford Illustrated Literary Guide to the United States.* New York: Oxford University Press, 1982.

GILBERT, SANDRA M., and SUSAN GUBAR. *The Norton Anthology of Literature by Women*. New York: W. W. Norton & Co., 1985.

KUNITZ, STANLEY, ed. *Twentieth Century Authors*. New York: H. W. Wilson, 1942.

LAUTER, PAUL, gen. ed. *The Heath Anthology of American Literature*, 3rd edition. Boston: Houghton Mifflin, 1998.

LEVINE, MIRIAM. *A Guide to Writers' Homes in New England*. Cambridge, MA: Applewood Books, 1984.

LOW, W. AUGUSTUS, and VIRGIL A. CLIFT, eds. *Encyclopedia of Black America*. New York: Da Capo, 1981.

MCGILL, FRANK, ed. *Cyclopedia of World Authors*. New York: Harper & Brothers, 1958.

MCQUADE, DONALD, gen. ed. *The Harper American Literature*, 2nd edition. New York: HarperCollins, 1993.

SHERR, LYNN, and JURATE KAZICKAS. *Susan B. Anthony Slept Here: A Guide to American Women's Landmarks*. New York: Times Books, 1994.

SNODGRASS, MARY ELLEN. *The Encyclopedia of Satirical Literature*. Santa Barbara, CA: ABC-Clio, 1996.

Webster's Dictionary of American Women. New York: Merriam-Webster, 1996.

GLOSSARY

allegory a literary work or visual imagery that functions on two or more levels of meaning by comparing objects to symbols outside the scope of the work.

alliteration the repetition of consonant sounds, even those spelled differently.

allusion a brief or indirect reference to something or someone known to most people.

analogy a literary parallel or comparison between like situations, objects, or ideas, often expressed as a simile or implied as a conceit, image, or metaphor.

anapest a metrical foot or unit formed of three syllables, two unstressed beats followed by a stressed beat (-- ').

anti-hero, anti-heroine a protagonist or central figure who lacks heroic qualities.

antithesis a balanced statement of contrasts that juxtaposes opposites in words, phrases, clauses, images, or themes.

apologia a literary defense of a person or situation, also an explanation or detailed accounting of an event or belief.

apostrophe an emotion-charged address to an absent or dead person, abstract quality, or object.

approximate rhyme words that come close to rhyme without copying the exact sound pattern, as in steer/stare, mud/could, and late/light.

archetype a recurrent character, setting, or pattern from early literature.

assonance repetition of a vowel sound, as with the *a* sound in ace/eight/say.

balanced sentence a sentence composed of equal elements on each side of a connector, which creates a pause to stress proportional comment on either side.

ballad a dramatic chronological story-poem.

bathos overstatement, excessive emotion, or anticlimax that stresses loss, sentiment, or tragedy to the point of creating humor or melodrama.

beast fable an amoral animal story or allegorical satire that features nonhuman characters in a comic action to reveal a character fault or weakness.

belles lettres   elegant writing.

blank verse   an unrhymed pattern of short and long beats into a five-beat line (- '/ - '/- '/- '/- '/).

cacophony   an arrangement of harsh or grating sounds to annoy or create conflict or tension.

cadence   a unified arrangement of phrases or sounds into a pattern.

caesura   a pause or interruption in a line of verse.

canon   an authentic body of writing by one author.

canto   a major segment or numbered section of a long poem.

character name   a method of revealing qualities of character or attitude through symbolic or descriptive names.

chiaroscuro   a deliberate contrast of light and dark elements.

climax   the turning point or height of a series of actions.

conceit   an elaborate comparison that teases the imagination to understand its logic.

consonance   the repetition of consonants, as in leaves/loaves.

context   the phrases surrounding a passage.

contrast   a strong difference between two elements in a comparison.

couplet   a pair of rhymed lines composed in the same meter.

dactyl   a metrical foot consisting of three syllables, a stressed beat followed by two unstressed beats (' --).

denotation   the literal definition of a word.

diction   the selection of words and phrasing.

elegy   dignified verse that praises, laments, or meditates on a subject.

end-stopped   the ending of a thought at the end of a line of poetry.

enjambment   thought that continues from one line of poetry into another.

euphony   a series of pleasant sounds producing a positive effect.

feminine rhyme   a pattern of words concluding on unstressed syllables.

foot   a unit of rhythm or cadence.

free verse   poetry written in a casual or unpatterned rhythm similar to spoken language.

griot   a storyteller or tribal historian.

hexameter   a poetic line containing six units, often broken into two groupings of three beats.

hyperbole   an exaggeration or overstatement.

iamb   a metrical unit that contains two syllables, an unstressed beat followed by a stressed beat (- ').

idiom   a phrase or expression producing meaning beyond the sum of the words.

imagery   a grouping of word pictures that create a single sense impression of sight, sound, taste, touch, or smell.

imagism   a free verse study of a single object and its use or purpose.

impressionism   style stressing personal response to an event or object.

internal rhyme   rhymed words within a poetic line.

irony   an implied discrepancy between the actual event or statement and what is meant.

juvenilia   literary works produced by an immature author.

lyricism   strikingly emotional verse that flows like a melody.

magical realism   free association of whimsy, dream, and fantasy with realistic detail.

masculine rhyme   an arrangement of stresses ending on an accented syllable.

metaphor   an implied comparison of unlike objects or thoughts.

meter   the pattern of stressed and unstressed beats in poetry to form a rhythm. The five standard meters are iambic (-'), trochaic ('-), dactylic ('--), anapestic (--'), and spondaic (''). The number of feet in a line gives a name to the rhythm, as in monometer, dimeter, trimeter, tetrameter, pentameter, and hexameter.

mood   the controlling atmosphere of a work, which may be tense, uplifting, sad, or a blend of atmospheres.

motif   an obvious pattern of events, characters, or themes.

naturalism   a type of literary study that depicts humans as animals controlled by heredity and environment, but not by supernatural forces or gods.

octave   a set of eight lines of verse; an octet.

ode   a lengthy ceremonial stanza that studies a single dignified subject and theme.

onomatopoeia   an echo word or phrase that imitates the sound it represents, as with gurgle, thump, hum, and snort.

paean   a tribute or praise song.

paradox   an unusual statement of truth through obvious contradiction.

parallelism   the use of similar grammatical structures.

pastoral   a literary work stressing rural events and characters.

personification   a phrase that gives human thought and feeling to an abstract idea, being, or object.

Petrarchan sonnet   a fourteen-line poem in iambic pentameter comprised of an octave to a sestet and rhyming in some variation of abbaabbacdecde.

pun   a witty remark comparing words with similar meanings or sounds.

quatrain   a four-line stanza.

realism   a literary re-creation of life in action, setting, atmosphere, and character.

rhyme scheme   the arrangement of rhymes at the ends of a series of lines.

rhythm   a natural arrangement of stresses in a line of verse.

satire   mockery that stresses human faults and weaknesses.

sestet   a six-line stanza.

Shakespearian sonnet   a fourteen-line poem composed in iambic pentameter rhyming abab, cdcd, efef, gg.

sibilance   alliterated s, z, or sh sounds.

simile   a comparison built around like, as, or than.

sonnet   a fourteen-line poem written in iambic pentameter.

spondee   a metrical foot composed of two stressed syllables (″).

symbol   a tangible object that represents an abstract idea or relationship.

theme   the main thought or idea of a work, such as patriotism, regret, or youth.

tone   the author's attitude toward a work and its audience — for example, cynical, earnest, or objective.

vignette   a brief scenario.

INDEX

A

"About Marriage," 179
abstract ideas, 10
"Academic Squaw," 223
"A Centenary Ode: Inscribed to
    Little Crow, Leader of the
    Sioux Rebellion in
    Minnesota, 1862," 197
"The Ache of Marriage," 179
"Adolescents-I," 232, 234
"After Apple-Picking," 23
"All the Beautiful Are
    Blameless," 198
allegory, 241
Allen, Paula Gunn, 222, 225
Allende, Isabel, 135, 234
alliteration, 10, 241
allusion, 241
"America," 187–188
Ammons, Archie Randolph, 74
    bibliography, 182–183
    chief works, 181–182
    life of, 180–181
"An Agony. As Now," 219–221
analogy, 241
analyzing poetry, 5–11
anapest, 241
"Anchorage," 227
"And Summer Will Not Come
    Again," 211
Anderson, Dame Judith, 67
Anderson, Sherwood, 15, 52, 100
Andrew Marvell, 76
Angelou, Maya, 122, 175
"Angina," 175
"Annabel Lee," 20
"The Anniad," 155
"An Octopus," 74
anti-hero and anti-heroine, 241
"Anti-Imperialist Writings by
    Edgar Lee Masters," 15
antithesis, 6, 241

"A Poem for Willie Best,"
    220–221
apologia, 241
"Apology for Bad Dreams,"
    67–68
apostrophe, 241
approximate rhyme, 10, 241
archetype, 241
"The Armadillo," 140–141, 142,
    162, 165
assonance, 241
"At Melville's Tomb," 113
"At the Executed Murder's
    Grave," 195
"At the Fishhouses," 139–140
Auden, W. H., 55, 59, 102, 143,
    190, 206
"Aurora Borealis," 233
"Autobiography," 228
"Autumn Begins in Martins
    Ferry, Ohio," 196, 198
"A Woman Alone," 178–179
"A World Without Objects Is a
    Sensible Emptiness," 169

B

*Babel to Byzantium: Poets and
    Poetry Now*, 172
balanced sentence, 241
ballad, 241
The Baptism, 218
Baraka, Imamu Amiri, 120
    bibliography, 221
    chief works, 219–221
bathos, 241
beast fable, 241
The Beautiful Changes, 166, 169
"Beauty and Sadness," 237–238
"The Bee Meeting," 211
The Beginning, 225
belles lettres, 242
The Bell Jar, 105, 212, 216

"Bells for John Whiteside's
  Daughter," 86, 89
Berryman, John Angus, 143,
  159, 190
  bibliography, 147
  chief works, 144–146
  life of, 143–144
"Between the World and Me,"
  204, 221
"Birches," 26–28
Bishop, Elizabeth, 72, 162,
  165, 224
  bibliography, 142
  chief works, 139–142
  life of, 137–138
"Bitter Fruit of the Tree," 122
"Bitter Strawberries," 211
"Black People: This Is Our
  Destiny," 221
"The Black Tambourine," 109, 113
"Blackberrying," 215
Blacks, 155
Blake, William, 97, 184
blank verse, 242
"Blue and White Lines after
  O'Keeffe," 236
"Blue Lantern," 238
"Blue Meridian," 100
"Blues Ain't No Mockin'
  Bird," 129
Bogan, Louise, 72
  bibliography, 106
  chief works, 103–105
  life of, 102–103
Bradstreet, Anne, 144, 146
"Break of Day," 122
"The Breath of a Rose," 125
The Bridge, 108, 110–112, 113
"A Bronzeville Mother Loiters
  in Mississippi," 156, 157
Brooke, Rupert, 23

**Brooks, Gwendolyn
  Elizabeth**, 39, 234
  bibliography, 157–158
  chief works, 156–157
  life of, 154–155
Brown, Sterling Allen
  bibliography, 122–123
  chief works, 121–122
  life of, 119–121
Browning, Elizabeth Barrett,
  35, 195
"Buffalo Bill's," 35
"Burning the Christmas
  Greens," 51
"Burnt Norton," 81

C

cacophony, 10, 242
cadence, 242
caesura, 242
"The Cameo," 91
Cane, 97–98, 99, 100
canon, 242
canto, 242
"Canto I," 57
"Canto XLV," 58
"Cape Hatteras," 112
"Carmel Point," 68
Carmichael, Stokely, 120, 218
*Caroling Dusk: An Anthology of
  Verse by Negro Poets*, 119, 132
Carter, Jimmy, 175
Catch-22, 82
categories, 6
Chaplin, Charlie, 109
"Chaplinesque," 109, 113
character names, 8, 242
"The Chaste Land," 115
"Cherrylog Road," 172–173
chiaroscuro, 242
"Chicago," 37–39
Chicago Renaissance, 36

The Children of the Night, 16
"The Children of the Poor," 156
Children Sing in the Far West, 169
Chills and Fever, 84, 89
"China Town," 238
"Christmas Eve," 182
"The City Limit," 181–182
climax, 242
collection, 5
"Colonel Shaw and the
    Massachusetts' 54th," 163
"The Colossus," 212–213
"Come In," 105
comparisons, 10
conceit, 242
concluding comments and
    questions, 11
"The Condor," 66
"Confession to J. Edgar
    Hoover," 195, 198
confessional, 6
Conrad, Joseph, 137
consonance, 242
context, 242
contrast, 242
"The Convent of the Sacred
    Heart," 79
"The Coora Flower," 157
couplet, 242
Crane, Harold Hart, 47, 52,
    58, 97, 105, 118
    bibliography, 114
    chief works, 109–113
    life of, 107–109
"Credo," 69
Crisis, 124, 131
**Cullen, Countée Louis
    Porter,** 98, 119, 124, 129
    bibliography, 135
    chief works, 132–134
    life of, 131–132
cultural details, 8

cummings, e. e., 35, 47, 53,
    143, 154
"A curse Against Elegies," 204

D

dactyl, 242
"Daddy," 213–214
"The Dance," 113
"The Dark Tower,", 132 135
Davidson, Donald, 83, 115, 152
Day by Day, 160
"Dead Boy," 89
Dear Judas and Other Poems,
    66, 67
"Death in Mexico," 178–179
The Death Notebooks, 105, 200
"The Death of a Toad," 167
"The Death of the Ball Turret
    Gunner," 149, 152, 164–165
"The Death of the Hired Man,"
    23, 25–26, 29
"Deer Dancer," 228
denotation, 242
"Departmental: The End of My
    Ant Jerry," 28–29
"Departmental Ditties," 28
"The Desert Music," 52
The Dial, 54, 72, 108
dialect, 8
Dickey, James Lafayette
    bibliography, 175–176
    chief works, 172–175
    life of, 171–172
Dickinson, Emily, 137, 204
diction, 242
"Dirge Without Music," 94
"The Disquieting Muses," 175
"Diving into the Wreck,"
    209, 210
*Diving into the Wreck: Poems
    1971-1972,* 207
"Divorcing," 179

"Doc Hill," 14–15
Doolittle, Hilda (H. D.), 31, 35, 39, 47, 53, 71, 137, 216
  bibliography, 65
  chief works, 62–64
  life of, 60–62
Dove, Rita Frances, 189
  bibliography, 235
  chief works, 231–234
  life of, 230–231
"The Dragonfly," 105
Dream Songs, 145–143
"Dream Variation," 126, 127, 129
Dreiser, Theodore, 13, 52
"The Drunk in the Furnace," 191–193
DuBois, W. E. B., 98, 131
"Dulce et Decorum Est," 59
Dunbar, Paul Laurence, 119, 125
"Dusting," 233
"The Dwelling," 182

E

"Eagle Poem," 228
"Easter Morning," 181–182
Edgeworth, Maria, 72
Edwards, Bronwen Elizabeth, 222
elegy, 242
Eliot, T. S. (Thomas Stearns), 45, 52–53, 55, 59, 72, 108, 111, 119, 154, 160, 194
  bibliography, 82
  chief works, 77–81
  life of, 75–76
Ellison, Ralph, 97, 129, 154, 171
"Elmer, Herman, Bert, Tom, and Charley," 14
Emerson, Ralph Waldo, 184
"The Emperor of Ice-Cream," 43–44
end-stopped, 242
"England," 73

enjambment, 242
"Envoi," 58
epic, 6
"The Equilibrists," 88–89
"Eros Tuarannos," 19–20
"Euclid Alone Has Looked on Beauty Bare," 93
euphony, 10, 242
Evans, Mari, 122, 129
"Evening in the Sanitarium," 104, 105, 106
"The Ex-Basketball Player," 106, 142
explanatory notes, 11
Exultations, 54

F

"Falling," 173-174, 175
"Falling Asleep over the Aeneid," 165
fantasy, 35
Faulkner, William, 165
Fauset, Jessie Redmon, 97, 124, 131
"Fear," 92
feminine rhyme, 242
"Fever 103," 216
"Filling Station," 140, 142
Fine Clothes to the Jew, 126
"Fire and Ice," 23, 29
"The Fire Sermon," 80
"The Fish," 74, 139
"A Fixed Idea," 31
"The Flood," 225
"Flowers by the Sea," 35
"Fog," 39
foot, 242
"The Foot-Washing," 182
"For a Coming Extinction," 192
"For Alva Benson, and For Those Who Have Learned to Speak," 228

"For Anna Mae Pictou Aquash, Whose Spirit Is Present Here and in the Dappled Star," 228
foreign words, 8
"For John Berryman," 165
"For the Anniversary of My Death," 192–193
"For the Marriage of Faustus and Helen," 108
"For the Union Dead," 160 163–164, 228
Ford, Ford Madox, 54, 102
Foster, Joy Harjo, 225
free verse, 242
"From the Dark Tower," 133
"From the White Place," 236
Frost, Robert Lee, 16–17, 20, 39, 52–53, 55, 84, 105, 119, 148, 166, 175, 180, 206
 bibliography, 29–30
 chief works, 24–28
 life of, 22–24

G

"Geometry," 231
"Georgia Dusk," 99
"Gerontion," 79, 82
"The Gift Outright," 29
Ginsberg, Irwin Allen, 48, 60, 69, 95, 148, 198, 221
 bibliography, 189
 chief works, 186–188
 life of, 184–185
"Go, Lovely Rose," 58
"God's World," 91
"The Goldfish Wife," 169
Gordon, Caroline, 108, 115, 159
"Grass," 39
"A Grave," 73
griot, 242

H

H. D. *See* Doolittle, Hilda
haiku, 6
"Halfbreed Chronicles," 224
Hardy, Thomas, 17
Harjo, Joy, 118, 198, 210, 222
 bibliography, 229
 chief works, 226–228
 life of, 225–226
"Harlem," 126, 128–129
"The Harlem Dancer"
"Having Lost My Sons, I Confront the Wreckage of the Moon: Christmas, 1960," 196
"Hawk Roosting," 69
Hawthorne, Nathaniel, 160
"Heat," 35, 65
"Helen," 62–63
Heller, Joseph, 82
Hellman, Lillian, 166
Hemingway, Ernest, 53, 55
"Her Kind," 201–202, 204
"Here Lies a Lady," 85, 90
"Heritage," 131, 134, 135
hexameter, 243
"His Shield," 74
historical significance, 6
"Home Burial," 23, 25–26, 29
Hopkins, Gerard Manley, 143, 182, 195
"housewife," 202, 204
Housman, A. E., 131
Howl, 186, 188–189
"Howl," 185
"Huffy Henry," 145–146
Hughes, James Mercer Langston, 39, 97, 98, 122, 131, 154
 bibliography, 129–130
 chief works, 127–129
 life of, 124–126
Hughes, Ted, 69, 211

Hurston, Zora Neale, 120, 125
"Hurt Hawks," 68–69
"Hymn," 182
hyperboyle, 243

I

"I Am the People, the Mob," 39
"I expected . . . ," 224
"I Have a Rendezvous with
    Death," 134–135
"I Shall Go Back," 91, 95
"i was considering how," 35
"I Will Put Chaos into Fourteen
    Lines," 93–94
"The Ice House," 198
"The Idea of Order at Key
    West," 44–45
idiom, 243
"If I Am Too Brown or Too
    White for You," 223
"If We Must Die," 134
"Illustrious Ancestors," 178–179
imagery, 10, 243
imagism, 31–32, 35, 243
impressionism, 243
"In a Station of the Metro," 54
"in Just-," 35
"Incident, 132–133
Style, 319
internal rhyme, 10, 243
"In the Cage," 159
"In the Village," 142
"In the Waiting Room,"
    141–142, 142
Ion, 61
irony, 243

J

jamb, 243
James, Henry, 137
"Janet Waking," 87–88

Jarrell, Randall, 83, 138, 159,
    160, 164, 171, 175
    bibliography, 152–153
    chief works, 149–152
    life of, 148–149
Jeffers, John Robinson, 59
    bibliography, 69–70
    chief works, 67–69
    life of, 66–67
J-E-L-L-O, 218
"The Jerboa," 74
"The Jilting of Granny
    Weatherall," 175
Johnson, James Weldon, 98,
    119, 125, 154
"The Journey," 197
Joyce, James, 53–54, 97
"Justice Denied in
    Massachusetts," 92, 95
juvenilia, 243

K

Kafka, Franz, 184
"Karintha," 99, 100
Keats, John, 32, 34, 45, 47,
    89, 131
Kennedy, John F., 29
Kerouac, Jack, 184, 185
Khanshendel, Chiron, 222
Kingston, Maxine Hong, 234, 238
"Kitchenette Building," 157
Knopf, Alfred A., 42, 125
Kooning, Willem De, 51

L

"Lachrymae Christi," 113
"Lady Bates," 150
"Lady Lazarus," 214–215
La Fontaine, Jean de, 72
"Lais," 35
Lancelot, 17

language, 5, 10–11
"The Last Quatrain of the
     Ballad of Emmet Till," 156
Lawrence, D. H., 31, 53, 61, 62
"Leda," 64
"Leda and the Swan," 64
Lee, Ulysses, 120
Le Figaro Litteraire, 115
"The Leg," 152
"Lenore," 20
Levertov, Denise, 48, 60, 201
     bibliography, 179
     chief works, 178–179
     life of, 177–178
Lewis, Sinclair, 15
"Life, Friends," 146
"Life's Rendezvous," 134
"Lightning Bugs Asleep in the
     Afternoon," 198
"Lilacs," 35
Lincoln, Abraham, 13
Lindsay, Vachel, 13, 17, 125
literary movement, 5
Locke, Alain, 98, 124
Lorde, Audre, 210, 216, 227, 238
"Losing a Language," 193–194
"Lost Sister," 238
"Love Calls Us to the Things of
     This World," 169
"The Love Song of J. Alfred
     Prufrock," 77–78, 82
Lowell, Amy Lawrence, 53, 159
     bibliography, 35
     chief works, 33–34
     life of, 31–32
**Lowell, Robert Traill Spence,
     Jr.,** 20, 48, 83, 114, 138,
     140, 146, 149, 198, 200,
     211, 228
     bibliography, 165
     chief works, 161–164
     life of, 159–160
"Lucinda Matlock," 14

"Luke Havergal," 15–16, 18, 20
*A Lume Spento [With Tapers
     Quenched],* 53
lyric, 6
lyricism, 243

M

"Ma Rainey," 121–122
"Madam's Calling Cards," 128
"Madonna of the Evening
     Flowers," 33–34
magical realism, 243
"Mail Call," 152
"The Man-Moth," 139, 142
masculine rhyme, 243
Masefield, John, 13
"Master and Man," 122
Masters, Edgar Lee, 39, 100,
     119, 122
     bibliography, 15
     chief works, 14–15
     life of, 12
Melville, Herman, 160, 161, 184
"Memories of West Street and
     Lepke," 163, 165
"Mending Wall," 23–24
"Merry-Go-Round," 129
Merwin, William Stanley
     bibliography, 194
     chief works, 191–193
     life of, 190–191
metaphor, 243
meter, 243
Millay, Edna St. Vincent, 20,
     28, 131, 198
     bibliography, 95–96
     chief works, 93–95
     life of, 91–93
"The Mills of the
     Kavanaughs," 165
"The Mind Is an Enchanted
     Thing," 73–74

"The Mind-Reader," 678–169
"Miniver Cheevy," 15, 17
Monroe, Harriet, 31, 41
mood, 8–9, 243
Moore, Marianne Craig, 52,
    55, 108, 137, 148
    bibliography, 74
    chief works, 72–74
    life of, 71–72
"Morning Song," 213
Morrison, Toni, 120, 228
"The Mother," 156
motif, 243
"Mr. Flood's Party," 15, 19–20
"My Butterfly: An Elegy," 22
"My candle burns at both
    ends," 92
"My Grandmother's Love
    Letters," 107
"My Kinsman, Major
    Molineux," 160

N

"Naming Power," 224
"Nantucket," 35
narrative, 6
Nash, Ogden, 29
The Nation, 103, 177, 190
naturalism, 243
"The Negro Artist and the
    Racial Mountain," 125
"Negro Hero," 157
"The Negro Speaks of Rivers,"
    124, 127
"Neon Scars," 224
"New Orleans," 226–227, 228
"Newborn Woman, May 7,
    1948," 224
"Next Day," 150, 151–152
"Night," 105
"Night Bird," 175
"Night Clouds," 35

"No Swan So Fine," 74
"A Note Left in Jimmy
    Leonard's Shack," 195
notes and comments, 11
"Notes on Commercial
    Theater," 129

O

"O to Be a Dragon," 72 74
octave, 243
"October-November," 107
ode, 243
"Ode on a Grecian Urn," 45,
    89, 135
"Ode pour l'Election de Son
    Sepulchre" ["Ode on the
    Selection of His Tomb"],
    55–57
"Ode to the Confederate Dead,"
    116–118, 152
*Of Woman Born: Motherhood as
    Experience and Institution*,
    207, 210
"Oh My People I Remember," 224
"Old Paddy Beck, my great-
    uncle," 197–198
Olson, Charles, 48, 177
Ommateum, with Doxology, 180
"On Hearing a Symphony of
    Beethoven," 95
onomatopoeia, 10–11, 244
"On Thought in Harness," 94
O'Neill, Eugene, 125
opening and closing lines, 7
Opportunity, 119–120, 125, 131
"The Oriental Ballerina,"
    233–234
original language, 5
"Out, out . . . ," 29, 52
"The Owl," 69
Owl's Clover, 42

P

"A Pact," 57
paean, 244
Palimpsest, 61
"The Paper Nautilus," 74
paradox, 243
parallelism, 244
"Parsley," 230
passage of time, 7
pastoral, 244
"The Pasture," 24, 27
patriotism, 29
"Patterns," 31, 33
"Pear Tree," 39, 65
personification, 10, 244
"Peter Quince at the Clavier,"
    42–43
"Petit, the Poet," 14
Petrarchan sonnet, 244
"Philomela," 85–86
"Piazza Piece," 86–87, 89
"Pity Me Not," 95
Plath, Sylvia, 65, 93, 105, 146,
    152, 175, 200, 203
    bibliography, 217
    chief works, 212–216
    life of, 211–212
Poe, Edgar Allan, 20, 107
*Poem and Prayer for an Invading
    Army,* 93
Poetry, 103, 108, 160
poetry, analyzing, 5–11
point of view, 5
Porter, Katherine Ann, 175
"Portrait in Georgia," 100
"Portrait of a Lady," 49, 52
Pound, Ezra Loomis, 31, 47,
    60, 62, 71, 72, 75, 79, 154,
    175, 180, 190
    bibliography, 59
    chief works, 55–58
    life of, 53–55

"Pouters and Fantails," 71
preface, 11
Pre-Raphaelites, 34
"Psalm of Those Who Go Forth
    Before Daylight," 39
pun, 244
"Purdah," 216

Q

"The Quaker Graveyard in
    Nantucket," 161, 164, 228
"Quaker Hill," 112
quatrain, 244
"Queen Anne's Lace," 50, 169
A Quinzaine for This Yule, 53

R

Ransom, John Crowe,
    115–116, 148, 154, 159,
    160, 195
    bibliography, 90
    chief works, 85–89
    life of, 83–85
"The Real Revolution Is Love,"
    228
realism, 244
"Recuerdo," 92
"The Red Wheelbarrow," 39,
    49, 51, 52
"A Refusal to Mourn the Death,
    by Fire, of a Child in
    London," 89
"Renascence," 91
repetition, 6–7
"The Return," 93–94, 95
rhyme scheme, 10, 244
rhythm, 9–10, 244
Rich, Adrienne Cecile, 194, 201
    bibliography, 210
    chief works, 208–209
    life of, 206–207

"Richard Cory," 15–16, 18–19
Rilke, Rainer Maria, 102
"The River," 111–112
"The River-Merchant's Wife: A Letter," 58
"The Road Not Taken," 26
Robinson, Edwin Arlington, 119, 122, 131
  bibliography, 21
  chief works, 17–20
  life of, 16–17
Roethke, Theodore, 104, 172, 195, 200
"The Roman Fountain," 104, 106
Ronsard, Pierre de, 56
Rose, Wendy, 210, 225
  bibliography, 224
  chief works, 223
  life of, 222–223

S

Sandburg, Carl Augustus, 13, 55, 119, 125, 135
  bibliography, 39–40
  chief works, 38–39
  life of, 36–37
satire, 244
"Sea Poppies," 65
"Sea Rose," 62
"The Seamstress," 238
"The Second Coming," 59
sense impressions, 10
"Serepta Mason," 15
series, 5
sestet, 244
"Sestina," 142
"Seventh Street," 99–100
Sexton, Anne Gray Harvey, 65, 93, 105, 146, 152, 159, 211, 212, 216, 224, 234
  bibliography, 204–205

chief works, 201–204
life of, 199–201
Shakespearian sonnet, 244
She Had Some Horses, 225, 228
"Sheltered Garden," 65
Shenandoah, 115
"Shine, Perishing Republic," 59, 67, 69
sibilance, 10, 244
significant facts, 8
"Silence," 74
Silko, Leslie Marmon, 222, 225
simile, 244
Simple books, 126
"Sister Lou," 122
"The Sisters," 31, 35
Skinner, Cornelia Otis, 29
"Skunk Hour," 162–163, 165, 298
slang, 8
"Slim in Hell," 121–122
"Small Frogs Killed on the Highway," 197–198
"Snapshots of a Daughter-in-law," 208–209, 210
Snapshots of a Daughter-in-Law: Poems 1954-1962, 206
Song, Cathy, 234, 237–238
"Song for a Dark Girl," 128
"Song for Ishtar," 179
"Song of the Son," 100
sonnet, 244
"Sonnet xcv," 95
"Sonnet xli," 95
sound pattern, 10
Sources, 207
"Southern Cross," 112
speaker, 7
spondee, 244
Spoon River Anthology, 12–15, 39, 100
"Spring and All," 50

Stevens, Wallace, 58, 72, 108, 154, 180, 206
   bibliography, 45–46
   chief works, 42–45
   life of, 41–42
"Stings," 211
"Stopping by Woods on a Snowy Evening," 23, 27–28
style, 6
"Sunday at the Mintons," 211
"Sunday Greens," 233
"Sunday Morning," 43, 45
"The Sundays of Satin-Legs Smith," 157
"Sunflower Sutra," 187
"A Supermarket in California," 69, 186–187
supplemental materials, 11
"The Swarm," 211
"Sweeney Among the Nightingales," 78–79, 82
"The Swimmers," 118
"Sylvia's Death," 203–204
symbol, 244

T

Tan, Amy, 135, 238
Tartuffe, 166–167
Tate, John Orley Allen, 83, 102, 107–108, 125, 148, 159–160
   bibliography, 118
   chief works, 116–117
   life of, 115–116
"Tell all the Truth but tell it slant," 204
"Theme for English B," 126
themes, 9, 244
"There Sat Down Once," 146
"Thirteen Ways of Looking at a Blackbird," 45
"This Is Just to Say," 51

Thomas, Dylan, 89, 172
Thoreau, Henry David, 180, 184
"Three Songs," 112
"Three Thousand Dollar Death Song," 224
Thurber, James, 29
time, passage of, 7
titles, 6
"To a Brown Boy," 131
"To a Man Working His Way Through the Crowd," 71
"To a Snail," 74
"To Aunt Rose," 189
"To His Coy Mistress," 89
tone, 8–9, 244
"To Negro Writers," 126
Toomer, Nathan Eugene (Jean), 47, 97–101
   bibliography, 100–101
   chief works, 99–100
   life of, 97–99
"To the Hopi in Richmond," 224
"To the Soul of Progress," 71
"The Touch," 204
Tracks, 228
"The Truth the Dead Know," 202–203, 204
"The Tunnel," 112, 113
Twain, Mark, 13
Two Gentlemen in Bonds, 84, 89

U

"Ulalume," 20
"Ulysses," 157
"The Unknown Citizen," 59
Updike, John, 106, 142

V

Van Doren, Mark, 116, 143
Van Vechten, Carl, 42, 125

"Vanishing Point: Urban Indian," 224
Vega, Lope de, 53
"Venus Transiens," 34
vignette, 244
"A Virginal," 55
"Virginia," 112
"Vision," 228
Voltaire, 166
"Vulture," 68–69

W

"Waialua," 238
Warren, Robert Penn, 83, 116, 148–149
The Waste Land, 59, 76, 79–82, 111
"We Real Cool," 156–157, 234
"The Weary Blues," 125, 127–128
"What the Mohawk made the Hopi Say," 224
"When the Negro Was in Vogue," 126
"The White Porch," 237, 238
Whitman, Walt, 13, 47, 57, 97, 107, 125–126, 137, 144, 148, 180, 184, 186
Who Owns America?, 84, 116
Wilbur, Richard Purdy
bibliography, 169–170
chief works, 167–169
life of, 166–167
Wilde, Oscar, 107
"Wild Swans," 94–95
Williams, Tennessee, 52
Williams, William Carlos,
35, 39, 47, 71, 103, 148, 154, 159, 169, 180, 184, 185
bibliography, 52
chief works, 49–51
life of, 47–48

Wilson, Edmund, 103, 144–145
"The Windhover," 182
"The Wine Menagerie," 108
Winesburg, Ohio, 15, 52, 100
Winnie, 155
"Winter Remembered," 89
"With the Shell of a Hermit Crab," 198
"With Usura," 58
"The Woman at the Washington Zoo," 150–151, 152, 175
The Woman at the Washington Zoo: Poems and Translations, 148–149, 150
"The Woman Hanging from the Thirteenth Floor Window," 226
"Women," 103–105
Wordsworth, 34
Wright, James Arlington,
118, 210, 224
bibliography, 198
chief works, 196–197
life of, 195–196
Wright, Richard, 97, 129, 154, 204, 221

Y

Yeats, William Butler, 53, 59, 64, 102, 143, 206, 212
"Yet Do I Marvel," 131, 133–134
"The Young Housewife," 49
"The Youngest Daughter," 238

Z

Zola, Emile, 17